♠ THE COMPLETE ♥ GUIDE ♣ TO WINNING ♦ POKER

by Albert H. Morehead

A FIRESIDE BOOK
Published by Simon & Schuster
New York London Toronto Sydney

CONTENTS

INTRODUCTION		7
1.	*About the Game of Poker*	13
2.	*How to Run a Poker Game*	41
3.	*What Every Poker Player Must Know*	49
4.	*How to Play High Poker*	81
5.	*How to Play Low Poker*	117
6.	*High-Low Poker*	143
7.	*Dealer's Choice Games and How to Play Them*	185
8.	*Poker Probabilities*	215
9.	*The Mathematical Theory of Games and Its Application to Poker*	229
APPENDIX		
	The Evolution of Poker	235
	The Laws of Poker	240
GLOSSARY		255
INDEX		279

INTRODUCTION

POKER HAS BEEN CALLED the American national game. Actually, poker comes as close to being international as any card game possibly could. It probably originated in Persia; it developed in Europe; it did attain its present form in the United States — probably in the 1830s — but today it is played in every country where playing cards are known. Nevertheless, since the world considers poker to be the national game of the United States, every American — if only from patriotic pride — should know how to play an acceptable game of poker.

THE BASIC PRINCIPLE

No one knows surely *where* poker originated, *when* it originated, or how it got its name. The basic principle of poker is that the most unusual combination of cards is the winning hand. This is such an obvious basis for a game that there may have been ancestors of poker stretching back to the year 894 A.D., when playing cards were invented (by the Chinese). At least 400 years ago the Persians had a game called *As Nas* in which there was a 20-card deck, four players, five cards dealt to each, and wagers on which player had the best hand. Since no cards were left over,

7

there could be no draw; and the idea of stud poker had not yet been thought of. As early as the 1600s the Germans had a game they called *pochen*, their word for "bluff" or "brag," and from this game developed the early English game *Brag* and the French game *Poque*. It cannot be proved, but it is irresistibly plausible, that our name, poker, derived from the French *Poque*.

Until the Louisiana Purchase in 1803, New Orleans and the entire Mississippi River valley were French territory. The people spoke French, and if they played card games they played French card games. After the Louisiana Purchase, thousands of English-speaking citizens of the new United States poured into the territory and took over the city of New Orleans and the Mississippi Valley, but they could not help being influenced by the French customs and terms. So they adopted the French game *Poque* but changed its name to the familiar English word poker. That, at least, is the logical assumption; and while no one can prove it, all poker historians have accepted it.

We are all familiar with the prototype (and stereotype) of the Mississippi River steamboat game which was introduced in the 1830s and flourished at least until the Civil War. The rules were simple. Each player was dealt five cards face down, and after the deal everyone could bet on whether or not he had the best hand. There was no limit, and either of two customs governed the betting (it is hard, here, to differentiate between fact and legend): A man could bet anything he wanted to, and his opponent, according to some stories, could always "call" ("have a sight") for as much money as he had with him; or, according to other versions, his opponent was always given 24 hours to raise the money required to call.

The entire history of poker since that time is the history of repeated efforts to pep up the game, to encourage players to "stay in" and bet. Mathematically, a man playing straight poker (no draw) in a two-handed game should bet against his one opponent if he has some such hand as a pair of fives. Psychologically, it doesn't work out that way. The hand just doesn't look good enough. So, first the element of the "draw" was added, giving a venturesome player the hope of "improving" when he wasn't dealt a good hand originally; then a few extra winning hands, such as the "straight," were added; then the "ante" was added, so that there would always be something in the pot for a player to shoot for; then came wild cards, and then stud poker. Next came "freak games" of all kinds, and now it has reached a point at which there are probably thousands of different games called poker.

These games are all related, yet no two are exactly alike. Therefore, you can make few general statements that apply to all games; in fact, you can make few general statements that apply to even two or three forms of poker.

WHY POKER IS SO POPULAR

Poker became the national card game of the United States because it so well suits the American temperament. It is a game for the individual. Each player is on his own, the master of his fate.

There are other reasons why poker is such a timeless favorite. It fits any situation, whether it is a serious game among experts or a hilarious game for the entertainment of family and friends who just want to have a good time. Almost any number of persons can play in the same game. Poker is easy to learn, and once learned is never forgotten. And the cost of the equipment is inconsiderable; there is no more economical form of recreation than card-playing.

Public opinion polls have shown in recent years that poker, despite the almost universal popularity it already enjoyed, has been growing in favor more rapidly than any other game. More persons are playing poker, and are playing it more often, than ever before.

Every American should understand poker. Nearly every American does understand poker, or wants to. And it is part of the charm of poker that it is so easy to understand.

POKER IS A GAME OF SKILL

Since its earliest days, people have made the mistake of considering poker a gambling game. It seems to be a gambling game because it is usually played for money, and in fact it is not a good game if there are no stakes. Nevertheless, poker is farther from a gambling game than almost any other card game you can think of, even contract bridge. Despite the fact that there are innumerable forms of poker and that the strategy differs in all of them, good players will almost always wind up winners, and poor players, losers. As these pages unfold I will give many bits of advice on how to be a skillful and winning player rather than a losing one, but I can sum up the whole principle with my first bit of advice, which is as follows:

If you aren't beating the game, you are being outplayed. There is a reason why you lose, even if you can't figure it out.

Mathematically, all things are possible. Out of a hundred thousand players, there will be two or three good players who consistently hold bad cards and lose when they should win, and there will be two or three poor players (to balance them) who consistently hold good cards and win when they should lose. It is a form of self-deceit, and flying in the face of probabilities, to think that you are one of the unlucky few if you are losing when you think you should be winning. For nearly all players, the cards even up in the long run. They do not come out exactly even — that would be as unusual, over the course of a lifetime, as for a player always to have ten per cent the better of it — but they come close to even. Most players will hold somewhere between 48 per cent and 52 per cent of all the good cards they are entitled to. That creates a range of four per cent. The minimum advantage of the good poker player over the poor player is ten per cent, and in a game where there is a wide disparity — as when one very good player plays with palookas — the advantage can be 25 per cent or more. Therefore, a consistently bad card-holder (who gets only 48 per cent of the good cards) will still have enough percentage to be a winner. If he is a poor card-holder he may win a little less than he should, and if he is a good card-holder he may win a little more, but he will still win.

The conclusion is this: When you have read this book, and put its precepts into practice, and when you are convinced that you are playing the game as well as possible, then, if you still lose, your only recourse is to find a different game to play in—one in which the other players are not quite so good.

ABOUT
THE GAME
OF
POKER

T HIS BOOK IS DESIGNED for all classes of poker players, from neophyte to expert. In order to bring the beginner up to date, I will present a brief outline of how poker is played. The inexperienced player should consult the Appendix (The Laws of Poker) after reading this section, and familiarize himself with rules and procedures. A thorough knowledge of the laws is essential both for the serious player who wishes to be successful and the casual player who wishes to avoid social embarrassment. All but the most hardened poker addicts are urged to review the structure of poker and solidify their understanding of how the game is played.

HOW POKER IS PLAYED

While poker is played in innumerable forms, it is really necessary to understand only two basic points:

1. The values of poker hands.
2. The principles of betting.

A player who understands these can play without difficulty in any type of poker game.

OBJECT OF THE GAME

In poker, everyone plays for himself (in fact, partnerships of any sort are strictly forbidden by the laws) and the object of each player is to win the pot. The pot is the accumulation of all bets made by all players in any one deal. Every chip a player puts in the pot means he bets so much that he has or will have the best poker hand around the table. After the betting is over, the hands are shown (called the *showdown*) and the best poker hand wins the pot.

THE POKER HANDS

A poker hand consists of five cards.* The value of a hand depends on whether it contains one of the following combinations:

Royal flush, the highest possible hand: the five highest cards (ace, king, queen, jack, ten) in any one suit.

Straight flush: all five cards of the same suit, in sequence, as, the 6, 7, 8, 9, 10 of diamonds.

Four-of-a-kind ranks next under a straight flush; as, four aces, or four sixes. It does not matter what the fifth, unmatched, card is.

A *full house* is three cards of one rank and two cards of another rank, as 8-8-8-4-4. Such hands rank next under four-of-a-kind.

A *flush* is five cards of the same suit, but not all in sequence, and ranks next below a full house.

A *straight* is five cards in sequence, as 5-6-7-8-9, but not all of the same suit. It loses to a flush or higher hand, but beats anything else.

Three-of-a-kind ranks next under a straight.

Two pairs, as Q-Q-7-7-4, rank next under three-of-a-kind.

*This, of course, refers to the basic and simple forms of the game, draw poker and five-card stud.

One *pair* beats any hand containing no pair but none of the higher-ranking combinations named above.

And below the rank of hands containing one pair are all the no-pair hands, which are rated by the highest card they contain, so that an ace-high hand will beat a king-high hand, and so on. If the highest cards of two hands are equal in rank, the next highest cards (and so on down the line) determine the rank of the hand. Thus, A-K-6-4-3 outranks A-Q-J-9-8.

The first thing a beginning player should do is to learn and remember these combinations and their relative values. For, in poker, one hopes to hold a higher-ranking hand than anyone else, and one bets on his hand if he thinks it is the best, or throws it away if he thinks someone else has him beaten.

The ranking of poker hands, given above, is not arbitrary. The less likely you are, mathematically, to receive a certain hand, the higher it ranks and the more likely it is to win if you do get it. For example, you should expect to be dealt a straight flush only once in 65,000 hands; but you should be dealt two pairs once in every 21 hands, and you should have at least a pair once in each two hands you hold.

THE BETTING

In the course of each poker deal there will be one or more *betting intervals*.

Before the cards are even dealt, the rules of the particular poker game being played may require that each player put an initial contribution (called an *ante*) of one or more chips into the pot, to start it off.

Each betting interval begins when any player in turn makes a bet of one or more chips. Each player in turn after him must either *call* that bet (by putting into the pot the same number of chips); or may *raise*, which means that he puts in more than enough chips to call; or he may *drop*, which means that he puts no chips in the pot, discards his hand, and is out of the betting until there is another deal and he receives a new hand.

When a player drops, he loses all chips he has previously put into that pot. Unless a player is willing to put into the pot at least as many chips as any player before him has put in, he must drop.

A betting interval ends when the bets have been equalized — that is, when each player has put into the pot exactly as many chips as each other player, or has dropped. There are usually two or more betting intervals for each poker deal. After the final interval, each player who has met all the bets shows his hand face up on the table, and the best hand takes the pot.

If at any time a player makes a bet or raise that no other player calls, that player wins the pot *without showing his hand.*

Check is a poker term that means the player wishes to remain in the pot without betting. In effect, it is "a bet of nothing." A player may check provided no one before him in that betting interval has made any bet. If any other player has bet, he must at least call the bet, or drop. If all players check, the betting interval is over.

In each betting interval one player is designated as the first bettor, according to the rules of the game. The turn to bet moves clockwise (from player to player to the left), and no one may check, bet, or even drop, except when his turn comes.

THE TWO MAIN TYPES OF POKER

It is best for the beginner to learn one type of poker first, then the other variants, one by one. The main types of poker are two: draw poker and stud poker. In draw poker, all cards are dealt face down. In stud poker, a player receives one or more cards face down and his other cards face up. (This does not clearly determine his hand for the other players; for suppose a player has two queens, a six and a four, face up, and one card face down. Without knowing what his face-down card is, you cannot tell how good his hand is. If it is a queen, it gives him three queens;

if it is a six or a four, it gives him two pairs; if it is any other card, he has only a pair of queens.)

In draw poker, each player is dealt five cards. Then there is a betting interval. After this, each active player may discard any of his cards and the dealer gives him other cards to replace them (called the *draw*). There is then a second betting interval, after which there is a showdown among the active players, and the highest hand takes the pot.

In stud poker, each player is dealt one card face down, called his *hole card*, then one card face up. There is then a betting interval, after which each active player is dealt another face-up card. Another betting interval, another round of face-up cards; another betting interval, and a final round of face-up cards. Each round of new cards is dealt only to players who have not dropped. Each of these players now has a full five-card poker hand, with one card face down and the other four face up. There is a final betting interval, and then a showdown in which each active player turns up his hole card and the highest hand takes the pot.

PRELIMINARIES TO THE POKER GAME

Type of game to be played. The players should first decide (unless the host or club has established the custom) what game is to be played—for example, draw poker with an occasional round of stud; or whatever else best suits the majority. The decision, made, should not be changed except by unanimous consent. The number of players affects the choice of game. For example, ten players could readily play five-card stud, but seven-card stud (a variation in which each player receives seven cards) would be almost impossible and draw poker would be unwise.

Laws. A code of poker laws should be adopted and should be final for settling all questions. No poker laws are universally followed, there being many local customs and preferences; but the laws in this book have been prepared to suit the widest possible following and are recommended for adoption. Any exceptions made to these ("house rules") should be written down in advance and posted or put in the book.

Time limit. Before play begins, the players should set a time limit and stick to it. Violation of this principle may eventually break up the game, or turn pleasant sessions into unpleasant ones.

The kitty. By unanimous agreement the players may establish a special pool, to defray the cost of playing space, equipment, refreshments, or any other expense incidental to the game.

Penalties for infractions of rules, when payable in chips, are paid to this "kitty"; and, if such payments are insufficient, one white chip may be "cut" from each pot and placed in the kitty. A maximum limit should be put on the kitty, with no other payments made to it after this maximum is reached.

No player owns a proportionate share of the kitty unless, at the time the game breaks up, there is a surplus after allowance for all expenses. Any such surplus is divided among players who are still present and who are in the game at the time the kitty reaches its maximum amount and payments to it are suspended.

Ethics. Approved poker ethics, in various groups, range from the hard-boiled code in which anything short of cheating is permissible, to the strict standard that is traditional in such games as bridge. A survey of alternative customs in this respect is given later in this book. Players should agree on the customs they will follow, and so mark the book that there can be no misunderstandings later.

Cards. The ordinary pack of 52 is used, with the cards in each suit ranking: A (high), K, Q, J, 10, 9, 8, 7, 6, 5, 4, 3, 2. There is no rank of suits.

Wild cards. Any card or cards may be designated, by unanimous agreement, as *wild*. The holder of a wild card may designate any other card for which the wild card will stand: when deuces are wild, the holder of ♣ 2 ♡ Q 9 7 4 may designate the ♣ 2 as ♡ A.

The joker. It is quite usual to play with a 53-card pack including the joker, which is wild.

The bug. The joker in a 53-card pack is often called the *bug.* The bug is a wild card with limitations: It may be counted as an ace, and it may be counted as a card of any suit or rank necessary to make a *flush* or *straight.* In special forms of poker (to be described later) the bug may take on other functions.

Natural and wild cards. It is optional to rule that as between two hands that would otherwise tie, the one containing the fewer wild cards is the higher-ranking poker hand. (This means that in competition for "low hand," as in "high-low poker," such a hand would lose; in competition for high, it would win.) The question of naturals vs. wild cards must be decided by agreement before the game, unless covered by house rules. In the absence of such agreement or rule, naturals and wild cards count the same.

Five-of-a-kind. When there are one or more wild cards, the highest-ranking poker hand is five cards of the same rank or so designated. Such a hand ranks higher than a royal flush.

Chips. Seven or more players should have a supply of at least 200 chips—usually, 100 whites, 50 reds and 50 blues. The white chip is the unit, one red being worth five whites and one blue being worth ten whites or two reds. (These proportions may be, and often are, varied to suit the convenience of the players.)

Banker. One player must be designated as banker, to keep the stock of chips and the record of how many have been issued to each player. Players should have no private transactions or exchanges among themselves; a player with surplus chips may return them to the banker and receive credit for them, while a player requiring more chips should obtain them only from the banker.

Betting limits. There are different ways of fixing a betting limit. Some limit is conceded to be necessary. Once fixed, the limit should be unalterable throughout the game. The limit may be any of the following popular ones:

1. *Fixed limit.* No one may bet or raise by more than a stipulated number of chips; for example, two or five or ten. Usually,

this limit varies with the stage of the game: In draw poker, if the limit is two chips before the draw, it is usually four after the draw. In stud poker, if the limit is one in the first three betting intervals, it is two in the final betting interval (and, often, two whenever a player has a pair showing).

2. *Pot limit*. The limit for any bet or raise is the number of chips in the pot at the time the bet or raise is made. (This means that a player who raises may count as part of the pot the number of chips required for him to call. If there are six chips in the pot and then a bet of four is made, the total is ten chips; it requires four chips for the next player to call, making 14; and he may then raise by 14 chips.) When pot limit is played, there should still be some maximum limit, such as 50 chips.

3. *Table stakes*. This, and especially table stakes with pot limit (i.e., table stakes with betting *also* restricted by the amount in the pot, as above) has become one of the most popular forms of fixing a limit. The limit for each player is the number of chips he has in front of him: If he has only ten chips, he may bet no more than ten, and he may call any other player's bet only to that extent. No player may withdraw any chips from the table (except if the game agrees otherwise), or return them to the banker, until he leaves the game. A player may add to his stack, but only between the showdown (or the time that he drops) in one pot and the beginning of the next deal.

The custom of table stakes, in which a player may "call a sight" (that is, stay in for the showdown) for all the chips he has, produces occasional side pots (see diagram).

FOR EXAMPLE: A has 40 chips, B 80, C 150, D 200. A bets 20; B calls; C raises 50. This bet *taps* A (requires him to put up all his chips to call). C puts only 40 chips in the pot, 20 to call, 20 to raise; the 30 chips which represent the remainder of his raise go into a side pot. D calls, putting 40 chips in the main pot and 30 in the side pot. A calls, putting his remaining 20 chips in the main pot. Now A can stay through to the showdown, regard-

Player		A	B	C	D
Chips		40	80	150	200
First betting interval	Main Pot	20	20	20	
				20	40
		20	20		
	First side pot	(tapped)	30	30	30
Second betting interval	First side pot		Check	10	10
			10		
	Second side pot		(tapped)	40	40
				Players in 2nd side pot	
			Players in 1st side pot		
		Players in Main Pot			

less of the additional bets of other players, and if he has the highest hand he will win the main pot. B calls, putting 20 chips in the main pot and 30 in the side pot. In the next betting interval, A is not concerned. B checks and C bets 50, tapping B. Of C's 50 chips, 10 go into the first side pot and 40 begin a second side pot. D calls, putting 10 in the first side pot and 40 in the second. B calls for 10, closing the first side pot. At the showdown, the highest of the four hands will win the main pot; the highest hand as among B, C and D will win the first side pot; the higher hand as between C and D will win the second side pot.

But when a player drops he loses interest in all side pots. Suppose, in the example just given, there is still another betting interval, in which C bets 30 chips and D drops. By dropping, D loses his interest in the main pot and the first side pot as well as in the second side pot; for he has conceded that C has a better hand, and therefore C succeeds to D's rights in all pots.

Limits on raises. It is common to limit the number of raises any one player may make to three (in some circles, two) in each betting interval. Almost equally common is to have a limit of three raises—no matter by whom—in any one betting interval. (This type of limit is most often applied in high-low poker.)

IRREGULARITIES

The laws of poker are not designed to prevent cheating, for which there is no remedy except to refuse to play with the guilty party. The purpose of the laws and penalties for infractions thereof is to protect innocent players from loss because of irregularities committed by other players because of carelessness or overanxiety to win. Poker has suffered as a club game because standard penalties were not adopted and followed. with good grace, as they are in bridge. Adoption of standard laws should reduce arguments, prevent ill-feeling, and thereby make the game more pleasant.

HOW TO BECOME A GOOD POKER PLAYER

The first step is to learn the values of the poker hands and to study the principles of betting until you are sure you understand them thoroughly.

Then deal out hands, face up—the hands of six or seven players, as they would be dealt in a game. Notice the poker combinations. Decide what you would discard and how many cards you would draw if you were playing draw poker. Observe how many poor hands and how many good hands show up; this will give you an idea of what to expect other players to hold in an actual game.

Read the rules of the various games on the following pages, and the advice on skillful play.

Most important of all, play poker in actual games. No amount of study compares with participation.

The Forms of Poker

As mentioned previously, there are innumerable ways to play poker. All have some features in common, such as the rank of the hands and the basic fact that each hand eventually consists of five cards; all have their points of difference that affect not only the procedure of play but also the strategy. The selection of a game is not wholly a matter of taste. Some games are definitely more suitable to a particular group or a particular setting (such as a home or a club) than other games. I will list the main subdivisions of the game and make some observations on their suitability for particular groups and occasions.

The main division of poker games is into two large classes: closed or draw poker, in which all cards are kept face down until the showdown; and open or stud poker, in which some cards are exposed to all players as the betting progresses.

DRAW POKER

Jackpots. Draw poker in which a pair of jacks or better are required to open. This game is usually played "pass and back in," that is, you can pass or check free before someone bets, and then come back into the pot. Although it has not been gaining in popularity as fast as some of the other forms, jackpots is the standard form of draw poker played in homes and family groups, and it is proper that it should be. It is easier in such a game for a casual or inexperienced player to figure how good his hand is, because he is given a standard, the pair of jacks, as a starting point.

Draw poker. Open on anything, pass and out — that is, in every turn you must either bet (at least the minimum, the lowest bet permitted, or a call) or you must drop. This is the game most often preferred in places where games are conducted professionally. By a professional game I mean one conducted for the profit of the proprietor, who either cuts the pot or charges for seats by the hour. The pace is faster because there is more betting when the artificial standard of a pair of jacks is removed, and it is easier to keep track of who is in and who is out when a player cannot check and then come back in. Further, there are no hands passed out because players with strong holdings are waiting to trap others into the pot (*sandbagging*). Most of the legal games in California (where draw poker, but not stud, is permitted by state law) are run on this system.

Blind opening. The player at the dealer's left must open the pot and (usually) the next player at the left must raise. This game is necessarily played "pass and out" before the draw but is usually played "pass and back in" after the draw. This is the form of the game favored in men's private clubs throughout the United States from coast to coast, and it is almost the only form of poker played in countries other than the United States. In fact, many American servicemen returning from World War II overseas called it "English poker," "Australian poker," and so on. It is the appropriate game for clubmen, who by definition are well-to-do and like a lot of action. When you start off the pot with anywhere from two to ten times the amount it costs a person to play, the odds offered by the pot are so attractive that usually several players stay in. There is a fallacy connected with this (which I will reveal later) but the fact remains that it gives big bettors an outlet for their gambling instincts.

STUD POKER

Five-card stud. The first card is dealt face down, all others face up. No game has lost popularity as rapidly as this. Thirty years ago two-thirds of the professional games were five-card stud; today, not one-tenth of the games are. Five-card stud, the original and basic form of open poker, is a game for serious and conservative players. It was created to provide more rounds of betting (there can be only two in draw poker, before and after the draw; in stud poker there are four rounds). But five-card stud does not fulfill the player's emotional desire for good hands (the average winning hand is no better than a pair of kings); and except for die-hards the game has no advantage over seven-card stud, and several disadvantages. In seven-card stud the average hand seems better; there are five betting intervals instead of four; and the scope for skill is, if anything, even greater.

Seven-card stud. The first two cards are dealt face down, the next four up, the last card down, with each player selecting five of his seven cards to use as his poker hand in the showdown. This is the pet game of rich men, celebrities, socialites (who usually play it high-low), and men's clubs where the players happen to like stud better than the usual blind-opening draw game. The true professional dotes on seven-card stud, because in no other form of the game does observation (important in all stud games) or close figuring (important in seven-card games) play so big a part. Nevertheless, it is not a widely played form of poker.

FREAK OR SPECIAL GAMES

Lowball, or low poker. This is any form of draw poker in which the *lowest* poker hand instead of the highest wins the pot. Perhaps because most players consider themselves poor cardholders, this form of the game has had a tremendous rise in popularity since the late 1930s, but almost solely on the Pacific Coast. The low-hand principle creates a lot of action because there are many more "good" one-card draws to otherwise worthless hands than there are in other forms of poker.

High-low poker. Any form of draw or stud poker can be played high-low; the high and low hands split the pot. The true expert, playing in an average game, has a really tremendous advantage in high-low poker. Barring the most unusual bad breaks, it can almost be said that the best player cannot lose in a high-low game! Yet, the average player almost never realizes this, and welcomes a high-low game because he thinks it gives him a better chance to overcome the luck of the deal.

Wild-card games. These are principally ladies' games; the serious poker player usually scoffs at them. Many serious players do use the bug—the joker considered only as an extra ace or as a filler in straights and flushes—but they too sneer at any greater extension of the wild-card principle. It is true that the use of wild cards is most suitable to purely amateur games, but make no mistake about one thing: the greater the number of wild cards, the more freakish the game, the greater the expert's advantage becomes. Mathematically, luck can play no greater part in one form of poker than in another, and the more complicated the game, the greater is the part played by judgment as to what constitutes a good hand and what a losing hand.

Special hands. Even the most serious players sometimes choose to introduce special hand-values that have no place in poker tradition—dogs, cats or tigers, skeets, skip straights, four-flushes, and so on. The purpose is to enliven the game by providing more combinations to which even a conservative player may choose to draw. These hands are played chiefly in men's clubs and in home games among more or less serious players. They do not hurt the game if a player can bring himself to remember that all poker values are relative and that you stand to win if you play only good hands and to lose if you play bad hands. The traditional gambler who bet his pile on a pair of sevens against one opponent on a Mississippi steamboat was no worse off than the club player who bets his pile on a little dog or the stud player who bets on ace-high. Whatever the form of poker, the pot is usually won by the hand that figures to be better than anyone else's, whether that hand is ace-king-high or four-of-a-kind.

The Two Main Forms of Poker

DRAW POKER

In the original poker game, each player received five cards face down, did not reveal any of them until the showdown, and never had a chance to improve beyond the five cards originally dealt to him. This was "straight poker."

Draw poker was the first of a long line of innovations designed to speed up the game and create more betting action. Each player was given hope beyond his original five cards, for he could discard any number of them and receive new cards to replace them.

Continued attempts to liven up the game by encouraging betting led to eventual adoption of a rule that in certain circumstances (as after a passed-out deal, or after some player held a big hand) the next pot should be a "jack," meaning that the stakes would be jacked up by raising the limit and increasing the amount of the ante. This created bigger pots, and so that no very weak hand could win such a pot by default, the rule was added that the betting could not even be begun on a hand weaker than a pair of jacks. The resultant game, jackpots, eventually came to be played in the United States almost to the exclusion of other forms of draw poker. In countries other than the United States, an earlier form of draw poker known as "Blind and Straddle" continues to be more popular.

JACKPOTS

The ante. Before each deal, every player in the game antes one white chip. (By unanimous agreement, each dealer may ante for all players. This comes to the same thing in the long run and saves a great deal of trouble.)

Players. Seven make the best game, eight make a full table. When eight play, the dealer may sit out each round. (When the dealer takes cards, it is sometimes necessary to shuffle the discards before completing the draw; but many players would rather do this than force the dealer to be idle for a full deal.) Each player receives five cards, all face down.

Opening the pot. The first betting interval starts when the deal is completed. Eldest hand (the player to the dealer's left) has the first turn. He may either:

(a) *Open* the pot by making a bet, if he has a pair of jacks or any higher-ranking poker hand; or

(b) *Check,* meaning that he does not make a bet at the time but reserves the right to call or raise a bet later. (Instead of "check" many players say "pass" to signify inability or disinclination to open the pot on the first round. When this is permitted, the game is "pass and back in." In all other forms of poker the rule is "pass and out," that is, to pass is to drop out without the right to re-enter later.) A player may check whether or not he has as good a hand as a pair of jacks.

If eldest hand checks, the next player in rotation may either open or check; and so on. Once any player makes a bet, the pot is open, and each player in turn thereafter must either drop, call or raise.

Deal passed out. If every player, including the dealer, checks on the first round, the deal is passed out. Each player antes another chip. The next player in turn deals. (If dealer is anteing for all players, only the next dealer in turn antes.)

The draw. When the bets in the first betting interval have been equalized, dealer picks up the undealt portion of the pack. Each player who is still in the pot, in rotation beginning nearest the dealer's left, may discard one or more cards, face down, at the same time announcing the number of cards he has discarded. The dealer then takes an equivalent number of cards from the top of the pack and gives them to that player, to restore his hand to five cards.

Each player in turn receives the full number of cards demanded before the next player discards and draws.

Dealer draws last, and must announce the number of cards he discards.

Standing pat. A player who does not wish to draw to his original five cards must so signify by announcing the fact or by knocking on the table when his turn to draw comes. Such a player *stands pat.*

Limiting the draws. When there are six or more in the game, no player should be permitted to discard and draw more than three cards.

Splitting openers. The player who opens the pot is permitted to discard one or more of the cards essential to the combination which permitted him to open, and need not announce that fact. He is permitted to place his discard face down in the pot, so that it may be referred to later as evidence that he held proper openers. In fact, it is a good idea to establish a policy that the opener *always* puts his discards into the pot. In this way, the first bettor need not reveal whether or not he has split openers — a revelation which might subsequently be to his disadvantage.

Disposition of discards. The player next in turn to deal should gather in all cards as they are discarded, keeping them face down and not looking at the faces of any of them.

Shuffling the discards. If dealer has given out the next-to-last card of the pack, and if the demands of the players in the draw are still not satisfied, he must shuffle together the bottom card and all cards previously discarded, have them cut by the player who will next receive a card in the draw, and proceed with the draw with the new partial pack so created. The discard by the opener and the discards by the players still to receive cards are not included.

Reviewing the draws. At any time during the draw, until the first legal bet has been made thereafter, any player may demand that each other player state the number of cards he drew, and the other players must so state, truthfully. (Many games allow a review of the draws at any time.)

Final betting and showdown. When the draw is completed, the player who opened the pot must either check or bet. If this player has dropped, the next player in the pot to his left has the first turn. Each other player in turn may then check, or, if any bet has been made, may either call, raise or drop until the bets are equalized.

When all players have checked, or when all bets are equalized, every player who has not previously dropped shows his full hand in the showdown, and the highest-ranking poker hand wins the pot.

Proving openers. Before his hand is discarded for any reason, the opener must prove that he held sufficient strength to justify opening the pot.

If the opener's hand is in the showdown, he must show his entire hand and may add his discards, if necessary, to indicate which original cards represented his openers.

If the opening bet is not called, or if the opener drops after opening, or if the opener makes the only bet after the draw and is not called, he must show face up enough cards (combined with his discards) to prove that he held openers, and he must show his other cards face down to prove that he held no more than five cards.

Inability to prove openers is subject to penalty — see "false openers" below.

False openers. If the opener cannot prove on demand that he held openers, his hand is fouled. If all other players have dropped, each other player may withdraw from the pot any chips, except his ante, that he has contributed. The antes and any chips contributed by the opener remain for the next deal.

If, at any time before the bets in the first betting interval are equalized, the opener announces voluntarily that he does not have openers, all bets except antes and except the opener's chips are withdrawn from the pot. The players in turn to the opener's left may open. If no one opens, the remaining chips go over to the next deal. If anyone opens, the false opener may play, but chips he previously put in the pot are forfeited.

The opener is deemed to lack openers if his hand contains more than five cards.

PROGRESSIVE JACKPOTS

This is the same game as jackpots, except that when a hand is passed out and everyone antes again, at least a pair of queens is required for openers in the next deal. If this is passed out, at least a pair of kings is required in the next deal; if this is passed out, at least a pair of aces in the next deal. The sequence is seldom carried beyond a pair of aces. This form of the game has the effect of raising the stakes somewhat.

STRAIGHT DRAW POKER

This game is sometimes referred to as "pass-out" and sometimes as "bet or drop." It differs from jackpots as follows:

No minimum holding is required to make the opening bet before the draw.

In each turn, a player must either bet—at least one white chip, usually called a "white check"—or drop. Once he has dropped he may no longer compete for the pot. If any bet has been made before him, he must at least call to stay in.

BLIND OPENING

This form of draw poker is known by many different names — blind tiger, tiger, English poker, Australian poker, pass and out — and is played in many minor variants, but none is materially different from any other.

The laws of draw poker are followed except in the following respects, which concern principally the first betting interval and the showdown.

1. *The blind.* Whether or not there was any ante before the deal, at the conclusion of the deal the player at dealer's left (called the *age*, or the *blind*), without looking at his hand, must make an opening bet of one chip.

2. *The straddle.* The player at the left of the blind must *straddle* by betting two chips. In effect, he raises one chip. The player at his left may then straddle again, if he has not looked at his hand, betting four chips; or this player may look at his hand before taking action. (The advantage of straddling is to gain position; the last player to straddle becomes the last bettor in the betting interval after the draw. Unless this rule is followed, there is no purpose in straddling.) If the voluntary straddle of four chips is made, the next player, still blind, may straddle by betting eight, etc.; usually some limit is put upon the number of straddles permitted. A player who has looked at his hand may not straddle, except in the case of the first straddler, who is forced to do so.

3. *Betting.* After the last straddle, each player may look at his hand. In turn to the left of the last straddler, each player must either pass or bet. If he passes, he is out, and he may not come back in that pot. The first player to bet must raise the last straddle by the amount of the limit — which is usually the amount by which the last straddler raised. Once any player has made this voluntary bet, each player after him in turn may either call, raise or drop; the age (i.e., the blind opener) counts his opening bet toward his call, and each straddler counts his previous bet

toward his call. If all other players have dropped when it comes around again to the blind, he may call, raise or drop, and so may each successive straddler.

4. If no one calls the amount of the last straddle, that player takes the pot, which includes the blind, his own chips, and any straddle up to his. If anyone calls, as soon as bets are equalized there is a draw and then a second betting interval. The limit after the draw is usually the amount by which the last straddler raised.

(For example: G deals; A bets one blind; B straddles, betting two blind. C looks at his hand and drops. D plays, betting three. E and F drop. G plays, putting in three chips. A plays, putting in two chips. B raises, putting in two chips, one to call, and one to raise, since that is the limit before the draw. D, G and A put in one chip each, calling. After the draw D will bet first, since he is at the left of the straddler. The limit after the draw will be one chip.)

5. *Optional rule.* There may be no more than two straddles, and the limit for a raise is always two chips before the draw and four chips after the draw, regardless of the number of straddles.

6. *Rank of hands.* In addition to the ordinary poker hands, the following hands have value:

Big cat, or big tiger: King high, eight low, no pair. Loses to a flush, beats any lower-ranking hand.

Little cat, or little tiger: Eight high, three low, no pair. Ranks next below a big cat.

Big dog: Ace high, nine low, no pair. Ranks next below a little cat.

Little dog: Seven high, deuce low, no pair; ranks next below a big dog, beats a straight or any lower hand.

As between two cats or dogs of the same rank, ties are broken as between any two no-pair hands. That is, K Q 10 9 8 would beat K J 10 9 8; 7 6 4 3 2 would beat 7 5 4 3 2.

(The object of using cats and dogs is to increase the number of hands worth drawing to and so bring more players into the pot, enlivening the game. Such hands, and other special hands which are defined in the glossary, are encountered in any type of poker game, but most often in blind-opening games. Some — but only a few — players rule that since a cat or dog beats a straight, a cat flush or dog flush beats a straight flush and becomes the highest-ranking hand. This is subject to agreement in the particular game before starting to play.)

Stud Poker

FIVE-CARD STUD

Dealing. After the preliminaries, the dealer gives one card face down to each player in rotation; then one card face up to each player.

A player's face-down card is his *hole card*, and it is not exposed until the showdown.

After these cards have been dealt, the pack is temporarily laid aside and the deal is interrupted for a betting interval. When the bets in this interval have been equalized, the dealer gives another face-up card, in rotation, to each player who has not dropped. The deal is again interrupted for a betting interval. After this, a third face-up card is given to each player who has not dropped, and after another betting interval each such player receives a fourth face-up card, completing his hand of five cards. Now there is a final betting interval, after which each player who is in the showdown turns up his hole card, and the highest hand takes the pot.

Betting. There is no ante in stud poker, except by agreement. When an ante is used, it is usually one chip by the dealer (as opposed to one from each player, or the equivalent paid by the dealer, in draw poker).

In the first betting interval, the player with the highest card showing must make a bet; if two or more players tie for the highest card showing, the player nearest the dealer's left (that is, the player who received his card first) bets first.

In any subsequent betting interval, the highest poker combination showing designates the player with the first right to bet. Thus, a player whose first two cards are A and 6 will bet first, as against a player whose first two cards are K and Q or A and 5, or as against a player whose first two cards are also A and 6 but who sits at the left. A player whose first three cards are 2, 2, 3 will bet ahead of a player whose first three cards are A, K, Q.

After the first betting interval, it is not obligatory to bet. The first bettor may check, and any player thereafter may check if there has been no previous bet.

The betting is governed by the standard laws.

Dealer's obligations. The dealer is expected to designate the player who must bet first in each betting interval, as by pointing to the proper player and saying, "First queen bets." If dealer is in error, any player may demand a correction until at least two players in rotation have checked or bet.

The dealer is also expected to call attention to combinations of three showing cards which make it possible that the holder will eventually have a straight or a flush (but not a straight-flush). Thus, if all three of a player's showing cards are hearts, the dealer should announce: "Possible flush." If a player's first three cards are 9, 8, 6, the dealer should announce: "Possible straight."

Betting limit. It is customary in stud poker to have one limit for bets and raises during the first three betting intervals, and a higher limit for the final betting interval, and also for any earlier betting interval in which any player has an "open pair."

In some circles the limit is graduated round by round—one chip in the first betting interval, two in the second, three in the third, and four in the fourth or in any betting interval when there is a pair showing.

SEVEN-CARD STUD
(Seven-Toed Pete, Down-the-River)

This form of stud poker is becoming increasingly popular. Each player receives three cards before the first betting interval—two face down, dealt one at a time, then one card dealt face up. There is then a betting interval. Next, three more rounds of cards are dealt face up, one at a time, with a betting interval after each. Finally, one more card is dealt face down to each player who has not dropped, after which there is a final betting interval and a showdown in which each player turns up his three face-down cards and selects five cards as his poker hand.

SIX-CARD STUD, EIGHT-CARD STUD

In six-card stud, the first card is dealt face down, the next four cards each face up, and the last card face down. There is a betting interval after each round of dealing from the second card on.

In eight-card stud, the first two cards are dealt face down, the next four face up, and the last two cards face down, with a betting interval after each round of dealing from the third on.

In each case a player chooses any five of his cards to be his poker hand in the showdown.

About the Laws of Poker

It has often been said that poker has no official laws. I have been guilty of making that statement myself, but when I reconsider, I realize that exactly the opposite is true. Poker has innumerable sets of "official laws."

There is no disagreement about the laws of *correct* procedure. Everyone agrees on the rank of the cards, the order of play, the method of betting, etc.

The only disagreement is on irregularities and what should be done about them. The ethics in a "tough" club game are entirely different from the ethics in a polite parlor game. If a player miscounts his chips and puts into the pot more than he should, a group of strangers might make him leave them in; a private men's club might slap on a penalty of a chip or two; and a group of personal friends would let him withdraw the excess without any question. If a player acts out of turn, a gambling house will let him get away with it, because to inflict a penalty might offend the player and lose a customer; a group of his friends might penalize him in a good-natured way; a mixed group of husbands and wives in a family game probably would not even notice it.

If a man says he has filled a flush, bets, and then is found to be bluffing, in a family game he is considered a trifle dishonest. In a men's club he is considered to have played exactly according to the traditions of the game.

To sandbag—that is, check and then raise when someone bets into you—is considered the essence of poker by the majority of serious players, but it so enrages most people that professional clubs have had to make a rule against it.

In a tough game, one can make the most outrageous statements about his hand, and the practice is not only tolerated but is sneered at as kid stuff that has no chance to fool anybody; but in the refined purlieus of a society living room it is considered less than nice.

You can imagine what the general attitude would be in a game among experienced players if someone, before betting, asked, "I've forgotten—does a full house beat a flush?" But in the casual family game such a question is not too unusual and no one draws any particular conclusions from it. It would not even arouse comment unless the woman who asked happened to hold neither a full house nor a flush, in which case she would probably be gossiped about as being a bit too sharp for her own good.

In the game of poker these dilemmas are solved by the fact that every club, group, or even individual social game, has the right to make its own rules. The rules can be and are made to conform to the temper and preferences of the participants.

Nevertheless, it is not only desirable but almost essential that such rules be written. Then, when any misunderstanding or question arises, the players can consult the written rules and stick by them, whatever they say, so that there can be no hard feelings.

The poker laws in the Appendix of this book are recommended

for adoption by any game or group of players. These laws follow those adopted by principal clubs and gambling houses throughout the United States, and especially from Nevada westward. There are several other admirable codes of poker laws, and from a practical standpoint it does not make a great deal of difference which code is adopted as long as the players abide by some code.

Since a poker game is "every man for himself," poker players are by nature rugged individualists. "Serious" players seldom see why anyone else should be permitted to make laws for them. They prefer to make their own, or at least to look over the available prescriptions and select the ones they like best. There is nothing wrong with this as long as every player in the game clearly understands the procedure to cover each particular case, and as long as the laws are written so that there can be no misunderstandings about them.

The Nature of Poker

I hope that through these introductory pages has run one recognizable thread of thought: All forms of poker are games of skill, and one form is no more skillful than any other (although the *margin* of advantage of the better players varies somewhat from game to game). The player who complains that in the freak games, or ladies' games, the palookas are always drawing out on him, condemns himself as a poor player. True, it hurts to lose a pot you thought you had won, but the more others try to outdraw your best hand in any form of poker, the more you figure to win.

The greatest of all fallacies is the one so solemnly pronounced by California law: that draw poker is predominantly a game of skill and stud poker is not. Superficially, it would seem that the absence of information in draw poker increases the difficulty of judging the relative value of a hand, but precisely the contrary is true. The more information there is, the greater the scope for reasoning to replace blind guessing. In addition, the expert player of stud poker requires both the drudgery and the imperviousness to distraction that go with remembering all the cards that have been shown and folded. These cards affect the possibilities of the hands that may be made. Without remembering at least a certain number of these cards, one cannot play stud poker well. (That is why a stud dealer in a professional game is never supposed to announce a possible straight flush—his occasional failure to do so might give a player the benefit of his observation that a card essential to the straight flush is already dead.)

I have no desire to criticize or to influence California legislators. I am as happy as any other poker player that in at least one state, at least one form of poker has been recognized as a game of skill, as it should be in all states. My object is only to point out that all forms of poker, including deuces-wild and Spit-in-the-Ocean, are games in which luck can be overcome and skill be made paramount.

I repeat: If you are losing consistently, you are not unlucky— you are being outplayed.

HOW TO RUN
A POKER GAME

THE ENJOYMENT OF A POKER game can be greatly increased if certain particulars are decided on in advance. Not only will the game run more smoothly if the "ground rules" are known and agreed to by all the players, but arguments will be kept to an absolute minimum. (It is overly idealistic to expect a poker game to run with no disagreements whatsoever, but there is no reason not to minimize the number of disturbances.)

If a game is played on a regular basis, it is also a good idea to write down the rules which govern play. This provides an authority which can be referred to in case of dispute, and also enables a new player to be added without a lengthy explanation (perhaps subject to error or omission) of the house rules. A new player can simply be given the agreed rules and the regular players can answer any questions.

Needless to say, each poker game will create its own code — both for rules of play and for proper behavior. In this chapter I will list the topics that should be covered in advance if you are to insure the smoothest possible game. Although it is virtually impossible to suggest specific rules which would be found satisfactory by any large group of players, I will give a few general suggestions and include a few examples which may provide useful hints as to the form of rules to be enacted.

The most important function of this chapter is to provide a list of topics that should be discussed. By covering all the items in this list (as well as any others that may occur to the players), you will guard against the vast majority of potentially unpleasant situations likely to arise.

In order to apply this to your own game, discuss each individual item with your poker circle (or the group of persons you hope to start a game with) and come to an agreement on each particular item.

This list is also valuable when you are invited to a strange game. Bring along a checklist of these topics, and be sure to find out how the game treats each one before you start to play. This will reduce your disadvantage as an unfamiliar player, and will avoid the possibility of your being involved in a hassle stemming from faulty or unclarified house rules.

TOPICS TO BE COVERED IN HOUSE RULES

1. *Time.* Perhaps the greatest danger to a poker game is that it will continue indefinitely at some sessions. It is wisest to fix a closing hour and adhere to it strictly. In a regular game, it should be easy to state a time at which the game will end. (This is often stated in the form that the last round—each player deals once—begins at a certain hour.) On occasion, the time limit may be extended, but *this must be decided before play begins.* Once again, in a regular game, it is dangerous to extend the closing hour too frequently, lest it become a standard procedure, thus essentially ending the game at a later hour.

The importance of fixing a closing hour can best be understood by considering the feelings of the players at a vaguely decided closing time. The losers are all anxious to continue so that they will have a chance to recoup. Frequently, the winners too are anxious to continue, either because they are enjoying the game or (for the most bloodthirsty) because they realize that a player who is losing is likely to play well below his usual level and even to take desperate chances in an attempt to get even.

If the closing time is extended, there may be new losers anxious to continue when the new time is reached. Thus, there is the danger that the game will be extended again, and even again, until the players decide they might as well stay up all night, and so forth.

As a corollary to keeping a firm closing time, the starting time should be made as early as possible so as to allow a suitable period for the game. Players should be encouraged to come early by reaffirming the adherence to the strict closing time.

2. *Money.* Poker is played almost universally for stakes, however small. Definite arrangements should be made at the beginning of the game for the settlement. The best procedure is to require that all debts be settled at the end of each session, or, if this cannot be achieved, that no player may take a seat at a later session unless he has settled his accounts for all previous games. Often the players will want to carry out transactions through "transfers." (A owes B, B owes C, B asks C to collect from A.) Unless such transfers are carried on under the house rules (settled at the end of a session, or before the next session, or whatever) they are likely to lead to a confusion of accounts and a great deal of hard feeling. Guard against such difficulties by insuring that whatever the form of transaction among the players, the rules of the game are satisfied.

Other possible ways to prevent money difficulties are to require each player to bring or deposit a certain amount, and to play directly for cash. It may also be desirable, in social penny-ante games or serious games with sizable stakes, to set a limit on the amount each player can lose during one session. Poverty poker (in which a player is given a second stack—to be paid for by the winners if necessary—after losing all his chips) is a good way to limit losses and yet maintain the social aspects in a small limit game. In any event, try to avoid the possibility that anyone may lose more than he is prepared to lose.

3. *The Players.* Most poker games entail certain restrictions on the number of players. With too few, interest in the game is

apt to diminish. With too many, it may be awkward to play certain games (such as draw poker or seven-card games) or may simply crowd the table and lead to discomfort. Therefore, it is wise to establish both upper and lower limits for your game. If there is danger of "standing room only," the players should be encouraged to reserve their seats in advance or to announce when they will be unable to attend.

It should also be an established policy of regular poker games whether or not "strangers" shall be allowed to take seats. Very often, one of the players will wish to invite a visiting friend from out-of-town. While some players might accept this without a second thought, others may register violent objections. To preserve harmony, such matters should be settled in advance and written into the house rules. When the game usually meets at the home of a "host" (presumably one of the players), it is often left to this person's judgment who may be invited to sit in on the game.

4. *Chips and stakes*. These are being treated together because, to a great extent, they are interdependent. The ratio of the denominations of the chips can affect the size of the stake (in general, the lower-valued the chips, the freer the game), and the desired stake can often be achieved by a judicious choice of chip values.

If the game is to be a limit game, it is most important to have a great number of the smallest (and perhaps second-smallest) units available. To have a wide range of chips will result only in an endless string of transactions in which one player makes change for another. There are no big bets in a limit game, so only a few different denominations (perhaps three) should be needed. The larger denominations should be used only to save space when one player collects a great many chips.

In a pot limit (or table stakes) game, it is best to have a wide variation in the rank of the different chips to be able to handle the varied money situations easily. Experience has shown that the most convenient ranks of chips in a pot limit game are those in which each successively higher-ranking chip has a value several times that of the closest lower-ranking chip. (Thus, in a "nickel ante" pot limit game in which the lowest chip represents one nickel, the next chips might stand for 25 cents and one dollar rather than 10 cents and 25 cents or 25 cents and 50 cents.) In games of this form, five denominations of chips are usually distributed.

The form of stake to be used should be chosen to suit the game. Casual players will prefer a limit game. This enables a player to see a lot of cards at a relatively low price, and to keep a limit on the maximum losses without too much special attention by the players.

More serious players prefer pot limit (or pot limit with a ceiling on the maximum allowable bet), or table stakes. The best poker players usually adopt "pot limit table stakes" — betting is restricted both by the amount in the pot and the amounts the players have on the table — or straight table stakes.

When table stakes are played, the house rules should state clearly whether or not a winner may remove his winnings from the table; also the minimum amount a player must keep in front of him, the minimum "takeout" or starting stake, and so forth.

When pot limit is the preferred form of betting, it is usually wise to set some sort of upper limit on any one hand (based on the amount the players can afford to lose), lest things get out of hand on one sensational deal. A very large loss is always likely to injure the game as a whole, not only because it may deprive the game of the big loser but because some of the other players may fear a similar calamity. Setting a maximum loss on one hand in pot limit play is one way to avoid such difficulties.

5. *The ante.* The ante should be agreed upon in advance and is usually a function both of the chip denominations and the form of betting. It is a good idea to vary the ante if both open and closed poker are being played. In closed poker, when there are few betting rounds, it is usual to have each player ante one unit; in open poker, only the dealer is required to put in an ante. When the game is such that every player must ante on every hand, it is a good idea to have the dealer ante for everyone.

This avoids a lot of fingers protruding into the pot, arguments about whether or not Jones has put his chip in, and so on.

6. *The games.* The house rules should state which forms of poker are allowed, or how it is to be determined whether or not a game suggested by one of the players is acceptable. In most games it is customary to let the dealer choose the form of poker for his deal (or, perhaps, for each player in turn to choose for a round of deals). The rules should state either that the dealer may choose from a specified list of games, or that he may select any form of poker he wishes. (Some more casual games do not always restrict the choice to a form of poker.) If the dealer is allowed latitude, it should be specified in the house rules how many objections must be registered to require that a different game be chosen. Depending on the personalities involved, some poker games will require a rule that one objection vetoes the choice of game; other groups will be more liberal.

Care must be taken with "dealer's choice" in one situation. When both draw and stud poker are being played, the players calling draw poker will be at an advantage if they are given the privileges of the dealer (to bet last) at draw poker. Since this is a considerable advantage (see Chapter 4), it is customary to have a marker (called the "buck") passed from player to player after each hand of draw poker.

Although the player whose turn it is to deal actually gives out the cards, the betting starts with the player to the left of the player with the buck. In other words, the buck marks the "draw dealer." In this way, no player can gain an advantage through calling draw poker in his turn. (This need not be taken into account in stud poker because the position of the dealer is of very little importance.)

7. *The rules of play.* It is most important to agree on a code of play. This code must cover both the technical side — the actual rules — such as improper number of cards, cards exposed during the deal, and so forth, as well as a code of behavior. As there is no universal set of poker rules, the easiest way to agree on this matter is to take some set of rules (such as the one given in this

book) and make whatever modifications are necessary to suit the players. The house rules can then state that a certain published set of rules is the authority except for specified exceptions. This method is also valuable in that it sets an authority which can be consulted, with no question of interested parties offering opinions.

The code of behavior is equally important. Some poker games will allow a player to say just about anything. Other games will frown on "coffeehousing" — giving possibly misleading information through gratuitous conversation. In any event, for both social and technical reasons, it is vital to set down in advance what a player may or may not say or do during the course of the game.

Finally, any special rules which are to be used must be made a part of the house rules. The rules given in this book cover most of the possible irregularities which may occur, and also set down methods of dealing with specific situations (side pots, splitting the pot at high-low, proving openers at jackpots, etc.). There may, however, be special rules which your particular game may wish to adopt. As always, it is of the utmost importance to have any such rules agreed upon and written down in advance.

WHAT EVERY
POKER PLAYER
MUST KNOW

No MATTER WHAT kind of poker game you are playing in, there are certain things you must know. I list them and comment on them below. They are listed in order from the simplest to the most complex. The more of them you are capable of digesting, the greater your chances of winning. Therefore, I start with obvious "kid stuff" that any poker player worth his salt knows as a matter of second nature, and I progress to factors that may not even occur to anyone but players of the highest order.

1. *The rank of the hands.*

Don't scoff at this—75 per cent of all poker players have difficulty remembering.

2. *What constitutes a good hand, a fair hand, a bad hand.*

All these are relative values and vary in accordance with the game you are playing, but it is essential knowledge you must take into any game. In jackpots draw poker, a pair of sevens is a weak hand not worth playing; in blind-opening draw poker, in certain circumstances it might be a good hand worth a stay and even a bet. A pair of tens and a king in the first three cards constitute a good hand in seven-card stud but are not worth a play in seven-card high-low stud, in which a good starting hand (for low) is something like 7-3-2. Later on I discuss good hands, fair hands, and bad hands in every one of the principal forms of poker.

Before you go into a game, make sure that you have a very clear idea of this, whether you get it from experience, from intuition, from this book, or from any other source.

3. *Your chance of improving.*

As I will explain later, poker is not a game of higher mathematics. All you need are rough approximations of the accurate figures. Nevertheless, you have to know generally what your chance is of improving the hand you were dealt. To take an extreme example, if you did not know this you would be as likely to play an inside straight (in which the odds are nearly 11 to 1 against you—odds you are seldom if ever offered by the pot) as a double-end straight (when the odds are less than 5 to 1 against you—odds frequently offered by the pot).

4. *What you stand to lose or win.*

At this point we begin to approach expert stuff. The ultimate phase of mathematical figuring in poker is the number of hands you will win and *how much* you will win on them, and the number of hands you will lose and *how much* you will lose on them. You know the chestnut about the man who had three farms and lost them all in poker; he lost the first two by drawing to inside straights and not hitting, and the third by drawing to an inside straight and hitting. It is not enough to know that when you draw three cards to a low pair the odds are 8 to 1 against making three-of-a-kind. The necessary next problem is: What are the chances that I will win if, in that one case out of nine, I do make three-of-a-kind? If your three-of-a-kind, once you make it, has only an 85 per cent chance of winning the pot, then, to be mathematically sound, you must deduct your losses on the other 15 per cent—the times you improve but still don't win.

5. *The best hand probably held by each opponent.*

This comes even closer to the expert level, and if (as in stud poker) it involves discounting all cards that you know about, it becomes super-expert. I will give you a simple and over-simplified example. In a stud game you have a pair of kings. Your opponent has an ace showing. What is the chance that he has a pair of aces? If you have watched all the cards that have been folded, and if three aces have shown, you know that the chance is zero. If two aces have folded, you know that the chance is remote; if one ace has folded, you know that there is a distinct danger; if no ace has shown, there is a substantial probability that your opponent has aces. All of this is modified by your appraisal of the opponent himself. If he is the sort who probably would not have stayed unless he had an ace in the hole, then, regardless of the mathematics of the case, he is likely to have aces. The true expert in a stud game must watch every card dealt, remember every card folded, and judge every opposing hand in accordance with the cards the opposing player cannot have or probably does not have in the hole.

6. *What the opponent thinks he has.*

This again approaches the highest degree of skill. After all, your opponent may bet into your three aces when he has queens-up, because he honestly thinks that queens-up will be the best hand. So remember, when the opponent bets, that he may be wrong! Your bets and especially your calls will be based on your estimate of how good a hand the opponent *thinks* he has.

7. *How to fool or outguess the opponent.*

This is as far as you can go in poker skill. It is the highest expert or super-expert level of skill, and it probably cannot be taught, cannot be measured, cannot even be defined. Anyone who has the knack or ability to outguess his opponents probably has such an aptitude for poker that he doesn't need a book to help him win. Furthermore, he probably knows quite well that he doesn't need a book, or my advice, and no doubt if he and I played poker together he could beat me.

Yet the finest poker player, or any player, can profit from reading books on poker. When he reads such a book he is reading about what other good poker players have done and the methods they have found effective. *I have never seen a bad poker book.* Many of them are badly organized, yes; usually they are incomplete; analyze them as a whole and they consist mostly of tips that apply to specific situations and not to the game as a whole. Nevertheless, they are all worthy publications—helpful, admirable. If you tried to write everything that is known about poker in all its forms, you would fill a 25-volume encyclopedia. Many of the finest poker exploits are inspirational and intuitional. They won't necessarily occur even to the most expert player at the strategic moment when they will be most helpful. But if that player has heard about them through books that recount the experiences of other players, he doesn't need inspiration or intuition or even practical experience in a game — they become part of his own experience.

To illustrate this, I will cite a couple of the chestnuts of the game, the stories that don't lose their validity because they are so classic or because the situations involved are so rare.

FIRST POKER CHESTNUT

Five-card stud. Table stakes. Last betting interval.

Player A had Q, J, 10, K showing, plus his hole card.

Player B has 6, 10, 8, 4 showing, plus his hole card.

Player A has taken the lead throughout; Player B has played along, outlasting other players. Player B has a six in the hole, giving him a pair of sixes.

On the last card Player A bets out, perhaps half his stack.

Player B knows that there are six cards that would give Player A a cinch hand: A, K, Q, J, 10, or 9. But Player B *taps*.

Player A calls and loses. His hole card is a seven.

There was nothing unusual in the fact that Player B figured the bluff of Player A. Every sucker in the land does that several times per session. The significance of this case is in the fact that Player B tapped and that Player A called.

The unimaginative player, in B's position, would be proud of the fact that he had detected the bluff, would call, and would win the pot. This particular Player B went further. He trusted not only his own judgment but also his estimate of his opponent, and thus violated the precept, "never bet into a potential sure thing."

Put yourself in Player A's position. You have bluffed when

the odds heavily favored your having a cinch hand. Your opponent, who has stuck around through three previous rounds of betting, has not been content to call you but has bet everything he has on the table. Why should he do this if he has simply detected your bluff? He could content himself with calling, and take in an easy pot. So the only logical explanation for Player B's bet is that he has detected the bluff, but unfortunately (for him) he cannot beat the board. Therefore, his only chance to win the pot is to let you know that he has detected the bluff, in the reasonable expectation that you, caught bluffing, will fold your hand and give up.

On this basis, Player A calls and fully expects his K-Q high to beat Player B's king in the hole. (Of course, B's previous calls with a pair of sixes were doubtful, and for him to have played along with a king in the hole seems most unusual — but that is not part of the story.)

As I said before, this is a matter of inspiration. The exact circumstances will probably never present themselves to you if you play poker all your life. Nevertheless, you should not underestimate the value of knowing about this and dozens or hundreds of other poker situations that some good players have encountered and mastered. They are all part of the well-rounded education the finished poker player must have.

SECOND POKER CHESTNUT

Draw poker, jacks to open. $10 limit. Ante is $7 ($1 each).

Player A (next to dealer) opens with two aces. Player B plays. All other players drop.

Player A draws three cards and makes four aces. Player B draws one card.

Player A bets out, Player B raises, Player A reraises, Player B reraises, Player A drops.

This is the only case on record in which a player dropped four aces after raising once. It is unlikely that it could ever actually happen, because poker players are human beings, and a human being would not drop four aces. (Player A certainly could have *called* the final raise, especially in a limit game.) But the situation is entirely logical.

Player B would not have stayed on a simple draw to a straight or flush, and he would have raised with two pairs, so he was marked with a draw to a straight flush. He knew that Player A knew this, so that he would not have given his second raise if he could merely beat a full house, on the assumption that any full house by Player A would be better than his (because Player A went in with a single pair of openers). Consequently, it must be figured that Player B made his straight flush and Player A's four aces are no good.

It is all inescapable logic, however unrealistic it may be.

Advice to All Poker Players

Now I am going to take up the general considerations that apply to all forms of poker. Sooner or later in this book I will treat each of the principal forms of the game and give specific advice about each, but first I consider it more appropriate to discuss certain important considerations that apply to every form of poker.

1. The ethics and etiquette of the game.
2. The mathematics of the game.
3. Psychology and bluffing.
4. Position.
5. Money-management.
6. Card memory and analysis.

ETHICS AND ETIQUETTE

Poker is not a sociable game but it is distinctly a *social* game. That is, it is a game one must play with others, and we may assume that every human being would rather be popular than unpopular, and also that every group will soon reject a player who is generally disliked by the other players. Therefore, if you are playing in a poker game and you want to keep on playing, it behooves you to conform to the social customs and make sure that the other players do not hate you enough to kick you out.

It is notably unprofitable to be recognized as a good fellow in poker games, but it is almost as bad to be characterized as a prime sonofabitch. The object of the winning player is to steer a middle course. He wants to be known as a tough but fair opponent, as a ruthless but honest adversary. The problem is: "How to be honest and yet a winner." My advice is as follows:

1. Sandbagging is a logical part of the game to the thinking player, but, as I said before, for some reason it enrages the average player. Many professional games have been forced to introduce the house rule that you cannot check and then raise. Find out what the custom of the game is and observe it. If it makes the opponents angry for you to check the best hand and then raise, don't do it. It may slightly restrict your style, but it doesn't really have a great effect on your winnings or losses in the long run. In fact, much money is lost by failure to bet the best hand in the vain hope that someone will bet into you.

2. In some games, any comments you make are taken with a grain of salt, in other games the "gentlemanly code" is adopted, and you are not supposed to say that you have a bad hand when you have a good one, or that you filled a flush when in fact you didn't, etc. In such games, don't compromise your popularity by violating the customs. You won't lose anything by keeping your mouth shut; the bet speaks for itself, anyway.

A woman wrote to Dorothy Dix and said, "Dear Miss Dix: A man wants to marry me but he doesn't know I have false teeth. Should I tell him?" Dorothy Dix answered with classic succinctness, "Keep your mouth shut."

Since the poker player would be a fool to tell the truth about his hand, and since he may win undying unpopularity by playing the gay deceiver and chatterbox, Miss Dix's advice is sound for the poker player too.

3. Be just a little more conservative than the standard estab-

lished in the game. In all except the toughest games in the country, the majority of players are more "liberal" (venturesome) than they should be. From curiosity or boredom or sheer ignorance, they play along too often, raise too often, and call too often. It is neither winning style nor good etiquette to become known as the Rock of Gibraltar in such games. However, if you play them just a little closer to the chest than the average conservative player in the game, but stick your neck out with a gambling move now and then, you will maintain your chances of winning and avoid being stigmatized as a greedy soul who likes money better than good fellowship. It is true that conservatism pays in poker, but don't try to make it pay too much.

4. Conform to the pace of the game. Old-fashioned poker players like to take every step with the greatest deliberation, with close figuring before betting and excursions into psychological analysis before deciding whether or not to call. In distinction to this, the public game in a licensed club or gambling house moves with machine-like precision, and if you pause for as much as ten seconds you will be subjected to impatient prods from the other players. If you are by nature a slow thinker, you may suffer a bit in the fast games, but not as much as from violating the custom of the game.

5. Don't be a stickler for the laws in an amateur game. The players commit the most horrible crimes known to poker: they drop out of turn; they want to look at your hand when you bet and didn't get called; they relinquish a pot and then want to reclaim it when they find out they had the best hand after all.

Let them get away with it. I assume your principal desire is to be a winning player (that is the purpose for which this book was written), and in such a game you will win just by avoiding the more horrible of the mistakes that are made all around you. Be content with that. They will eventually kick you out of the game because you win too much, but if you don't hurt their feelings by insisting on strict interpretation of the laws, you will last quite a while longer.

6. Lose a few arguments! For example, if you have put in your

ante and someone says you haven't, why not put it in again? On this subject I would like to make one pointed observation: if you argue and then give in reluctantly, you have done as much damage to yourself as if you had argued and never given in. In fact, you have done more damage; if you decide to stand on the fact that you are right, you may win the admiration of some players. Equally you will win their admiration when you give in fast and graciously although it is obvious that you were right all the time; it is apparent that you are not picayune about small amounts. So you must either stand on your rights or yield with no murmuring or muttering, and you shouldn't do either of them all the time.

7. The traditional problem of etiquette is saved for last: Can you quit when you are a big winner?

Here again the answer depends on the game. In a public game you should have no qualms at all; in a club game you should simply take care to give ample advance notice, such as a half-hour or an hour; and in a truly social game you mustn't. You can nurse your stack and you can refrain from doing anything that would keep the game going, but you can't give the impression that you are in there for the money and not for the sheer fun of it. At least wait until someone else quits, and then go along with him.

MATHEMATICS OF THE GAME

You don't have to be a mathematician to be a good poker player. It doesn't even help.

True, poker offers some of the most fascinating of mathematical problems and for that reason has engaged the attention of the best mathematicians. Some of their researches invade the highest levels of the higher mathematics. Their findings are published in books. You can trust these books.

I have read dozens of poker books, and as far as I know, Oswald Jacoby's is the only one written by a master mathematician. Yet, I have never seen a poker book in which the quoted odds are wrong by more than some insignificant fraction or percentage. But you do have to have a knowledge of simple arithmetic, a memory for the simple odds that you read about in books, an understanding of what these odds mean, and a quick eye for appraising the size of the pot. It is considered neither cricket nor poker to stop and count the pot every time your turn comes and you have to make a decision, although this procedure is usually tolerated if a big decision arises at table stakes, and it is sometimes necessary at pot limit.

The basic mathematical principle, subject to very few exceptions, is: Don't play unless you think you have every other player beaten.

Reference to the tables of percentages (Chapter 8) will furnish a guide to the relative infrequency of the various poker hands, and so to the probability that any such hand will be the best hand dealt. These tables will also show that the best hand before the draw (in draw poker) or the best holding in the first cards dealt (in stud) stands to win, and that (with rare exceptions) an inferior hand playing against the best hand will lose in the long run.

When you have the best hand around the table, and you know or feel sure that you have the best hand, mathematics doesn't enter into it at all. You simply shove your money into the pot. You may take some comfort from the figures elaborately prepared by mathematicians, proving that the best hand going in is usually the best hand coming out, but what would it matter? Who ever heard of dropping the best hand?

So the only mathematical questions arise when you may not have the best hand going in. In any such case you must improve to win. You must then ask yourself three questions: 1. What are the odds against my improving? 2. What are the odds offered me by the pot? 3. What is the chance that I will win if I do improve?

The first question is answered by tables of odds that you can quickly and easily commit to memory; nearly every case that may confront you is treated in Chapter 8 of this book. The second question—the odds offered by the pot—is a matter of an eyecheck of the pot or knowledge of how much is already in it and how much you have to put in. The third question—your chance of winning if you do improve—is answered partly by the tables of probabilities and partly by your knowledge of the game. Here are some (slightly simplified) examples to clarify this third question:

FIRST EXAMPLE

Draw poker, seven players, blind opening. Dealer (G) antes one, A at his left opens blind for one, B raises blind for two. C bets three. D, E, F, G, A drop. B can stay for one.

B holds 10-9-8-7-K. The odds are 39 to 8 (about 5 to 1) against him making a straight. The odds are only 27 to 20 (almost even) against his making a pair of sevens or better.

The pot has seven chips in it and B can stay for one. B is offered 7-to-1 odds by the pot.

If B fills his straight he has at least a 90 per cent chance of winning—that is, not once in ten times will C have or draw a hand better than a ten-high straight. On this basis only, B should play; because the odds are only 5 to 1 against making the straight and the pot offers him 7 to 1.

Notice that the amount of money a player has put into the pot previously has no bearing on the issue.

B's chance if he makes a pair depends entirely on what kind of player C is. In a good game B would reject the chance of winning on a low pair, because C would not have bet with less than aces or at least kings. In a liberal game C might have bet with a four-flush or bobtail straight. In this case a low pair might win; but about 15 per cent of the time B might lose even if he makes his straight. Here we must assume a tight game, however, because in a liberal game all the other players would not have dropped.

SECOND EXAMPLE

Draw poker, seven players, jacks to open, pass and back in. The ante is seven chips, the limit two before the draw, four after the draw. Dealer is G. A, B, C, D pass. E opens for two and all players from F through C drop.

D holds 10-9-8-7-K. The odds are still 5 to 1 against his making a straight. The pot offers nine chips against the two he must pay to call, or $4\frac{1}{2}$ to 1. He cannot win by pairing, because E has at least jacks. The odds against him are greater than the odds he is offered, so he throws in his hand.

These are the simplest possible examples (though both of them happen frequently) and in most cases closer figuring will be necessary. The examples were purposely made simple to illustrate the basic theory of the application of mathematics to poker. Mathematics can be very useful — in fact, some knowledge of the odds is essential — but nothing can be more damaging than placing slavish reliance on the mathematical probabilities. Events always alter the *a priori* assumptions. For example, in a seven-hand game of draw poker it is useful to know that two aces would normally be the best hand before the draw; but if you hold the aces and three players have already come in before you, you must assume, or at least suspect, that your two aces are not the best hand; and if one of those players has raised, you can be fairly sure they are not.

There is the further factor, at times, that after you decide to stay, some other player will raise, and the odds offered by the pot will go down. So the percentages are modified by your position (which determines the danger that the pot will be raised after you), and by your appraisal of the other players and what they hold. (This point is discussed in more detail under "Money-Management.")

In table-stakes play, percentage will usually operate in favor of a player who has only a few chips left. When he stays in for this number of chips, the pot is usually giving him large odds, and his loss is limited to this one bet. Only such a case, as a rule, justifies a "freak draw."

The mathematical expectancies must also be modified by a further question you must ask yourself: "Is there any point to betting?" For example, you are against one other player in a draw poker game. He draws three cards, and you draw three cards to two jacks. You make jacks-up. The odds are $2\frac{1}{2}$ to 1 that he did not improve his pair, so mathematically you have a good bet. But the realities are that if he did not improve he probably will not call, and your bet becomes pointless, whereas if he did improve and calls, he can probably beat you. Therefore, mathematics or no mathematics, you do not bet. If you had made three jacks you would have bet, because mathematics tells you that the odds are 8 to 1 against his having made three-of-a-kind, and you may get a call if he made aces-up or kings-up.

When you are deciding whether to stay or drop, and when betting is normal, mathematics is an excellent guide. When players begin raising and reraising, mathematics goes out the window.

Nevertheless, every poker player who aspires to be accomplished should know the odds against improving on various draws, and he should not forget to compare those odds against the odds offered by the pot. This may seem so fundamental that it is hardly worth mentioning, but not one poker player in a hundred bothers with these figures, and the vast majority of all losses suffered in poker games can be attributed to sticking around when the pot offers shorter odds than the odds against improvement.

PSYCHOLOGY AND BLUFFING

I wish I could write something useful on the subject of poker psychology, but I cannot. I have read literally thousands of pages on the subject, and learned nothing. It is interesting for a poker addict to read about this or that type of player; what their habits are and how to detect them; but from a practical standpoint it is all bosh.

Poker psychology is a matter of special aptitude. You have it or you don't. If you have it, nobody has to teach you, and if you don't have it, nobody can. All I have ever been able to say on the subject is this: If you are being consistently outguessed, you aren't going to be able to do too much about it. It is no disgrace to lack the knack, but there is no remedy. I will give advice on bluffing, but it will be very general. Only through experience can one really master the art.

Fortunately, it is possible to be a consistent winner in a poker game even if one or two other players surpass you in the intuition (or whatever it is) that gives one player ascendancy over another. If you have better technique (knowledge of the game and application of that knowledge) and if you are more conservative (which means playing only when it is mathematically sound to do so) you can still beat the intuitive player who tosses his chips away in curiosity or overoptimism. If the majority of your opponents are equal or superior to you in technique and can also outguess you, that is simply no game for you!

Part of what I said about psychology can also be applied to the art of bluffing, and it *is* an art, never think it isn't; but bluffing does lend itself to a considerable amount of advice and standard rules, which I will discuss here.

First, and most important, you *must* bluff sometimes. I know that some players are temperamentally unsuited to bluffing and find it repugnant, but it is an essential part of the game. If you never bluff, that fact soon becomes noticed, and you do not get called on your good hands. If you never get called on your good hands, you are unlikely to win.

The literature of poker takes a standard attitude toward bluffing. "Bluffing is advertising," it shouts. "When you bluff, expect to lose; your reward is that you will then get called on your good hands."

I have always agreed with the conclusion but I have never been able to stomach the premise.

In my opinion, every bet you make in poker should be made for one purpose only: To win the pot. I admit that bluffing is a losing game at best, because in poker the best hand usually wins the pot, but I still feel that every bluff should be so designed as to have the best possible chance to win.

There are two purposes to bluffing: (1) To create constant doubt in the minds of opponents, so they cannot be sure you have a good hand when you bet and will call the bets you make legitimately on strong hands; and (2) to win the pot because the bluff succeeds and all other players drop.

Bluffing pays dividends even when you show no profit on those hands, because it accomplishes purpose (1); but if in the long run you lose more than a very small amount by your bluffs, it is better not to bluff at all.

My advice on bluffing policy is as follows: At the start of the game or session, do not bluff. If you are getting called on your good hands, continue not to bluff. After two or three cases in which you do not get called, begin to bluff. After two cases in which you have bluffed and have been caught, stop bluffing until again you find that you are not being called on your good hands.

Scientific bluffing requires a knowledge of position, which I will discuss next. Most of all, however, it requires a certain amount of conscious thought. It is not a matter of inspiration.

The primary question to ask yourself before making any bluff is: Is this precisely the way I would play the strong hand I pretend to have, if I really had it? If the answer is no, and the game is fairly strong, you will lose by bluffing.

Plan your bluff in advance. Imagine a particular hand you would like to hold and imagine the most skillful way you could play that hand. Then, assuming that you hold the hand you wish to represent, bet throughout as if you held that hand. The most frequent bluff, by far, is also the most futile bluff. A player draws one card to a straight or flush possibility, fails to fill, and stubbornly bets anyway. This is a bad bluff for a liberal player. It is a good bluff only for a conservative player who almost never draws to a straight or flush possibility, and even that player must be careful not to bluff into a hand that may comprise two fairly high pairs, because his one-card draw will usually be figured for a two-pair hand. He will get a call that is not simply suspicious but is quite valid.

The next most frequent bluff—and almost as futile for a good player—is the one in which a player with a single pair fakes three-of-a-kind by raising before the draw, drawing two cards, and then betting. If it is a planned bluff, he may have a two-card draw to a flush or straight rather than to a pair. Before considering this bluff, make sure that if you actually did hold three-of-a-kind you would play in exactly the same way. A bluff must almost always be planned from the start of the hand. If it is based on a later impulse it is not apt to fool a good player, because he will find some inconsistency in the way the hand was played at the start.

This brings us to another cliché of poker, but it is a valid one: It is easier to bluff a good player than a poor player. For example, a poor player will often stay in on a low pair and draw two cards to that pair and an ace kicker. Don't try to bluff him by drawing two cards—he will be too suspicious of an unsound act he is capable of performing himself.

Always most effective among bluffs is the pat-hand bluff. It is most effective if you have simply played without raising when you are close to the opener, or when there is obviously a chance that several players may stay or even raise after you. For this kind of bluff, if you do get a later opportunity you must raise, and if the pot has previously been raised, you must reraise. It is logical with a pat hand to try to "suck in" as many players as possible, and if there is any false note—if you would not have played a genuine pat hand in exactly the same way—it is a bad bluff.

The pat-hand bluff is fortified by an occasional instance in which you stand pat with three-of-a-kind or perhaps with aces-up or kings-up. The odds are 9 to 1 against improving three-of-a-kind, which usually will win without improvement anyway, and 11 to 1 against improving aces-up, which also will usually win without improvement. So, if you have been caught with one or two pat-hand bluffs, you help to keep the opponents guessing by repeating your action when you have a fair hand that will probably win on its own. But the important thing to remember is that all these stratagems are designed to keep the opponents guessing—not to be an integral part of your effort to win. The basic objective in poker is still and will remain the effort to win as much as possible when you have the best hand.

You will often hear it said that bluffing depends largely on the stakes in the game—that you cannot bluff successfully in a low-limit game, and that you can bluff successfully in a high-limit or table-stakes game. There is not a great deal to this. Perhaps, in a wide-open low-limit game among relatively poor players, it is hard to get away with a bluff when there is perhaps $15 or $20 in the pot and all you can bet is $2. But in a good game this does not necessarily apply. A good player doesn't want to waste any chips, no matter how few. The mathematical considerations that apply to staying in the pot do not apply to calling a final bet. If there is $20 in the pot and you can draw cards for $2, you are getting odds of 10 to 1, and your chance of improving is likely to be considerably better than that. But when it comes to calling a final bet, there are no odds except those offered by the pot against the chance of a bluff. Either the player has what he represents, or he hasn't. If he has what he represents, any chips put in the pot are thrown away. The difficulty in bluffing in a good game is that a good opponent is all the more likely to read your bluff and call whether the pot is big or small.

However, the *amount* of a bluffing bet is important. Too small a bet will seldom have the desired effect. A very large bet is too risky; if the player you are trying to bluff happens to have made a big hand, you will be called, and your loss will be all out of proportion to your possible gain.

For example: There is $30 in the pot; you are playing table stakes, and both you and your opponents have ample chips. You bet $100. This is too much to risk to win $30 (the best you can do, for if you are called, you lose). Both Jacoby and Coffin, in their books on poker, advise betting the size of the pot; in this case, $30. This is a normal bet and should not in itself arouse suspicion; and if you have at least an even chance, in your estimation, of winning by your bluff, you have made a reasonable bet because you stand to win as much as you stand to lose.

In a low-limit game, a bluff will seldom succeed unless it is planned from the start; usually this means a pat-hand bluff. For example: A passes, B opens, C plays, E plays and all the others drop. B draws three cards, C stands pat, E draws three cards. B checks and C bets. C has played exactly as he would play a pat straight or flush; he would not raise immediately because he would not want to drive other players out. This bluff, if it is one, has a good chance to succeed.

A bluff rarely succeeds against more than two players, and then (in draw poker) only when each drew three cards. However, the opener can often succeed in the following bluff: C opens, D, E and F play. C draws one card, D and E draw three each, F draws one. C bets; he has drawn one card to a pair of queens and is bluffing. D or E might call if it were not for F's one-card draw, but each is afraid F has filled and can raise. D and E drop, F has not filled (or has two low pairs) and drops, and C wins. (How did C know F had not filled? He knew, that's all; and a player who does not know should not try such bluffs.)

The big-bet bluff does usually win, simply because it isn't worth while for a serious player to call it. If you bet a $50 or $100 stack to win a $10 or $12 pot, you will get away with it more often than not. The difficulty is that even if your bluffs are not detected, every now and then you are going to run up against a hand that is good enough for a call on its merits, not on suspicion, and you are likely to lose back more than you pick up in that succession of small pots.

Bluffing in stud is different from bluffing in draw poker in one important respect. In stud, your bluff must represent some particular hole card with which you would have played as you did.

A bluff in stud poker can be either a planned bluff or an unexpected bluff that develops from the end situation.

In the planned bluff, the player represents a certain hand throughout and never deviates from the course he would have followed if he had actually had that hand.

In the unplanned bluff, the player winds up with a losing hand but suddenly realizes that he would have played the same way on a different, winning hand. He then bets as though he had that winning hand. For example, A has a six in the hole and 6-10-8-A showing; B has a king in the hole and J-10-K-5 showing. A bets and B drops. This is a semi-bluff, because A might actually have the winning hand (but if he has, he will not get a call anyway). B is justified in figuring A for an ace. If more than one ace has shown, this bluff may lose; if A has raised previously, the bluff should not be attempted. If B is a poor or a wild player who doesn't do much thinking, the bluff will probably lose.

When you are trying to spot another player's bluff, you have to depend on your judgment of the player more than on anything else; but one principle to keep in mind is this: You can't always trust the man who bets or raises, but you can nearly always trust the man who calls. Suppose you are C, the third man to speak. A, the first man, bets; B calls. Before worrying about beating A, pause to wonder if you can beat B. *He* isn't bluffing.

WHEN TO BLUFF

Do bluff against: (1) A player who was losing earlier, but now is ahead. (He won't risk becoming a loser again.) (2) A player who has lost successively, by close margins, on the type of hand he probably has this time. (3) A player who does not customarily call in the situation you find yourself in at the moment. (4) A good player whom you have successfully bluffed before.

Do not bluff against: (1) A player who has called well over half the previous bluffs against him. (Assume he can "read" you, even though you do not know how.) (2) A player who may be able to beat the hand you have represented yourself to have.

(3) A suspicious or curious player who consistently calls. (Usually this means any poor player. A good player can often be bluffed, a poor player seldom can.) (4) Anyone, when you are losing heavily.

Even when you have built up your bluffs skillfully, and though you choose your victims carefully, you will lose many of your bluffs — enough to get yourself the "advertising" that brings you calls on your good hands. If you can win half your bluffs, or nearly so, it is winning practice. If you lose substantially more than half your bluffs, quit bluffing.

When a player bluffs and wins, he should rarely show his hand, no matter how strong the impulse to gloat. There will be plenty of time to show his bluffing hands when he loses.

I will have more to say about bluffing from time to time as we go along. At this point I want to repeat a statement that may not have received enough notice when I said it the first time: You are unlikely to be a winning poker player if you never bluff; you must bluff from time to time, win or lose. But whenever you bluff, try to win. (For a different outlook on the theory of bluffing, see Chapter 9.)

POSITION

Position in poker is a matter of the number of players who can still act after you. Playing position is a matter of taking into consideration what those players may do before you decide what to do yourself.

Position is a mystery to most poker players. But, next to the relative value of your hand, it is the most important matter for a poker player to think about in the game.

In a poker game you will have bad hands, fair hands, and good hands. The bad hands you will throw away. The very good hands will win for you, but you will not hold them often. The winnings on them will be of great importance only in certain rare cases when you will be lucky enough to hold a very good hand against a hand that is almost as good, such as four-of-a-kind against a high full house — and remember that such a case can go against you as easily as for you. The fair hands represent the bulk of your winnings and losses, and your success in playing such hands will depend largely on your understanding of position.

Cases arise constantly when you must consider your position as well as your hand, but at all times there are two main positional objects: (1) you want to be the last to act, if possible; (2) you don't want to get caught between two players who may have betting or raising hands. In a close case, play along when your position is good, and drop when your position is bad.

Take a case in draw poker in which there will be at most three active players, A, B, and C. A has opened and B has raised. C should usually either reraise or drop. If C simply calls, his position is bad. The normal process will be for A to check after the draw and for B to bet. Now, if C calls, even though he may think he has B beaten, he risks the danger that A can beat him and may even raise back. However, if C reraises before the draw, he makes his position good because, normally, A and B will check to him after the draw and he can have a free checkout if he has not improved.

In a similar game, A opens, B and C call, and D raises. It is probable that there will be no players after D, in which case he will have the advantage of being the last to speak.

In stud poker, good position is to the right of the high "board" (cards showing) since you will then be last to act.

The player who is last to bet invariably has an advantage. Skillful play consists largely in watching for opportunities to make your decision as late as possible; and dropping in all doubtful cases when other players will make their decisions after you.

At the start, the dealer in draw poker has the best seat; the player at his left has the worst and is said to be "under the guns."

Coincidentally, the opener of a pot accepts the worst position after the draw. For this reason it is best not to open a pot if it is possible that another player will do so.

In draw poker, because it is an advantage to be last, you should try to avoid opening (betting first) if you can get anyone else to do it for you. The closer the opener is to your left, the better your position will be after the draw. The closer the opener or the last raiser is to your right, the worse is your position after the draw, because the more likely you are to find yourself between a betting hand on the right and a doubtful quantity on the left.

The best seat is in front of players who open freely and raise freely, and behind any sandbaggers (players who pass strong hands and then raise when someone else opens). "Openers to your left, sandbaggers to your right." This is especially true in a limit game.

A player should make no bet, raise or call without considering how many players still have a chance to act, and what they may do. In general, do not play on a hand that is barely good enough when someone after you may raise.

For example: Draw poker with seven players. A passes, B opens, C holds a pair of kings. C should drop. There are five players behind him (including A, who has another chance). If C plays and anyone raises, he will not be strong enough to meet the raise and will have lost what it cost him to play.

But if A passes, B opens, C and D drop, and E and F play, G should play on queens. If G drops, A should play on jacks. G will be last bettor after the draw if A drops, which is likely; A will surely be last. As last bettor, either will have the opportunity to judge the strength of the other hands before making a decision after the draw.

Whenever a player raises before the draw (in draw poker), or in any case in stud poker, the next player is in a poor position, and as a general rule should drop unless he too would have been strong enough to raise.

PLAYING POSITION

In stud poker, the player who takes the lead sacrifices a positional advantage. The exception is when all the active players speak before him. For example, A has the high hand showing, and it seems likely that he will continue to have. B and C are in

the pot. D is the last of the active players. He sacrifices no position when he bets or raises, because the tendency thereafter will
be for the other players to check to him and he will have full freedom of action.

Remember that position, important as it is, should affect your
play only on hands that are already questionable. When you have
the best hand in either draw or stud, you usually have to bet it
regardless of your position.

Here are some everyday examples of position play.

In most draw poker games, a player in an early position should
seldom open unless he is so strong that he wants to invite a raise
so that he can reraise, and even then he is usually better off to
pass in a "pass and back in" game.

When the opener is at your right, you ordinarily just play along
on a very strong hand, such as a pat straight, because you do not
want to drive out other players; yet if you are one of the last to
speak, you raise. In either case you are playing position.

The converse case is the one in which you hold a fair two pairs
next to the opener, and raise to drive out other players, on the
grounds that a two-pair hand is usually the best before the draw
but is hard to improve, and it suffers a sharp diminution of winning chances every time another player comes in. With this hand,
you would not necessarily raise if you were in a late position, so
again you are playing position. In fact, your position is so poor—
you cannot stand a raise either before or after the draw—that if
the nature of the game makes a raise potentially unprofitable, you
should probably *drop* two pairs (up to tens) when next to the
opener. It is exactly the same in stud poker. When you are next
to the high hand showing, you will simply call or check, but if
you are far away from the high hand you will raise; again you are
playing position.

A good bluff depends more on position than on any other
factor. Strangely enough, it is not the usual "good" position that
you want for a successful bluff; more often you should choose
what would ordinarily be bad position. For example, when there
are four players in the pot, the last player is in good position for

playing a fair hand but in bad position for bluffing. Those other three players, who checked to him, all have the right to call, and because they all checked, none will be afraid of the others. (However, at table stakes, where the *amount* of a bet may be varied, "good position" is also good bluffing position.)

The most successful bluff is one that makes the most dangerous opponent think he is "in the middle." He may then drop the only hand good enough for a call, for fear that one of the next players can beat him.

For example: Draw poker, seven players, pass and out. A and B drop. C opens, D drops, E stays, F raises, G and C stay. E now raises, and he stands pat and bets after the draw. F is likely to drop a fair hand because he cannot tell what G and C will do. G and C are likely to drop against a pat hand anyway. (In this case, however, if the game is conservative, E's bluff is dangerous, because there may be many strong hands around the table.)

MONEY-MANAGEMENT

Seasoned poker players will usually assure you that money-management is at least as important as any other factor in skillful play. Many of them say that it is the most important single factor. I am going to start this section with a few general but absolutely essential statements.

Courage is perhaps the most important single factor in the make-up of a poker player. While courage alone cannot transform you into a good player, you can *never* hope to be a winning player if you are cowardly in your approach to the game.

You should play poker to win; playing to avoid a loss puts you at a disadvantage. An ultraconservative player who does not back his good hands to the limit is a sure loser in the long run, for he will never take maximum advantage of his skill.

Poker is a game of percentages. To be a winning player, you must increase the amount bet when the odds are in your favor. But don't expect to win every hand you contest! You are bound to lose some of your good hands to better hands. There will also be many hands which you must throw in. These represent a loss — the amount you must pay in antes (your "overhead"). You must overcome these two forms of loss by winning as much as possible on your good hands. You give up just as much by winning less than the maximum, as by losing more than necessary on your bad hands. An overcautious player is under a tremendous handicap once he starts losing. He either lives in fear of further losses and tends to drop out too quickly, or he calls too often in a desperate attempt to recoup.

I cannot teach you courage, but I can tell you how to reduce the evil of fear through proper money-management. You cannot play well if the stakes are dangerous for you. Therefore, if the amount involved in a particular game frightens you away from your normal style, you must make certain adjustments (or else avoid such games!).

At the outset, set aside the amount of money you are willing to lose. Be honest with yourself in this respect. You must be able to play through the game as if your stake were unlimited. Allow yourself full freedom of action to the extent of your financial capabilities. If you should lose your stake, quit the game!

If you manage your stake carefully and honestly, you will avoid losing through fear, and you will be over the first hurdle on the road to winning.

This brings up the factor of *the amount you are willing to risk.* Proprietors of gambling houses used to say that their principal advantage came from the fact that "a sucker will sit and lose more than he will sit and win." It is necessary to limit your losses. When you are losing, you are probably playing poorly anyway; your standards are distorted in your anxiety to get even. The most widespread mistake in money-management is to quit a game when ahead and to sit out long hours of a futile losers' game when behind.

Figure what your capital is. In any one game you should not lose more than five per cent, or at the very most ten per cent, of that capital. The game selected should be one in which you will get a fair early play for your maximum appropriation — perhaps one or one and one-half or two stacks, but when you have lost that amount you should quit the game. When you are winning, you should stay as long as you want to, or as long as you can keep on winning. Suppose your capital is $500. You should join a game in which you can probably play for an hour or so on $20 to $30, even if you are holding nothing, but in no case should you let yourself lose more than $50.

Having gotten ahead, you should salt away your capital and play from that point on the other fellow's money. At the very least it is psychologically disturbing to wind up a loser after having been well ahead; and any psychological hazard reduces your effectiveness.

Always use the same method of money-management. A method of play is either right or wrong. If the method isn't right, you shouldn't adopt it in the first place. If it is right, you shouldn't deviate simply because you are feeling down in the dumps because of your unlucky streak, or overconservative because you want to hang on to your winnings. A good rule is this: If, midway in the game, you find that more than once you are doing something you wouldn't have done on the very first hand, such as playing when ordinarily you would have dropped, or failing to bet or raise or call when ordinarily you would have done so, that is a good time to quit the game. And remember to be honest with yourself!

Now, as to your money-management in a particular game, there are two main approaches to the question of betting. One type of player likes to wait for a big hand and play it for a killing. He tries to build up the pot when he is pretty sure he will win it. If he can't build up the pot, he doesn't particularly care how much he wins. The other type of player looks for a lot of action, and plays whenever he thinks he has the odds in his favor. He is in many more pots than the first type, and of course wins more pots, but he invests more going into pots he doesn't win. I don't mean that he plays bad hands (because then he wouldn't win), but he is content with a succession of small profits.

Since good poker players have followed both lines, obviously there is something to be said for each of them. Much more, however, depends on the game you are playing. In some games, you are forced into one line of play or the other.

Take a draw poker game with a low limit and an ante every pot, or a blind opening — say a blind-opening game in which the dealer antes $1, the next player opens blind for $1, the next player raises to $2. It costs you $4 per round just to sit in the game. In such circumstances you cannot be too conservative. You must be in there every time the odds favor you, even slightly.

For example, in an eight-handed game, a pair of aces is likely to be the best hand going in, and the best hand going in is mathematically likely to be the best in the showdown. If you hold aces or better, you have to open even if you sacrifice some position by doing so, because you must get your full share of the $4 pots that start off every deal. There are two reasons why this is forced upon you. The cost per round will eat you up otherwise, and the low limit prevents your being badly hurt even when someone has a better hand or draws out on you.

At the opposite side of the problem is the typical stud poker game. Here there is almost never an ante, so there is no overhead. You can afford to "play them very close," waiting for the best hand at the table before you bet at all. Assuming that you do not suffer socially, you can sit for an hour without ever playing except when you are high and must make the first bet.

In a table-stakes game, when the bets are usually low but can rise to extremely high levels, you have a choice of tactics. It is in such games that players who wait for a killing are the ones who flourish.

The basis of money-management is to avoid the occasional cases in which you are tempted to toss in a chip or two to see what will happen — on a hunch, or because you are bored, or because you just won a big pot. If a bet is unsound it figures to lose, and in the course of a long session you can throw away an appalling amount of money in these occasional lapses. Self-discipline is important to a poker player.

Many players waste their stacks of chips by failure to anticipate later developments. For example, you are playing in a
game with a high ante and a low limit, so that you find yourself
able to stay in for $1 or $2 when there is already $10 or $15 in
the pot. At the moment it seems very attractive, because you
are getting 7 to 1 or more, and you have perhaps a low pair that
has one chance in four or five to improve to the probable winning
hand. But if you know your game, you may know that the players
are liberal and that there are going to be two or three raises and
reraises before it actually comes to a draw. You have to decide
in advance if your hand is good enough to stand those raises.
Obviously, a low pair isn't good enough, and you save $1 by
getting out fast. ·

Another thing to remember is that every raise shortens the
odds. Here is a simple illustration based on the game mentioned
before. You have a $1 ante by the dealer, a $1 blind opening by
A, and a $2 blind raise by B. If C opens (in effect) by raising to
$3, and all the others drop, B can come in for $1 and get 7 to 1
on his money. There is $7 in the pot and he need put in only $1.
If another player raises to $4, the pot goes up to $11, but it
costs him $2 to stay and now he is getting only $5\frac{1}{2}$ to 1. And so on,
every time there is a raise.

Some authorities advocate adopting a strict system and sticking to it. That would be excellent if there were such a system,
but I'm afraid there isn't. A system can cover precisely the times
when you should play or raise or drop, but it can't cover the
questions of judgment that are bound to arise sooner or later—
whether or not to call, whether or not someone is bluffing or
underestimating his hand. You can lose enough by misjudging
these situations to offset the advantages of the system.

The most nearly foolproof system I have seen is the one
advocated by the excellent poker writer and player who writes
under the name of Jack King. He applies it to table-stakes stud.
If he plays at all, it is because he believes he has the best hand
at the time, and then he pushes in his entire stack. If his appraisal of his hand is correct (as it almost always will be), he has

the best chance of winning. This is a simple application of the rule that the best hand going in will probably be the best hand coming out. But there is the social drawback (in an informal game the other players probably won't like this system); and possibly they can beat the system anyway by calling only when they are pretty sure you have overrated your hand. If they learn to do this, your winning pots are mostly peanuts, and you can lose back a lot when you go wrong.

Nevertheless, table stakes creates a completely different set of standards in money-management. When circumstances are such that you can bet your entire stack, you assure yourself of a showdown without further risk or problems, and if other players have bigger stacks, one or more of them may have to drop out later on, when, if he had stayed, he might have outdrawn you.

I would like to add just one personal comment on money-management. Nothing upsets it so much as playing a "friendly game," in which there are certain players against whom you are not supposed to do your worst. To make the percentages work correctly, you have to be able to win the maximum when you have a winning hand, no matter whether the player with the losing hand is your friend or your enemy. It is unethical— worse, it is considered a form of cheating as bad as stacking the cards—to enter into collusion with another player to trap a third. Therefore, you have no compensating gain from your agreement. It isn't always possible to avoid such situations, but stay away from them as well as you can.

CARD MEMORY AND ANALYSIS

There is less of the drudgery of counting and memory in poker than in other card games of skill, but unfortunately you will need some counting and memory even in poker. If you aren't capable of it, you can still be a pretty good player but you won't be a master player.

In stud poker, memory of cards is important. In draw poker, you don't have to remember many cards but you do have to analyze the special values of certain cards. In both games you have to remember and analyze certain things your opponents have done. I will take these up one by one.

Memory in stud poker. The stud player simply has to remember what cards have shown and have been folded. Otherwise he won't know the chances that a particular opponent has a particular hole card. Also, he won't know his own chance of improving.

Here is an oversimplified illustration. (Maybe it wouldn't occur more than once in a hundred years, but related cases turn up every day.) You have four-of-a-kind. Your opponent shows 10-8-7-6, all hearts. If you don't know or don't remember that the nine of hearts showed and folded in another player's hand, you don't know you have a cinch hand. And, as a noted card authority once remarked, "You can't remember a card you didn't see." So you have to watch everything and remember everything. I will explain the practical application of this when I discuss stud poker.

Analysis in draw poker. From the cards in your own hand you can often draw conclusions about opposing hands. Suppose you stay against a player who opened — only the two of you in the pot. He draws three cards. You draw three cards to Q-Q-A-K-6. You make three queens. He bets, you raise; he probably had you beaten with aces or kings going in, but your holding of the ace and the king reduced his chance of making three-of-a-kind in either rank, and he probably bet on two pairs. If your hand had been Q-Q-8-5-3, you might have called instead of raising.

Watching the opponents' play. This is a special knack for some players, as I said in the section on psychology, but every player can cultivate the knack if he does so consciously. You must deliberately say to yourself (silently, of course): "Joe stayed against a showing ace when he had a six down and a jack up," or "Joe stayed against two opponents when he had a pair of sixes." If you don't notice and analyze this information consciously, you are far less likely to remember it.

In this connection it is a good idea to insist on one of the universal laws of poker: Every hand in the showdown, whether it wins or loses, must be shown. Though this is a universal rule, it is more honored in the breach than in the observance. In 99 per cent of all cases one player will say, "Kings-up," and flash his hand briefly; the other will say, "That's good," and throw his hand away without showing it. I admit that you will profit from doing the same when it is *your* hand that would have to be shown; but when it is somebody else's hand, you can legally ask to see it, and in most games you won't make yourself unpopular by doing so—especially if you pretend that you're just curious.

One should watch and catalog, as systematically as possible, the characteristics of every other player in the game. Even in a strong game, in which every player is supposed to know his way around, each of the following types will be encountered (for each represents a supportable style of poker play, depending on the temperament of the player):

The player who opens whenever he can, bets out (or raises) when he thinks he has the best hand, and in general tries to win as many pots as possible even if the winnings per pot are small.

The sandbagger, who seldom opens unless he is dealer or near to it, who calls or raises only when he is in good position to do so, and who checks strong hands after the draw in order to raise a bet. The general policy of this player is to build up his winning pots to large proportions, even though it means he will often win little—or nothing, if the pot is not opened—on his good hands.

The bluffer, whose general style may be either of the above, and who frequently bets a weak hand in precisely the same way that he would a strong one, from beginning to end. He won't stay in for a bad draw; but if he fails to fill, he'll often bet as though he had. Pointless bluffing is a losing game, but some players are sufficiently skillful at it to make it pay.

The free player, who almost always stays in on a high pair or a draw to a straight or flush, and who invariably stays in on two pairs. This is the one style of play, of those described here, that stands to lose in a game in which the majority of the players are more conservative.

Then too there is the sucker, who stays in from curiosity and calls "to keep the game honest." Such a player is seldom a problem. It is necessary only to remember not to try to bluff him.

It is probably futile to advise it, because so few players will follow the advice, but it is well worthwhile to keep a written record of the playing habits of each person against whom you play frequently, adding to it each bit of new evidence that has arisen in the most recent game. Writing such data down will probably fix the facts in your memory.

Against a strange opponent it is sometimes worthwhile to make a play that is somewhat unsound, when the information to be gained will offset the additional risk of losing. For example: You open a pot on queens-up. The stranger plays along, and you are the only two in the pot. You draw one card, do not improve, and check. He draws three cards and makes a moderate bet. You call, though it is a bad call, for you have two extrinsic advantages: (1) You see his hand and learn what sort of strength he bets on in such cases (including the possibility that he is bluffing); and (2) you give him the impression that you are a "small caller" and so discourage him from trying to bluff you on future hands. You will probably lose this pot, and for that reason would not call if his bet were a large one; but you may win.

I will have much more to say on the subject of card memory and analysis when I discuss the particular games, which I will now take up one by one.

HOW
TO PLAY
HIGH POKER

IN THIS CHAPTER I give advice on how to play both draw poker and stud poker for high. High poker, the original form of the game, still enjoys tremendous popularity despite the rise of the more modern forms. No player can be considered experienced unless he has completely mastered the basic principles of high poker.

At the outset I wish to issue a warning to the high players who, considering themselves satisfactorily prepared for this form of poker, may not pay proper attention to the material in this chapter, in their haste to reach the more complicated forms — especially high-low poker. There is no more important education for a high-low player than a firm grounding in the principles of the more basic forms. Do not skip over material here which seems "old hat." The firmer your understanding of each and every form of poker, the more capable you will be to become a winning player when you enter a game that is comparatively new to you.

DRAW POKER FOR HIGH

There are many forms of draw poker, and I will have something to say about several of them, but there are a few considerations that apply to every form of this game, and I will discuss these first.

1. *The draw.* If your object is merely to improve your hand, there is no question that you are best off making the maximum draw—that is, three cards when you have a pair, or two cards when you have three-of-a-kind.

That, however, does not resolve the entire question. Many times your object will not be simply to improve your hand. Perhaps you will need some specific degree of improvement, and perhaps it will be more important to deceive the other players than to improve.

First consider the case in which you need some specific degree of improvement. Suppose you know, no matter how, that you'll need two very high pairs—preferably aces-up—to have a chance of winning the pot. You have a pair, but it isn't high enough, even if you catch another pair. Your three unmatched cards include an ace. This is a classic case. Should you draw three cards to the pair, or should you draw two cards to the pair and the ace kicker?

If you hold the ace kicker, the odds are only about 4 to 1 against your getting aces-up or better. If you do not hold the ace kicker, the odds are about $5\frac{1}{2}$ to 1 against your getting aces-up or better. This is one of the rare cases in which it pays to hold a kicker. But you have to be quite sure that aces-up, specifically, is the hand you want. Every so often, when you do make aces-up by holding the kicker, your opponent will fill his full house and ruin you (this will happen almost precisely once in 12 times) and your three-card draw will give you about ten times as good a chance of making an even better hand and beating him on those few occasions. Holding the ace kicker is almost the only case I know in which a special draw has a mathematical advantage over the customary draw, and even here I know many good poker players who would rather draw three cards to the pair and take their chances on the many added opportunities to draw a still better hand—three-of-a-kind, or a full house, or even four-of-a-kind.

Now suppose your purpose is not to improve but to keep the opponents guessing. This case arises chiefly when your original hand is probably better than any hand another player will draw. The simplest possible example (but probably the least useful) would arise when you are dealt four-of-a-kind. (It is the least useful example because it will happen so seldom.) You have a choice between drawing one card and standing pat. Your decision depends entirely upon the betting before the draw. If the betting includes two or three raises, and you think there are strong hands out against you, your best chance is to stand pat. You will then be figured for a straight, since straights constitute well over 50 per cent of all the pat hands that are dealt. A player who makes a high straight, a flush, or a full house, will surely call a bet, will usually stand a raise, and with the better hands will reraise and then call your second raise. However, if you are up against weak hands before the draw and have simply raised once, you are better off to draw one card. You will then get a call on a high two pairs, a possible raise on three-of-a-kind, and tremendous action on a full house, especially if it is a high one.

As I said, knowledge of how to play a pat four-of-a-kind isn't going to be of much consequence in your practical poker play. Knowledge of how to draw to three-of-a-kind is going to be of tremendous importance.

If there were not so many exceptions—poker being a game of infinite variety—I would say flatly that for tactical purposes one card should always be drawn to three-of-a-kind even though mathematics favors the two-card draw. Very seldom do you have a chance to play three-of-a-kind any differently from two pairs before the draw. Getting called after the draw may depend largely on making the other players think your hand was two pairs rather than three-of-a-kind going in. A one-card draw represents a special advantage in draw poker, and any player who draws one card and is in any kind of good position will find the other players checking to him, giving him the maximum opportunity to make the best decision.

The important things to remember about three-of-a-kind are these: Unless you have more than three opponents, your hand will probably be best at the showdown even if you do not improve it. While a two-card draw gives you a much better chance to make four-of-a-kind and a slightly better chance to show some improvement, in most instances it would not matter if you drew one card or two cards or stood pat, you would still win.

Therefore, the draw to three-of-a-kind is partly a matter of your individual tactics and your recent history in the game. If you have not represented the hand too strongly before the draw, and if you are a player who has been detected once or twice recently drawing two cards to a pair and a kicker, then the two-card draw will be tactically best. Your chance of improvement is at the maximum and you are likely to get called by players who suspect you of bluffing.

Another time to draw two cards—to afford the maximum chance of improvement—is when your betting has revealed that you held triplets (for example: you have reraised before the draw). If you have been called on one or two pat-hand bluffs, that is an admirable time to stand pat on three-of-a-kind. You will probably win without improvement, and you may get a call. But, year in and year out, without background, the one-card draw will work out best.

A four-card straight or flush cannot possibly represent any problem. You draw one card. Ninety-nine per cent of the time, two pairs represent no problem either; you draw one card. There is a very slight exception in the case of two pairs. If you have two pairs that will probably win without improvement (for example, against one or two players who have not represented any great strength before the draw) and if you think they might suspect you of a pat-hand bluff, you might consider occasionally standing pat on your two high pairs, which should be no lower than queens-up. In fact it is good tactics to do this occasionally to lend variety to your game and to keep the opponents guessing, both when you have a genuine pat hand and when you are trying a pat-hand bluff. But be sure to treat this as a method of bluffing, not as a legitimate method of playing poker. Like anything unnatural in poker, it will not win if employed too often.

Aces occupy a unique place in poker. Against one opponent, and often against two, aces have a better-than-even chance to win unimproved. If you are the last man to speak before the draw, and two other players are in, and you have a pair of aces, you might consider simply staying in and drawing one card. This is especially effective as the aftermath of two or three conspicuous cases in which you have drawn to a straight or flush possibility and have failed to fill. If both players before you draw three cards, you draw one and bet. You may get a suspicious call from one of the three-card draws, even if he does not improve. The odds against your improving aces on a one-card draw are less than 5 to 1, while the odds are $2\frac{1}{2}$ to 1 against you even on a three-card draw. Such a mathematical disadvantage can often be sustained in the interests of better tactics. (However, don't sacrifice this much of your improvement potential unless the "set-up" — including past history — is perfect.)

Freak draws. In one sense, these should hardly be worth discussing. If you must make a freak draw, you shouldn't have been in there in the first place. Nevertheless, occasions do arise (some of them legitimately) when you have to make a freak draw, and the following general advice can be given:

A five-card draw is incredible, even when (as in many blind-opening games) you got 7 to 1 odds to go in against one opponent.

It is better to draw four to an ace (if the rules of the game permit a four-card draw) than to draw three to an ace-king.

It is better to draw to three cards in sequence, if A-K-Q or K-Q-J or Q-J-10, than to draw to a three-flush, such as J-8-7 of diamonds. One of the possibilities is that you will make one high pair or two pairs and will win, while the chance of making the actual straight or flush is almost too remote to be considered.

The draw of one card to an inside straight is nearly always wrong. The odds against filling are almost 11 to 1. Few are the hands that do not offer at least as good odds on making a single high or two pairs if you simply throw away all the unlikely cards and draw four cards to the highest card, or three cards to some freak combination such as a king and jack of the same suit. The inside straight is justly notorious in poker. Almost the only case in which you should draw one card to an inside straight is the case in which you hold something like 9-8-6-5 or lower and know that even pairing your high cards will not give you a chance to win. Even so, you can draw four cards to your highest card and have a 1-in-12 chance to make two pairs or better—the same chance as when you draw one card to an inside straight.

In Chapter 8 there are tables of the mathematical odds that give your exact chances on most of these combinations.

I have paid no attention here to the question of drawing when there is a wild card in the game, such as the bug or the joker, because all such cases will be taken up separately.

2. *The strength of your hand.* The first thing to remember in draw poker, and in nearly any poker game, is that the best hand going in is usually the best hand coming out. (This can scarcely be repeated too often.) The next thing to remember is that the more players who stay against the best hand, the fewer pots it will win but the more money it will win. The sole exception is the case of two low pairs—a special hand I will discuss separately.

The strength of your hand in draw poker depends entirely on the number of players who have not dropped.

This has proved to be a difficult concept for many poker players, and I will try to explain it in this way:

Mathematicians have worked out the hand that is likely to be highest in a game of any given number of players—for example, eight players or four players or only two players. When a player before you has dropped out, from the mathematical standpoint you can forget that he was ever in the game. *Consider only the players who are yet to speak.* As a simple example, in an eight-handed game of draw poker it takes two aces to have a better-than-average chance of being the high hand; but if you are the seventh man, and the first six have already dropped, and you have only the eighth man to contend with, the mathematics of the situation becomes precisely the same as if you were playing in a two-handed game and the first six players had never existed. In that case two deuces or an A-K will have a better-than-even chance of being the high hand. (Note that this is of practical significance only in a "pass-and-out" game.)

If you have absorbed that, you can follow the table below, which tells what you have to hold to have a good chance against any given number of players who are yet to be heard from:

NUMBER OF PLAYERS YET TO SPEAK	HAND WITH BETTER THAN A 50% CHANCE OF BEING HIGH
6 or 7	two aces
5	two kings
4	two queens
3	two tens
2	two eights
1	two deuces or A-K high

In certain games in which the overhead is high (as explained in the section on "Money-Management"), you must make the opening bet on these 50%-plus hands to give yourself a better-than-average chance to win. In games in which the overhead is low, you can afford to be more conservative, and winning players usually are somewhat more conservative. For example, you can refuse to open in any but the last three positions on anything less than aces, and you can refuse to open in the last three positions on anything less than queens. I do that myself, except in a jackpots game, in which I will open in last or next-to-last position on the minimum of jacks and take my chances on the possibility that some earlier player was sandbagging. If I do open on jacks, and an earlier player stays and draws three cards, I tend to draw one card and bet, representing two pairs and trusting that my opponent will not have the acumen to raise me and force me to drop if he does not improve. If he raises me and I have not improved, I usually drop. Occasionally I may lose to a bluff, but I more than make it up in the cases in which I actually did have my two pairs or better and can legitimately call the bluff.

Every mathematical figure in poker must be modified by later information. The mathematicians work on the basis known as *a priori*, meaning before the expected event has actually happened. Most of poker would be termed by mathematicians *a posteriori*, meaning that the calculations are made when actual information is already available. If you are the last hand in a seven-man game, and the third man has opened and the fifth man has stayed and the others have dropped, you must know (if the game is reasonably strong) that there is at least a pair of kings out against you. You will not stay on less than two aces or two low pairs, in spite of any number of mathematical tables that tell you that two eights stand a chance to win against two opponents. However, in a wide-open game, in which a player cannot bear to throw away a pair of tens or a four-flush, you may choose to stay on a little less than if the game were conservative.

In a good game, no one bets against a one-card draw with less than three-of-a-kind or aces-up, and if the one-card draw bets or raises, no one raises it without a flush. If the one-card draw reraises, he filled at least an A-Q or A-K flush or a possible full house, and his raise cannot be reraised without at least jacks or queens full. The profits in poker come from getting a call when you have a slightly better hand than your opponent; they are dissipated chiefly by the occasional chip thrown away in staying on a losing hand or calling on a doubtful hand, but they can be as easily dissipated, and much faster, by giving a very strong hand a chance to raise or reraise, and then calling.

Here so much depends on appraising your opponent that it is hard to generalize. A poor player will become overly enthusiastic when he has a good hand; he will become almost unrestrainable when he has made that good hand by drawing to it, as for example when he draws to four diamonds headed by the queen and catches another diamond. It might be the better part of valor merely to call him on a low full house, but it would be stupid to drop a low full house or an A-Q flush on his second raise, on the grounds that an intelligent player would have been fearful even of *calling* with his hand. A very good player, however, when he raises the bet of a hand that represented two pairs going in and drew one card, should not be called on less than jacks or queens full. Against such a player, there will be a net gain in the long run by throwing away a straight.

I would say that when there is action in the pot, there are three hands worth staying on: Two aces, but no lower pair; if the aces improve, they have an excellent chance of being high. A straight or flush draw if the pot offers substantially more than the odds against filling—that is, 6 or 7 to 1, as against the 4 to 1 or 5 to 1 odds against filling. And, third, a good hand going in—no less than queens-up or a low three-of-a-kind. A lower pair than aces, and especially two low pairs, are candidates for the trash can.

3. *The play of two pairs.* Some authorities have said that 90 per cent of one's winnings or losses in poker can be attributed to the play of two low pairs (no higher than tens-up). This is undoubtedly an exaggeration but it serves to emphasize an important point.

The basic principle governing the play of two pairs is this: Before the draw, the odds are nearly 2 to 1 (in any draw game) that any two pairs will be the highest hand. But the odds are 11 to 1 against improving.

Mathematically, two low pairs have a better-than-average chance of standing up (without improvement) against one or two opponents; they stand to lose if three or more opponents are in the pot. Queens-up is the lowest hand that stands to win against three opponents, and aces-up against four opponents. This takes into consideration the chance (12 to 1 against you) of improving the two pairs you are dealt.

From this knowledge has been derived a general rule that has almost become a poker precept: If you have two pairs, raise at once, so as to drive out as many of the other players as possible.

It should be noted that this rule was designed for high-overhead, low-limit poker games. Many players feel that if the game is pot limit or table stakes, so that the potential reraise is higher than the initial raise, there is little to be gained even by *calling* with two low pairs in a poor position.

It is true that a raise tends to drive out other players, and that you want them driven out when you have two low pairs. Nevertheless, the rule is faulty. You should raise only when you are the second man (next to the opener). You should merely stay when two players are in before you. You should drop two low pairs when there are three players in before you. When I say two low pairs, I mean in this case anything less than queens-up. I am also assuming that the pot is offering you no more than 6 to 1. In a reasonably tight game, with two low pairs against three preceding players, the odds are better than 2 to 1 that one of them will improve and beat you even if none of them has you beaten going in — and my experience is that one of them probably *has* you beaten going in, because there simply aren't enough high pairs around to give each of three intelligent players a high pair that would justify his playing.

Taking the other side of the medal, much money is lost by failure to back two low pairs strongly enough against one or two players who drew three cards each. If you have created doubt in their minds by an occasional unsound one-card draw or bluff, and if you have stayed after both are in, a one-card draw and a bet may get a call from a hand that did not improve. When two opponents draw three cards each, it is better than even money that neither of them improved, and when you have a better-than-even shot and can get a call from an unimproved hand, you have a good bet. But if you are known as a man who would not play "on the come" in second position, or if it is known that you would not open on a mere possibility, or if you are in a jackpots game in which you could not legally do so, do not bet — no one will call unless he can beat you. You have to be the third man to speak.

In playing two pairs, the thing to watch out for chiefly is the case in which the opponent will not call unless he improved and can beat you. For example, you open on two pairs and draw one card. One player stays and draws three cards. If you do not improve, a bet is futile. He knows you would not have opened on less than two pairs, and he will not call unless he has improved and has at least two pairs himself. Against a good player, betting out on the opening hand in such a position leaves you wide open to a reraise, which can be a very successful bluff if your opponent has you figured correctly.

Two low pairs should seldom be opened (except in a very late position) in a "pass and back in" game. The absence of high cards in the hand makes it more likely that another player will have a high pair and will open; and of all hands, two pairs is the hand on which you want if possible to be the last to speak. Queens-up or better may be opened, and should be opened if the overhead is high and the antes are worth grabbing, but many good players simply do not open on any two-pair hand under aces-up if they are earlier than fourth from the dealer.

In a "pass and out" game, you must open on any two pairs in any position. Your hand figures to be the best around the table and you cannot afford to toss in the best hand. Just remember to be oh-so-careful in playing them afterward. Except in a wild game in which players raise on single pairs and four-flushes, no two pairs lower than kings-up can stand a raise.

Why do I establish queens-up as the minimum for two "high" pairs? Because in most games I have observed players opening on jacks and staying on queens. If one of these hands draws a second pair, you will want to have a chance.

I will summarize the play of two pairs in the average draw game. In a "pass and out" game, open. Next to the opener, raise. Separated by more than one active player from the opener, never raise and consider (depending on the game) whether or not you should drop. Do not stand a raise in any case in which three players are in the pot ahead of you, and do not stand a raise on less than jacks-up unless the raise was made by the player next to the opener. Even then, proceed with extreme caution.

Play of three-of-a-kind. In a game of draw poker, any three-of-a-kind figures to be best four times out of five, before the draw. The advantage of three-of-a-kind is that it will usually win without improvement, and if improved it may win a big pot. The disadvantage of three-of-a-kind is that the odds are at best (with a two-card draw) about $8\frac{1}{2}$ to 1 against improving, and since three-of-a-kind can be played strongly before the draw, the loss is heavy whenever another player draws out on you. A low three-of-a-kind is not worth betting (after the draw) against more than two three-card draws or against more than a single one-card draw.

For this reason, a low three-of-a-kind (lower than tens) should be played before the draw about the same as a high two pairs. Raise fast, drive out other players, limit the number of other players who will draw against you.

I have discussed the draw to three-of-a-kind elsewhere; but, to repeat, a hand that is opened on a low three-of-a-kind and has not been raised should usually draw one card and bet. He will get calls from two high pairs, and he is likely to get a call rather than a raise from a straight or flush that has filled, for fear he too has filled (a full house) and can raise back.

A hand with a low three-of-a-kind that has been raised before the draw and has not raised back (and usually, low threes should not raise back) will do best to draw two cards, look at his draw, and bet. This is especially true if the raiser drew one card. The raiser may call on two high pairs, and he may figure the opener to have drawn to a pair with an ace kicker.

Three-of-a-kind, from jacks to aces, is worth a reraise before the draw. Having reraised, the hand almost must draw two cards for maximum chance of improvement. However, the action here is affected by position and the draw. If you are last to draw and speak with high threes, and if you are up against two two-card draws or one one-card draw, you might do worse than to draw one card and check, on the grounds that you might as readily have raised back with aces-up. You might then get a bet against you on any threes. If, having raised, you draw two cards and check, no one is going to bet into you (unless he can beat you); if you bet, low threes probably will not call.

With high threes (at least queens, preferably kings or aces) it may pay merely to call against two opponents or only one. You draw one card. The raiser will probably bet into you.

However, in a "pass and back in" game, any three-of-a-kind makes a good pass as first or second player after the dealer. Usually, nothing is lost except the antes if nobody opens. Your position after the draw is bound to be best, because you will be the last player from the opener to speak. You have an automatic raise if two or three players come in. You can choose instead to have an excellent positional advantage if more than three players are in—you refuse to raise, draw one card, and can be figured by every other player for a possible straight or flush draw (because there was so much money in the pot before you came in). This will give you a big pot when you hit a full and one or two players before you improved; it will often get you a call when you bet as last man, since your bet might be on a busted straight or flush draw; and you retain freedom to get out without further cost if there is much action before the betting reaches you.

With three-of-a-kind it is most important not to find yourself in the middle when the opener is on your right and there are one or more one-card draws on your left. Much of the money lost on three-of-a-kind can be attributed to betting in such a case. In bad position, you can only check three-of-a-kind. A bet is futile because the one-card draws have either busted and will drop, or have filled and will call or raise and win; or will bluff and put you in an uncomfortable position.

There is a further reason why it pays to check, rather than bet, when you hold threes in a bad position (with active players both to your left and to your right). If you check in that position, there will often be a showdown, and you will turn up with three-of-a-kind which you obviously had all along. Your opponents will remember this, and you will save yourself some problems when you have two pairs and wouldn't know whether or not to call a speculative bet.

4. *"Don't bet into a one-card draw."* This is the most useful and yet the most costly of all poker precepts. If you never bet into a one-card draw, you are unlikely to be a winner in a tight poker game. Yet, betting into a one-card draw is the most dangerous thing you can do in poker. The decision has to be a matter of discrimination, and of reconstruction of the opponent's probable hand.

Before deciding whether to bet or check (if permitted), consider the hand the opponent is most likely to hold. This must necessarily depend upon your appraisal of the opponent, but your appraisal can be a rough one—he is known to be a wild and gambling player, or a conservative player. Strangely enough, you are safer betting into the conservative player than into the gambler if you have two high pairs or better. Against the conservative player, aces-up and three-of-a-kind are often equivalent; he didn't stay on less than two pairs, and either of your possible hands will beat him if he calls. Against the gambling player, aces-up and three-of-a-kind are still equivalent. He may have drawn to a straight or flush; if he hit he can beat you, and if he didn't he will throw his hand away. The moral is nevertheless apparent. Against the conservative player, you can make money by betting because you may get a call on a fair hand. Against the gambling player, you can't make money by betting *because he won't call if he missed and will raise if he hit.*

Therefore, a bet into a one-card draw is probably justified against one or two opponents who probably stayed on sound hands; it is not justified against a player who is wild and might have stayed on anything, or against a player who stayed when there was already five or six times as much in the pot as he had to put in and who might therefore have gone in on a straight or flush possibility.

JACKPOTS
(Jacks Or Better To Open)

This game has several unique features. First, the pot seldom offers more than 2 to 1 odds in the early stages. In the classic game there are eight players, each antes a quarter, to start the pot with $2, and the limit is $1 before the draw, $2 after the draw (or any ante, first limit and second limit proportionate to those figures). Unless at least three players are in before you and no one has raised, you must throw away all bobtail straights and four-flushes. Since you know that the minimum hand is a pair of jacks, you can play no less than kings as second man, and you need at least aces thereafter. The game is usually played by casual, relatively unsophisticated players who stick around with any low pair and often with less. But if the game is played seriously, there is little action and it is chiefly a game of waiting for the big pot. After all, you will figure to hold a hand as good as aces only once in six or seven deals. The average winning hand after the draw is jacks-up.

Jackpots is a game for sandbagging. You should seldom open if you are earlier than fifth man, and then you should have kings; only the sixth or seventh man can dare open on jacks or queens. It is almost incredible that a man in first or second position can gain by opening, because with a fair hand (up to kings) he is likely to be beaten before the draw, and with a better hand he will do better by waiting for someone else to open and then raising if there are not too many players (or, in a wide-open game, even if there are). Three-of-a-kind or a pat straight is a good pass in the first three positions. If no one opens, don't grieve; probably your maximum gain would have been the antes if you had opened, and you are better off in the long run waiting for big action on good hands.

The foregoing assumes the usual rules—that the opener bets first after the draw. Therefore, the opener automatically endows himself with the worst position, and the player who checks before the opener and then comes back in will have good position. He will act last or nearly last.

I give you the record of a remarkable hand in one of California's best legal clubs, playing jackpots, simply to show to what lengths experienced players will go to avoid being the opener. The standard of play is not the highest but the application of the sandbagging principle is well worth noting.

Jackpots (usual limits as described above); eight players; pass and back in. A (worthless) checks; B (Q-Q-Q-6-6) checks; C (worthless) checks; D (9-9-9-8-3) checks; E (A-A-A-A-2) checks; F and G (both worthless) check; H, dealer (K-K-J-7-4) opens. A drops, B raises, C drops, D raises, E stays, F, G, H drop. B raises, D stays, E raises. B raises, D stays, E raises. B raises, D stays, E raises, B and D stay. No hand improves; B and D check, E bets, B calls, D drops. E wins.

It is noteworthy that not only the second player, B with a pat full, and the fourth player, D with three nines, refused to open, but even that the fifth player, E with four aces dealt to him, refused to open. The dealer, H, was justified in trying to steal the ante on his pair of kings, and he was very wise to drop when he saw what the situation was. D stayed rather longer than he would have if he had read the situation correctly, but many players would have done as he did! The hero of the hand was the fifth player, E, who was willing to let his four aces pass without profit if he could not make a killing on them. Mathematically, there was as much chance that there would be openers after him as that there were sandbaggers before him. This was a celebrated hand because the pot was relatively so large and the play was so unusual. Nevertheless, it is an example of the tactics used by many of the most successful players in jackpots.

The disadvantage of opening and the advisability of playing for a killing are, if anything, intensified when a jackpots game is played with table stakes, as it often is. In such a game the ultimate bet can be very large and the advisability of playing for the big pot is even greater.

I have played more in jackpots games of draw poker with high stakes or table stakes than in any other game, and my advice to a player in such games is: Don't worry about the quarters that roll away, round after round; they will not affect your winnings materially, even if the stakes are high and they happen to be dollars. Don't grieve when you have a big pat hand, have chosen not to open, and you see the hand passed out. You wouldn't have won much anyway. These are normal hazards of the game. There are many games in which the average pot is $3 or $4 and the extraordinary pot is $40 or more. A few of those big pots in the course of a long session will make a player a winner regardless of his results on the other pots.

But remember (as I said in the section on Money-Management) that this approach is mathematically unsound when the overhead is high, i.e., when the ante is high compared with the betting limit.

STRAIGHT DRAW POKER

This is the game in which you can open on anything and in each turn must bet or drop ("pass and out"). In each turn you must at least chip along, whereas in a jackpots game you could check free.

Much depends on the relative value of a white chip (the chip of lowest value; it may be blue). Some players make the white chip of nominal value only — say ten cents, when the limit is $1 before the draw and $2 after, and when the white chip is seldom bet except for perfunctory purposes. From such games came the entire present custom of checking free; "white checks" counted for so little that it seemed hardly worthwhile to keep a stack of them and bother to put them in.

But in the usual pass-and-out game, the white chip is twenty-five cents when the limit is $1 and $2. Also, in such games there is usually an ante of one white chip by each player, and in an eight-hand game this creates a pot of $2 before the first bet. Here the overhead is high ($2 per round), and the player must look for action on small pots as well as big ones, otherwise the overhead will ruin him.

To maintain your chance of getting action on fair hands, you have to toss in your white chip. Yet, there are at least two reasons for being conservative. First, the white chips do mount up. Second, if you are the first to toss in your white chip, technically you become the opener, and have bad position after the draw.

One thing many players tend to forget in an "open on anything" game is that although jacks or better are not required to open, there are going to be just as many good hands around the table as in a jackpots game. At the start the pot may seem to offer you 7 to 1 or 8 to 1 odds on your white chip, but before the betting is finished it is very likely that someone will raise, and it will cost you just as much as it would have cost in jackpots. If you wouldn't have opened or stayed in jackpots, you shouldn't usually open or stay in this game.

However, there are some important exceptions. For example, in the early positions you should toss in your white chip on an open-end straight or a four-flush. Otherwise it is usually unwise to play without a high pair (kings or better; many successful players say queens or better) or, of course, a better hand. With a really strong hand, one on which you might have sand-bagged by passing in a jackpots game, it is usually best merely to chip along in this game, awaiting some action in the betting and then raising when it comes back to you.

One important difference between this game and jackpots is that you can "play percentages" in late positions, even if you wouldn't have had openers in jackpots. I will repeat the hands it takes to have a better-than-even chance to beat a given number of players who have not yet been heard from:

HAND REQUIRED	TO BEAT
Any pair	1 opponent
Eights	2 opponents
Jacks	3 opponents
Kings	4 opponents
Aces	5, 6, or 7 opponents

That is, if you are next-to-last man—only the dealer yet to be heard from, the other players being out—you can make the limit bet with any pair. If you are third from end, your pair should be at least eights; if you are fourth from the end, it should be at least jacks; and so on.

However, there is more theory than practical value in such a table. Usually, one or more of the early players will have put in their white chips, and you cannot be sure whether they are weak or strong. Especially you must watch the position of the players who are in ahead of you. If the first or second man from the dealer has chipped along, it doesn't mean a thing; he may have anything. If the fourth or fifth man has merely chipped, he probably does not have a very strong hand. He probably would have bet the limit on a good hand.

In the late positions you can't afford to let the first round go by with nothing but white chips in the pot. From about the fourth man on (and certainly no later than the fifth man), you should almost invariably make the maximum bet if you have a pair of aces or two pairs — any hand that figures to be high before the draw. Every now and then you will merely chip along on such a hand, either because you have reason to believe there is going to be action later or for the purpose of "mixing up" your game and keeping the other players guessing. Such cases should be rare.

Both the nature of this game and human nature are such that there are many more draws to straights and flushes than in any other form of draw poker. In jackpots a player will (or at least should) throw away a straight or flush draw without hesitation when he is first or second man from the opener; he does not yet know how big the pot will be and it costs too much to come in. In this game, however, it costs only a chip; the pot already offers him excellent odds for that one chip, and he can make his final decision later.

At that later time he must chiefly consider two things: first, the size of the pot; second, his position. If a couple of players have merely chipped after him, they may be waiting to raise, and the price of his entry will go up. In such a case he should pocket his one-chip loss and get out. When no one can raise after him, he should stay if the pot gives him 5 to 1 or better.

The position of the opener is not too bad. If he fills, he can judge from the draws whether to bet out or merely chip and wait. If he does decide to chip and wait, at least he will have heard from every player before his time comes again. A player can be seriously embarrassed when the opener is at his right and bets, because he may be between a couple of raising hands and lose a lot of money instead of settling early for his one white chip.

BLIND OPENING

Of all forms of draw poker, this is one in which it is most important to play sheer percentages. I mentioned before that you cannot afford to sit back and wait for a killing or a cinch in this game, because the overhead per round is so high. When you have a better-than-even chance to win, you must be in there.

Although the blind-opening game was created to add to the amount of action, the game should actually be played quite conservatively because the average bet is so high. I am taking a typical game in which dealer antes $1, next player opens blind for $1, next player raises blind to $2, and the limit is still $1 before the draw and $2 after. There is $4 in the pot, but it costs at least $2 to come in (and usually the automatic first bet is a raise to $3) so that the first man in is getting at most 2 to 1 for his money and usually only 4 to 3—little better than even money. He has to have a pretty good hand for this. The first three men aren't going to have mere straight or flush possibilities; they are going to have very high pairs or better. Of course this game is necessarily pass and out, because the pot has already been opened, so you can always figure how many players after you are still alive and dangerous. In counting the players yet to speak you must, of course, count the blind opener and the blind raiser; but they were forced to bet, and until they have taken voluntary action you do not figure their hands to average higher than those of any other players who have not been heard from.

The following tables will tell you what you should have to make the first call or raise (when you are the first player to speak, which means a bet of $2 or $3), and to stay in when someone else has bet.

Blind opening; eight players; dealer (G) antes $1, A opens for $1, B raises to $2.

PLAYER	SHOULD CALL ($2)	SHOULD RAISE ($3)
C	Kings	Aces
D	Kings	Aces
E	Queens	Kings
F	Tens	Queens
G	Eights	Tens
A	Ace-high ($1)	Tens ($2)

A, of course, is in a special position because he already has $1 in there and is getting 4 to 1 from the pot if he merely calls.

PLAYERS AHEAD OF YOU WHO HAVE COME IN (NOT INCLUDING OPENER OR BLIND RAISER)	IF GAME IS CONSERVATIVE	IF GAME IS LIBERAL
1	Kings	Queens
2	Two low pairs	Aces
3	Queens-up	Two low pairs
4	Kings-up	Tens-up
5	Aces-up	Queens-up
6	Three threes	Kings-up

The play of straights and flushes is very important in this game. You will note that player A (the blind opener), when everyone except the blind raiser has dropped, should not draw to an open-end straight or to a four-flush. The pot is offering only 4 to 1, and for such a draw you should have 5 to 1 or better.

Because this game may otherwise tend to become dull, many groups seek to enliven it by the introduction of two or more of the special hands—dogs, cats or tigers, skeets, etc. In playing such hands you simply count the number of cards that will give you a straight or better, subtract that number from 47, and you'll know the odds against you. Though such a hand will usually win if you fill, you should still require substantially higher odds from the pot than the odds against you.

Here is an example of figuring those odds: You are playing dogs (the big dog being ace to nine with no pair) to beat a straight but to lose to a flush. Your hand is Q-J-10-9. There are 12 cards that will give you a straight or better—the four aces, any of which will give you a big dog; the four kings and the four eights, any of which will give you a straight. This is a 12-timer; you subtract 12 from 47 and find that the odds against you are 35 to 12, or almost 3 to 1. If the pot offers you 4 to 1 or better, you can afford to draw to such a hand. Against one opponent this is a good draw at any odds, because any of 12 other cards will pair you and any pair you make has a chance to win. I do not advise raising on such a hand, or on nearly any hand that must be improved to win, because every raise shortens the odds offered by the pot.

Sometimes, when you are playing the special hands, the inside straight comes into its own—the only time in the game of poker that this is so. For example, if you are playing both dogs and tigers, K-J-10-9 gives you the same 12 opportunities as K-Q-J-10. Except when these special hands are played, there is almost no conceivable case in poker in which it is wise to draw to an inside straight. (The only exception that comes readily to mind is progressive jackpots, where the pot may on occasion offer better than 12 to 1 odds for your money.)

One of the most frequent and therefore one of the most important situations in a blind-opening game concerns the play of player B (the blind raiser) when one other player has raised and everyone else has dropped. There was $4 in the pot originally; the raiser put in $3, making $7; and player B can stay in for $1, getting 7 to 1 for his money. Attracted by such odds, most players stay on almost anything. In fact, even in fairly good games it is not unusual to see a player toss in his dollar and draw five cards.

You will note that the odds offered by the pot, 7 to 1, justify drawing one card to a four-flush or an open-end straight, where the odds are 4 or 5 to 1 against filling; they are still against drawing to an inside straight, where the odds are 11 to 1 against filling;

they justify drawing four cards to an ace. Drawing four to an ace is very slightly better than drawing three to an A-K of different suits; about the same as drawing three to A-K of the same suit; and considerably better than drawing two cards to a three-card flush possibility or a three-card open-end straight possibility.

In general, even the 7 to 1 odds justify drawing only when you have an ace, or a K-Q of the same suit (to take advantage of certain freak draws), or three cards in sequence no lower than 10-9-8 (so that if you pair one of your cards you will still have a fair chance to win against an unimproved hand), or three cards of the same suit, of which at least two cards are ten or higher. In the long run, very little will be lost if you do not even pay your dollar to draw to less than an ace or a low pair, but of course it is fun to be in there drawing.

WILD-CARD GAMES

Deuces-wild. Many serious poker players will be horrified that I should discuss this game at all, but it is perhaps the most under-rated of all forms of poker — simply because it is played most often by women in their afternoon clubs or by others who do not take the game very seriously.

Actually deuces-wild is just as good as any other form of poker, and it presents its own peculiar problems.

The basis of the game is not to play unless you have at least one deuce, unless occasionally you are dealt three-of-a-kind or better. No two pairs and no single pair without a deuce are worth playing. The average winning hand is three aces. Three-of-a-kind lower than queens or kings should usually be thrown away fast if you have not improved them. They may win a dull pot, but almost never are they worth a call. In general, because of the high probability of improving, you should draw to your best hand rather than keep proven values.

A few problems arise in drawing. With two aces, a deuce, and two honor cards (ten or higher) of the same suit as one of the aces, such as ♠ A Q 10 ♡ A ◊ 2, it is better to draw to the two aces and the deuce than to the royal flush possibility. With a pair lower than kings, a deuce, and a straight flush possibility, such as ♠ A Q 10 ♡ Q ♣ 2, it is better to draw to the straight flush; the three or four of a kind may not win. A deuce plus three cards in sequence, or three cards of the same suit, are worth a play and are worth standing one raise but not two; if there are two or more raises, you should have a straight flush possibility, or if you have a pair and a deuce you should draw in an effort to make at least four-of-a-kind.

The big question is the number of deuces you hold. A pair of deuces is worth a raise and is worth meeting almost any number of other raises.

Figure that any deuce you do not hold is likely to be held or drawn by someone else, and get out fast when you do not hold deuces. When drawing to two deuces, hold an ace or a king and draw two; throw away any lower cards and draw three.

Draw poker with the bug. Introduction of the bug (joker) as a fifth ace and as a wild card in straights and flushes increases the number of good hands. Consequently, it requires slightly more to bet, raise or call.

Unless you have the bug, it is seldom wise to stay in (when someone else has opened) with less than aces, or to raise, when next to the opener, with less than queens-up. With a low straight, it is usually as good or better to raise immediately and take a chance on driving other players out, as to try to suck them in by just playing. Nevertheless, three aces will usually win a pot, and consequently a straight, a better hand, is dependable enough to permit a sandbagging policy if you prefer it.

A straight or flush including the bug is far more desirable than a natural straight or flush, because it reduces the danger of having a pat hand against you.

The bug has a damaging psychological effect on many players: when dealt it, they hate to throw the hand in. Almost never is it advisable to draw four cards to the bug; there is only one chance in seven of getting aces or better. A two-card draw to the bug and two cards in suit and sequence, such as B-◊9-◊8, offers no greater chance of improvement than a one-card draw to a four-flush or bobtail straight, and should be played just as rarely. (There is about one chance in five of improvement, the same as with a four-flush, and the average improvement does not give you as good a hand as a flush.)

However, the bug and a three-card sequence (in different suits) offers twice as good chance of improvement as a bobtail straight — for example, B-9-8-7, which will be filled by any of 16 different cards — so that the odds against improvement are only 2 to 1. The pot usually offers better odds than that, so such a hand should usually be played. Even better is a straight-flush draw including the bug; with, for example, B-♡6-♡5-♡4, there is almost an even chance to get a straight or better. Because of the possibility of winning a big pot, hands of this type are often worth a raise.

With the bug, an ace, and a face card of the same suit as the ace, a two-card draw is better than three cards to the bug-ace; but if the face card is of a different suit, it is better to discard it and draw three.

Since the bug makes a fifth ace, the expectancy of improvement by holding an ace (or bug) kicker with a pair is materially increased; when you hold the kicker, you have about the same chance of improving as when you draw three to the pair. Your chance of making three-of-a-kind is materially reduced, but your chance of making aces-up is increased more than enough to compensate for this, and you should hold the kicker when you think aces-up are pretty sure to win the pot.

Despite the extra ace in the pack, it is unwise to split aces-up in most cases. Draw one card as usual.

Having the bug with three cards of a suit, your chance of filling the flush is only slightly greater than when there is no bug in the pack (10 chances in 48 as against 9 in 47). It is seldom wise to play this hand when you would not play a four-flush in regular draw poker. Note also that with B-♡Q-♡9-◇8-♡7 you should throw the queen rather than the eight.

Draw poker with the joker. When the joker is included as a fully wild card, it dominates the whole strategy of the game. The average winning hand goes up to three-of-a-kind. The joker is almost always worth a play (unless the hand contains no pair or ace and the pot has been raised). The joker and a pair, or the joker and three cards in suit or sequence, or in near-sequence (as joker-8-7-5), is worth a raise; for to the ten or more cards that will turn such a hand into a straight or flush, as the case may be, must be added nine cards that will give you three-of-a-kind — a good enough hand to win most pots when you (rather than another player) hold the joker.

OTHER OPENING REQUIREMENTS

The following variations are sometimes played. They do not require further discussion.

Acepots. All the requirements are the same as in jackpots, except that a pair of aces or better is required to open. Even when there are eight players in the game, this restriction causes too many hands to be passed out unless the joker, the bug or other wild cards are in use. The strategy is roughly the same as in jackpots.

Four-flush to open. A player may open, as usual, with jacks or better; or he may open on any four-flush. The four-flush, if not improved, has no special value after the draw. (In some draw poker games, however, and in many stud games, a four-flush is played to beat a pair, but to lose to two pairs.) The object of making a four-flush open is to speed up the game; it is more likely that someone will hold openers, and other players are supposedly encouraged to come in on low pairs on the assumption that the opener may not even have a pair. However, since it is losing play to open on a four-flush, this special rule has little effect in a game among good players, though a one-card draw to a straight flush is worth opening on and that opportunity might be lost if the four-flush rule were not in effect.

Any bobtail to open. Jacks or better, as usual, or any bobtail (four-flush or double-end four-card sequence) suffices as an opener. All the comments in the preceding paragraph apply as well to this game. It must be remembered that a one-end sequence such as A K Q J, or an inside straight such as 9 8 6 5, does not fulfill the opening requirements.

Progressive jackpots. If, jacks being required, the pot is not opened, for the next pot queens are required, then kings, then aces (and, in some games, up to two pairs).

Stud Poker for High

FIVE-CARD STUD

Five-card stud poker depends on mathematics and self-discipline. The average winning hand is the lowest among all games of poker—a pair of aces or a pair of kings. Overhead is almost non-existent; there is almost never an ante, and you do not have to bet unless you have the high card showing on the first round. As a result you can sit in the game for literally hours and hardly spend a penny, waiting for a good hand to come along. The winnings almost always go to the players who are conservative at the start and bold when they think they have the best hands.

Stud poker offers some classic questions, which are easy enough to answer

1. The idea that you should not play unless you can beat or tie the board—i.e., you have a better hand than any hand showing, at the stage when you make the bet. I regret to say that this precept is almost entirely true. It is devastatingly boring, but it is true. You are unlikely to win in a stud game unless you bet only when you can beat anything showing. In all other cases you should get out of the pot.

2. The question of which is better, an ace in the hole (assuming no other ace showing) or a low pair, say up to fives or sixes. The low pair is much better. If the ace itself is not paired, you have the better hand at the start. You are even more likely to improve the pair than the ace-holder is to pair the ace. But much

depends on how you play a low pair after the first round or two. Probably the best method is to raise on the second round and see how many stay in. From that number, you can judge the possibility that you are up against other low pairs or high hole cards. From the next round of cards, you can judge the possibility that any of the high hole cards has paired.

Stud players are often prejudiced against low pairs back-to-back because they have lost so much on them. They have not lost by sticking around in the first place — that is when they get their killings if they improve — but by sticking around after it is apparent that some other player has hit for a higher pair. For example, a pair of fives unimproved is a bad fourth-round play against a strong player who showed an eight on the first round, has drawn an ace or a king later, and who bets strongly. He probably has you beaten at this point, and if so, you are going to lose in the long run by bucking him.

3. The one invariable rule of stud poker is not to stay against a pair showing unless you already have a higher pair. The number of "over" cards is of no consequence whatsoever. If he has you beaten at this point, he figures to beat you at the end, and he also has an advantage that you cannot possibly have — he can have a cinch hand and you cannot. If there is an open pair showing, be very wary of staying even when you have a higher pair. Stop first to consider the possibility that he was paired back-to-back at the start. This will depend upon your appraisal of the player and his habits, and also on the number of aces that have shown (or of cards higher than the high showing card at the start, as for example when the high showing card at the start was a queen and no kings have shown). A stud player must have the courage to get out on the highest showing hand when all the indications are that some concealed hand is better at this point.

Don't stay on straight or flush possibilities unless by pure accident you find yourself with a possible straight or flush with one card yet to come and the pot offers better than 5 to 1 odds for staying in.

One of the standard precepts of the game is: "Never bet into a possible cinch hand." But if you observe this rule you sacrifice much of your potential winnings. Stud poker is more a game of figuring than any other kind of poker. The opponent may show a possible cinch, such as a possible straight or flush, but you must consider the hole cards on which he might have stayed in so long. You must form your judgment on the hole card he *may* have rather than on the entire number of possible hole cards there are for him. A very important factor in making this determination is the *original upcard*. You then think about whether any of his possible hole cards will cause him to call a bet on a losing hand. When you think you probably can win, and also that he may call on a losing hand, you must bet. For example, you have queens-up and he probably has tens-up, but he may have three sixes, as in this case:

Five-card stud. You raised on the third round. At the final round only one opponent has stayed with you.

You have: Q down; 9, Q, 5, 5.

Opponent has: ? down; 10, 6, 8, 6.

If opponent has a six in the hole, he knows he has a cinch hand.

Opponent is high and checks. You must bet your queens up despite his possible cinch. It is too unlikely that he played at the start with a six in the hole and a ten up. His most likely hands are tens-up, or merely the sixes he shows, perhaps with an ace or other high hole card. But with either of these hands he can beat your showing fives, and with tens-up he can beat the nines-up that you are likely to have. So he will probably call a bet, and you will lose much of your potential winnings if you do not give him the opportunity.

Occasionally, you must bluff in such cases (when you have represented a hand that is probably two pairs but you do not actually have them). And occasionally the opponent will reraise as a bluff, and you must trust your judgment of his style to decide whether or not to call. All that is part of the game.

In stud poker you must look at every card dealt and every card folded, and remember them. They affect the chances that any particular opponent has a particular hole card. For example, two aces have shown and folded. You are against one opponent who catches an ace as his last card. You have two kings. You must ask yourself whether he would have continued to stay with an ace when the other two aces had already shown. If he is a very good player, figure him for an early pair—not aces paired on the last card. If he is a poor player, you might worry. But you cannot have any idea if you did not see and take note of those aces that folded. Incidentally, this is an oversimplified case; your success is going to depend on how many of the sixes and nines and queens you see, as well as the aces. Everybody notices aces.

When to play on the first round. The average winning hand is two kings or two aces. Many pots are won on less (such as ace-high) and many pots require more, as the upcards will reveal; but it is a basic principle to stay only when the odds against making two kings or better are lower than the odds offered by the pot. The following are minimum plays on the first round.

1. Any pair.

2. Ace in the hole; but if another ace is showing, the upcard should be a nine or higher.

3. King in the hole, when no ace is showing. If an ace or another king is showing, the upcard must be jack or queen, and no more than one other player can show a queen or jack (as the case may be).

The great fallacy is in staying on a hole card such as a jack simply because it is high—that is, in the occasional deals when all the original upcards are low. For example, the first upcards in an eight-handed game are 2, 8, 7, 10, 8, 5, 10, 6. You have the seven-up and a jack in the hole. You can "beat the board" but it is a bad play. The odds are 13 to 1 that another player has you beaten.

Raising in five-card stud. There are two arguments against raising early in a stud game. Once you have raised, you will get only minimum calls from the other players—unless one of them knows he has you beaten and raises back, in which case you are stuck with the odds against you and much of your money in the pot. The second argument against an early raise is that in most stud games the limit is higher on the last card, and if you can only raise once you might as well wait until the raise will win you the most money.

Now, despite these arguments, one must frequently raise early in a stud game. Following are some of the reasons for an early raise:

1. Assuming that you will soon be spotted as a tight player, the other players will figure you for an ace or a pair anyway. You might as well make them pay to stay around with you, and furthermore a policy of raising will open the way to a number of bluffs that will steal small pots at the beginning. Then too, since you are known to play conservatively, an early raise on a pair will put you in a very good position later if you happen to catch a showing ace. A higher pair than yours may very well fold.

2. If you are in good position (last man from the high hand) you may sometimes raise on the third card (the second upcard) to give yourself a free ride on the fourth card (the third upcard). After your early raise, everyone may check to you the next time and you can see your last card free. No doubt you would have had to call at least the minimum bet, anyway, to see that last card, and you might have been confronted with one or more raises.

3. Occasionally, when you have the second-best hand you may raise to drive the best hand out. This is a first-round raise. An ace that is forced high will not infrequently drop. If no more than two hands with small cards showing have stayed in against the ace, your raise on such a combination as K-Q may drive the ace out and leave you with a better chance to make a higher pair than the other players.

In all these cases a primary object is to vary your tactics. There are two basic ways to keep the opponents guessing in poker. One is to play different kinds of hands in the same way;

the other is to play the same kind of hand in different ways. If you are going to play only good hands in stud poker, then you have to play them in different ways so that you cannot be too easily figured.

There is one general exception to the principle of early raising. If the game is wide open—where the other players bet and raise very freely—there is seldom an occasion for you to raise early. On every round someone else is pretty sure to bet. The pot will be built up without your help. You might just as well wait until the end and make pretty sure you are going to win before you start putting unnecessary chips into the pot.

The play of an open pair. When you have the only open pair, every other player in the game is at a great disadvantage. You may have a cinch high at the moment, and if so it is pretty sure to stand up. Therefore, the policy of most stud players is always to bet the maximum on an open pair and make the opponents pay through the nose if they want to try to draw out on it.

In most fairly good stud games, no one is going to stay against an open pair unless he has a higher pair, or unless (on the next-to-last card) he has a straight or flush possibility. Even the straight or flush possibility is a pretty bad gamble unless the pot is already big. The pot should offer 5 to 1 odds unless at least three cards in the possible straight or flush are over the showing pair, and even then the pot should offer at least 4 to 1 odds.

In general, I subscribe to the idea of betting the maximum on the open pair, because only such a policy can maintain your chance of making a real killing when you actually do have three of a kind or two pairs when your open pair is showing. Nevertheless, discretion is sometimes the better part of valor. If you know there are likely to be a couple of higher pairs out (and sometimes you can tell this from the previous action), and if you know you aren't going to scare anybody out, you are simply betting a losing hand. If the other players are of the sort who will freely bet or raise on their higher pairs against your open pair, you are risking the loss of a considerable amount of money. In such cases it is no disgrace even to check the open pair; it is stubbornness never to do so. And, of course, you can still mix up your game by occasionally checking when the open pair has actually given you a cinch hand.

In any event you are under no obligation to bet the open pair on the last round. That is usually the time when you bet only when you do have the winning hand, and when you figure the other players to be too smart to bet into you.

As for playing against an open pair: You know, of course, that it is always dangerous. I am speaking only of the times when you have a higher pair, concealed of course. Only a losing player bets because he has a number of "over" cards which, if paired, will beat the showing pair. Except as a bluff, such hands should be dropped. In most cases the higher pair must not be dropped, but it is losing play to raise on it. The only time to raise is when you are alone with the open pair, when you have a lower limit before the last card, and you want to coax the open pair into checking to you on the last card. A bet by the only pair on the last round puts every other player on a terrible spot. There are few more effective bluffs against good players, because everyone knows that when a tight player gets a pair showing, there is a very good chance that he has two pairs or better.

Watching other cards. It takes a pretty good stud player to watch all the cards and draw the proper conclusions from them. Every player, however, can watch for the cards that most affect his hand. Sometimes simple observation leads you to some valuable conclusions. Suppose you have neither the temperament nor the aptitude for concentration to watch and remember every card, but you have observed the cards in general and have noticed that a "lot" of spades have shown. If you have a doubtful play on a spade four-flush for the last card, this observation will cause you to drop fast. If you have noticed an absence of showing spades, that might persuade you to stay in on your four-flush.

Much more important is to watch every card that pairs one of your cards. The appearance of those cards has a tremendous effect on your chances. For example, if you have an ace in the hole and no other ace has shown, the odds are 4 to 1 against your pairing it eventually. If one ace has shown, the odds go up to more than 6 to 1 against you. If two other aces have shown, for all practical purposes your ace is valueless except as a high card.

SEVEN-CARD STUD

In this game the average winning hand is a fairly high three-of-a-kind, such as three eights or three tens. There are quite a few straights and flushes. The worst mistakes made by the average player are: staying on a low pair, such as fours or fives; and staying more than one round on a three-straight or three-flush.

If there is another principal mistake, it is probably in playing a two-pair hand too strongly—unless you get your two pairs on the first four cards, in which case the odds are only about $2\frac{1}{2}$ to 1 against filling.

The nature of the game is such that there is considerable difference between a concealed low pair and a split low pair. (A concealed low pair is, for example, two fours down and a king up; a split low pair is a four and king down and a four up.) Of course your chance of improving is the same in both cases, but your chance of getting a big pot is far better with the concealed pair. In seven-card stud it is quite easy to have a full house with no pairs showing, and when you have such a hand a player with a straight or flush is very likely to bet into you, raise you, and ultimately call you, and you will win a big pot. With a split pair, if you make three-of-a-kind early, you show a pair, and the other players are automatically on guard. If the case card of that rank doesn't soon show, the other players must even keep in mind the danger that you have four-of-a-kind, and while this may occasionally put you in a good bluffing position, that is far less important than the fact that it will prevent your getting any action.

Legitimate plays in this game, on the first three cards (two down, one up) are roughly as follows: Any three cards of the same suit. Any three cards in sequence as good as 10-9-8. Any high pair, nines or better. Any concealed low pair. Occasionally, A-K in the hole if not more than one card of either rank (one ace or one king, but not one of each) has shown.

The key to the game comes when the fourth card has been dealt, so that you have two up and two down. At this point much depends, as it always must in any stud game, on what cards have shown around the table, but the following general principles should be observed:

An unimproved low pair should be dropped. The only exception is the case in which the other two cards include an ace, or a king and a queen, and in which not more than one of each of these ranks has shown. By a low pair here, I mean eights or lower.

A straight possibility should be dropped unless you have drawn a near card (as for example, a king or seven to a J-10-9) or unless you have paired. However, if two essential cards have shown, such as two eights or two queens in the case noted, the hand should be dropped.

A flush possibility should be dropped if the fourth card has not matched it, unless most of the cards of the same suit have not shown; or unless the flush cards are very high, including ace and king or queen; or the fourth card has paired the hand.

A high pair, queens or higher, should be played unless there is a great deal of action in the betting, with two players raising.

A pair should not be played against a higher open pair.

Neither two pairs nor a low three-of-a-kind justifies a raise against a high open pair. However, if no pair is showing, then two pairs or better in the first four cards call for a maximum bet or a raise. The principle is not much different from that of draw poker. The odds against filling are only $2\frac{1}{2}$ to 1, and rare will be the cases in which the pot offers smaller odds than that. The hand is probably the best at the moment, and the bet or raise will drive out hands that might have improved.

The best two pairs to have at such a time are "near cards," such as 10-8 down and 10-8 up. Opponents may then figure that the raise was made on some such combination as J-10-9-8.

If, later, you fill, and also get a card that looks as though it may have made you a straight, you may get a tremendous play from a flush and win a big pot.

The raise on such a two-pair hand is especially effective because any double-end straight or any four-flush made in the first four cards is worth a maximum bet or raise, and two or more reraises if the opportunity arises. (Only one reraise against an open pair that raises back.) It is about even money that you will fill the straight or flush in the next three cards, and the odds are $2\frac{1}{2}$ or better to 1 that you will win if you do.

Stubbornness and overoptimism are the main hazards to the player of seven-card stud. Very rare are the hands that can win without improvement. You might almost say that nothing less than a high three-of-a-kind in the first three cards is likely to win without improvement. The winning player must stay at the start when he has a good draw but must drop fast if he has not improved by at least the fifth card. To stick around with aces against three or four other players is futile. Hands run so high in this game that one of the other players almost surely has a better hand. One cannot repeat too often that in every form of poker, the best hand going in figures to be the best coming out.

The tactics of betting and raising in seven-card stud are almost exactly the same as in five-card stud. The only difference is that one can seldom be nearly so sure of having the winning hand, because with three cards down at the end, the hidden combinations are almost innumerable. Early raises are about the same in one game as in the other. Bets and raises on the last card are somewhat more dangerous in seven-card stud. Bluffing is less effective on the last card because it is so hard to know when a player may have a legitimate call, regardless of what he has represented in the past.

HOW
TO PLAY
LOW POKER

Low poker is played in the same manner as high poker, with one notable exception: the winning hand is the one which would be the "worst," i.e., the *lowest* ranking in a game of high poker.

Although there is little variation in the ranking of poker hands for high, low poker (a more recent game and an offshoot of the high form), being less steeped in tradition, grew up in many different ways. Thus, some players will treat the ace as the lowest card, while others treat it as the highest. Similarly, some groups treat a straight (e.g., 6-5-4-3-2) or a flush (e.g., ♡7-♡6-♡4-♡3-♡2) as a high hand — or, anyhow, higher than an ordinary unpaired hand — whereas in some low games it is agreed that straights and flushes do not count, meaning that the hand is valued only on the basis of the rank of its cards and it is irrelevant whether or not a player holds a straight or a flush.

Originally, aces were high, and straights and flushes were (comparatively) high hands. Thus, the best hand was 7-5-4-3-2 of at least two different suits. The more modern trend is to treat aces as low and not to count straights and flushes. In this case, the best hand is 5-4-3-2-A (usually called a "wheel"), followed by 6-4-3-2-A, 6-5-3-2-A, and so forth. It will be noted that, the treatment of aces, straights and flushes notwithstanding, the hand is

117

ranked from its *highest* card, then its second highest, and so on. Thus, 7-5-4-3-2 is a better hand for low than 7-6-3-2-A. The first hand is called a "seven-five low," while the second is a "seven-six low."

The modern trend to treat aces, straights and flushes as low is almost universally applied in lowball (draw poker for low, to be discussed in detail later in this chapter) and very often in high-low (see Chapter 6), where it adds much interest to the game.

Although in this book we will assume that aces, straights and flushes are all low (for purposes of making a low hand), very little adaptation should be needed if your game treats these cards and hands in the reverse manner. For example, if your game treats aces as high only, merely substitute the word "deuce" where I have given "ace" in the text; also read "three" for "deuce" and so on up the line.

It goes almost without saying that one must be certain to clarify the treatment of aces, straights and flushes before beginning play.

In this chapter I will discuss the two main forms of low poker, stud and draw. Low stud poker is played in several variations, depending on the number of cards given to each player. Low draw poker, which goes under the name "Lowball," and which has proved very popular in many areas, is given special attention. New ways which have been developed to spice up the low poker games are also covered.

Even if you feel you will not be interested in playing low poker, you should read this chapter carefully if you intend to play high-low, which is rapidly becoming the dominant form of poker in serious games. The failings of many high-low players are caused not only because they have not mastered the special techniques of this game, but because, never having played poker for low, they are unfamiliar with the basic principles of that category of the high-low game. Therefore, you should not brush off low poker merely because you find (as many confirmed high and/or high-low players do) it is not your cup of tea. It is not only essential to understand the principles of low poker in order to play high-low successfully, but the *comparison* of low poker with high poker may well increase your comprehension of the principles governing successful play for high.

Stud Poker for Low

Stud poker for low is often played by individuals who enjoy a large number of betting rounds but wish to relieve the monotony of high poker. Although low stud poker does not approach the popularity of lowball, it has been making small gains in recent years. (It should be noted that the fairest method of playing low stud is to have the *low* board act first within each betting round.)

Low stud poker is usually played with five or six cards. The six-card game is more popular for several reasons. First of all, the extra card provides an additional round of betting and therefore increases the action. More important, however, is the fact that in a five-card game for low, one bad card may ruin an otherwise magnificent hand. Poker players do not like the idea of holding a sensational hand and betting it strongly, only to lose through being "painted" (catching a picture card or a pair) on the last card. In a six-card game, a player who has a good hand all along has more chance to retain his advantage. One poor card need not ruin his hand—there is always a chance to recover.

Conversely, seven-card low is rarely played. Perhaps there are simply *too many* good hands in this game. This inflation of hand values causes unpleasantness in a different way. Just as a straight draw poker player is appalled to see that three-of-a-kind (which he has always considered a good hand) is only a moderate hand when, say, deuces are wild, so the confirmed lowball or five- or six-card low stud player will be very unhappy when he sees that low hands he considers good often lose in seven-card games.

Every form of low poker is more of a pure gamble than high poker. Whereas high hands can only be improved, low hands can become worse. In fact, a hand at draw poker for low *figures* to become worse (considering its potential) if a card is replaced or a new card is added. A low stud player may have a strong lead after four cards, only to see his hand ruined on the last card(s), whereas a high stud player is assured of permanent possession of certain values.

In high poker the best hand going in figures to be the best hand coming out. This, of course, is true in low poker as well, but there is an important difference. The degree of advantage of the best hand (at an early stage) of low poker is far, far less than the corresponding degree of advantage of the best hand (at an early stage) in high poker.

It is always a mistake not to back the best hand strongly, but it is also a mistake to count too heavily on your chances of winning when you have the lead in a low game.

Similarly, when you are behind in a low game, you require lesser odds from the pot to "chase" the best hand than in a corresponding situation in a high game. For this reason, low poker is always a game of tremendous action. A player with an inferior hand does not need very good odds from the pot in order to play. So the betting is comparatively loose, and sometimes even frivolous, with players backing wild chances. Such behavior is not as irrational as it may appear at first glance, since every play in a low game is essentially a gamble. A low hand may be ruined at any stage!

Because low poker generates so much betting activity, it is frequently played by poker enthusiasts anxious to be where the action is. Low poker players are not the type that enjoy the slow, cautious, calculating style of a high or a high-low game. Therefore it is not accepted practice in a low game to think too long before deciding on your action in a given situation. It is never good social practice to delay any poker game, but causing such delays is often regarded as a major sin in a *low* poker game.

HOW TO PLAY STUD POKER FOR LOW

Discussing the techniques of the various forms of poker, it is usual to give some idea of the values of different hands, along with tips on strategy. In stud poker for low, however, it is virtually impossible to set up a realistic table of hand values. Fortunately, it is also unnecessary. In low poker, above anything else, full force must be given to the cliché that a chain is as strong as its weakest link. In other words, the value of a hand is determined first and foremost by its worst card (potentially). When stud poker is played for low, so much of a player's hand is exposed that the value of the hand can vary wildly, depending on the upcards. In particular, the upcards determine the *zone* of the hand. Thus, a (potential) "ten-low" may or may not be a good hand. If no player has a pair or a picture card after several rounds, a ten-low will probably be nowhere near the winning hand. But if each player has a picture card . . .

Another factor in judging the comparative value of hands in low stud is the proportion of cards that are "busts." A bust in low poker simply means a bad card—usually a picture card, or a card that makes an exposed pair. Thus, in five-card low stud, a hand can never be better than its worst card. In six-card stud, one bad card can be overcome, but the odds on making a "good" hand are considerably shortened. In seven-card stud, one bad card may have little or no effect on the composition of (or chances to obtain) the final hand. Thus, the fewer the cards to be dealt to each player, the greater the effect of a bad card.

GENERAL RULES FOR EARLY-ROUND TACTICS IN LOW STUD

1. *Don't play with a bad card.* No matter how many cards are being dealt, it is unsound from every angle to continue playing a

hand of low poker if you have a bad card—*even one*! Mathematically, your chances of making a good low hand are greatly diminished. More important, from a pure poker standpoint, to play with a bad card is to inflict yourself with a handicap. The other players may (and probably do) have all "working" (i.e., valuable or potentially valuable) cards. If you do not have all working cards, you have less of a chance to win (eventually) than the other players. Why buck the odds? Players unfamiliar with low poker but familiar with high games should think of this as similar to getting out of a pot of high stud unless you can beat (or overlay) the board, or "not chasing an open pair." It is just as disadvantageous to play with an inferior hand when the game is played for low.

2. *In calculating the value of your opponents' hands, assume perfect-type hole cards.* This assumption is the only sound one to make because the "perfect" cards will almost always be there. There are two reasons for adopting this view. First, there is the obvious fact that unless your opponents are foolishly disregarding number 1, above, they will drop out as soon as they hit a bust. Second, it is easier to have "perfect" hole cards at low than at high, and since there is a good chance that your opponents were dealt such cards, there is every reason to assume it.

To illustrate this, let us compare the situations at high and low stud:

Suppose that at five-card stud for high you hold a king and a ten. Your king is exposed and another player has a jack exposed. For purposes of this hand, his "perfect" hole cards are jacks (best), aces (next), kings (lowest acceptable at this stage). This is a total of only 10 cards.

Now consider a similar situation in low poker. Your opponent has a low card—from five to ace—on board and one hole card. Even if you see a few of the potentially perfect cards for your opponent, there will still be more than 10 perfect cards he can hold. With, say, a three exposed, there are 16 potential cards (the aces, deuces, fours and fives) he can have which will give him two to a "wheel." (This calculation applies regardless of the hand considered the perfect low in your particular game.)

3. *Count the low cards.* It goes without saying that the more cards you can remember (in *any* stud game), the better. In low stud, however, there is obviously a greater emphasis on remembering the low cards which have shown. Not only is the memorizing of low cards at low stud of more value than remembering any other particular group of cards at high stud — it is also more likely to be valuable on any given hand. When the late rounds are played, you will want to know whether or not your opponent or opponents may have paired when they receive a low card at the end. If, for example, an opponent draws a "case" (last remaining) low card, you can be reasonably certain his bet is not a bluff. You can, however, suspect a bluff when he bets after hitting a "stranger" at the end. The odds are strong that he has paired his hole card.

4. *Elementary inferences about pairs.* One way you can count the low cards, in addition to counting those you can see faced on the table (plus, of course, your own hole card(s), which, let us hope, will be low! — see number 1), is to infer pairs. Why did Smith, with nothing but nice juicy low cards on his board, drop out on that round? The answer will almost always be that Smith's *last card paired his hole card*! Thus, if a player starts with a five exposed, then draws a three and drops out during that betting round, it's dollars to doughnuts he has a three in the hole. Such an inference, while easy enough, can be of considerable value in counting the low cards.

These special pointers, plus the general techniques dealing with bluffing, position, etc., covered previously, should give you a flying start in any low stud game. The rest is experience in judging hand values and general poker technique and psychology.

Lowball
(DRAW POKER FOR LOW)

This is a very new game, as poker games go; it is not much more than 50 years old. Its success has been phenomenal in some districts; in the legal games of California, there is probably as much lowball played as regular poker. The game has enriched the language of poker with many new terms: The best hand is a bicycle, or wheel. A relatively good hand of its kind is "smooth," and a relatively bad hand of its kind is "rough." For example, 9-8-6-3-2 is "a rough nine," while 9-5-4-3-2 is "a smooth nine." Lowball was the game which originally introduced the novelties that ace is low rather than high (or, with this principle extended to high-low games, *as well as* high), and that straights and flushes could be used as low hands.

The usual rules of draw poker apply — except, of course, that the *lowest* hand at the showdown wins the pot — with a few notable exceptions. The most important exception is that regardless of the position of the last raiser before the draw, betting after the draw starts with the first still-active player to the left of the dealer. This has a considerable effect on positional considerations, as I will discuss shortly. The other exceptions will be treated as they apply.

Lowball is usually played "pass and out" — before the draw you must either open or drop out if the hand has not yet been opened — so there is no sandbagging. Straddling (as in "Blind and Straddle" — see pages 32 to 33) is often permitted, and a moderate ante is common, making overhead a consideration.

Lowball is almost universally played with a fixed betting limit (which is usually doubled after the draw), and this leads to the fairly widespread practice of "semi-bluffing." By a semi-bluff, I mean a bet on a hand that does not figure to be the best if the other players have what they represented, but which may scare them out and may even be the winning hand. As we shall see, the special nature of lowball goes a long way toward explaining the frequency of such bluffs.

In lowball, where the ace is the lowest card instead of the highest, and in which straights and flushes do not count, the bug occupies a unique position. If there is no ace in the hand, the bug is simply an ace, the lowest card. If there is a natural ace in the hand, the bug never pairs that ace — it simply ranks as the missing card next-higher than the ace. Therefore, the hand 5-4-3-2-A (natural cards) cannot be beaten by the hand 5-3-2-A-Bug. These hands tie. But 6-5-3-2-A loses to 6-4-3-Bug-A, because the bug can be designated as the missing deuce. The bug is used almost universally in lowball games.

Throughout the following discussion it must be borne in mind that we are *assuming the use of a fixed limit for betting.* Lowball with pot limit or table stakes is quite a different game, but it is not played nearly widely enough to merit special consideration.

THE SEVENS RULE

In an attempt to avoid the possibility of sluggish action after the draw (which delay would reduce the enjoyment of the majority of the players), some lowball clubs have instituted what is known as "the sevens rule." This means that after the draw, if a player checks with a seven-low or better, he forfeits any further profits from the pot. He may still win the pot, of course, but if (for example) another player bets and the player with a seven-low calls and wins the pot, the player who made the bet is entitled to withdraw it.

Quite clearly, this rule reduces the number of plays that can be made after the draw and is thus to the disadvantage of the more skillful players. Therefore, if you feel you are a cut above the game you play in, try to join a game in which the sevens rule does not apply. If, however, you find that you are forced by circumstances to play where this rule exists, there is little that can be done about it. There simply is no advantage in "advertising" by refusing to bet when you have a seven-low or better—except that if you do not do so on occasion, when you do check you are marked as lacking the seven-low.

Thus, on occasion you must advertise by deliberately checking with a seven and forfeiting all further profits for that hand. To cover yourself, and especially to set up a potential killing on a hand you expect to win with an eight-low, it pays to check a seven occasionally when you suspect there will be little action after the draw in any event. However, as the advertising gain will be little even in the long run, such a play should be in the once-in-a-blue-moon category. The important thing is that you do it on occasion, however infrequent these occasions are.

Some Special Tips on Lowball

Lowball, as played in the poker clubs, with the action fast and furious, contains several elements which are not present in other forms of poker. In this section I will give advice on two aspects of playing lowball: first, how to manage yourself in this type of fast-action limit game; second, some special lowball strategy.

THE STAKES

When it comes to judging whether or not a particular lowball game is "your speed," be sure to consider the stakes with great care. You may be used to a limit poker game for high; the same limit (of a bet on each round) in lowball will make the game approximately twice as expensive! This is not so much because of the nature of lowball but because of the nature of the people who play it. Lowball is a game of action, as opposed to a game of careful computation and analysis. The lowball player is drawn to the table by the same fascination that grasps the horse player and (especially) the crap shooter. So great is the craving for action that if a player takes more than a few seconds to decide his course at any particular point, he is likely to draw adverse criticism.

For the present, however, I am concerned only with the nature of lowball as it applies to the stakes. When you learn the stakes of a lowball game, double them in your own mind to judge the size of the game. Of course it is *always* a good idea to watch a poker game before playing in it. In any game, the particular players determine the size of the game. However, should a situation arise in which you want to make as accurate a guess as possible as to the size of the game without having watched, the "double" rule will suffice in a large percentage of cases.

MONEY-MANAGEMENT

In a way, this is perhaps the most important factor in maintaining a winning philosophy in lowball. Money-management (see pages 72-77) is important in any game, but many players hit the rocks in lowball because it is so different in this area from any other form of poker.

Lowball is, first of all, a low poker game. As we have already stated, any form of low poker is, in general, more of a gamble than the corresponding form of high poker. The advantages of the better hands are minimal in low poker and the better player cannot expect to win as often, or with as much certainty, as he does at high or (especially) at high-low poker. In addition, as we will see, proper play at lowball involves backing a *potentially* strong hand to the limit. Whereas at high poker a man with three aces knows he has certain assured values — whether or not he has a chance to improve them — and can bet on these values, the lowball player who waits for a "made" hand to do strong betting will not only be an eventual loser on a mathematical basis, but he will find that there is no one playing against him when he has one of his rare good hands. Remember that lowball, being a game of action, necessarily requires chance-taking. In other words, a player must give action to get action. It has been said that a conservative lowball player is just as sure a loser as a free-wheeling high player.

Since it is necessary to take chances playing lowball, and since even when you have the advantage you cannot expect to win as often as when you have the advantage in high poker, the lowball player must be prepared to accept more frequent losses than the high player. In other words, no matter how good a low-ball player you are, you cannot control your own destiny as much as you can in a high (or high-low) game.

Therefore, money-management becomes important. You must make especially realistic estimates of the amounts you are willing to put up for a session, or, as extended sessions of lowball tend to have a stultifying effect on a player's capabilities, for a portion of a session. Experience with lowball games in poker clubs indicates that stacks tend to build up and become depleted with almost unnerving rapidity. The seasoned high player, accustomed to keeping a careful watch over his stack, must adopt a completely new set of standards for lowball. While it is just as certain that the better players will win at low-ball in the long run, there is no assurance (as exists to a very large degree in high poker) that a player will wind up on top during a particular session or sitting (portion of a session). Furthermore, there is no way to protect winnings or to guard against continued losses.

Thus, as regards money-management, the only way to play winning lowball is to become inured against the occasional losses you cannot guard against. In lowball, more than any other (common) game of poker, it takes the long, long run for every-thing to get evened out — so be prepared to wait for it.

RISK STRATEGY

I have previously mentioned one of the basic forms of play at lowball that might well be called "risk strategy." This means that it is important, as a general rule, to back potentially strong hands to the limit. Such a situation exists only in very modified forms in high poker. For example, with an open-end straight flush (such as ♠Q-♠J-♠10-♠9) at draw poker for high, there is a certain fixed chance of big improvement and a player need judge only whether or not the pot offers satisfactory odds to warrant staying in for the draw. (See pages 57 to 61.)

A corresponding hand at lowball is something such as Bug-4-3-2 with an odd (useless) card. It will be observed that this hand is fairly weak as it stands, yet has enormous potential. The draw of *either* an ace or a five will yield a wheel (the best hand), while the draw of a six, seven, eight, etc., will give the smoothest possible hand (sometimes called a "nothing," such as "seven nothing" for 7-4-3-2-A, or a "nut," such as "six nut" for 6-4-3-2-A) of the rank of the card drawn. Furthermore, if such a hand is made, it will be as the result of drawing a card, and the holder of this hand may be in position to get a lot of action after the draw. Since lowball is a game of big hands (when there are multiple raises and reraises), it is essential to bet strongly on this hand — even to reraise before the draw.

Now the risk comes in, because it is not overly likely that you will draw an outstanding hand in any one trial. There is always a strong chance of pairing or drawing a picture card which will yield a relatively poor hand. Consequently, if there are several other players in the pot, this hand, without significant improvement, figures to lose — either to a pat eight or nine (or even better pat hand) or to one of the players who drew one card.

Therefore, the winning lowball player must be willing to throw money into the pot on hope. That this is the best percentage strategy and will win for the player in the long run does not alter the fact that such machinations are unfamiliar to the experienced high player. Indeed, they would be considered unsound by a high player uneducated in the ways of lowball, for the very good reason that this type of play is losing strategy in high poker!

To summarize, in part, what has been said thus far about the potential switch from more solid forms of poker to lowball, there are two factors to bear in mind:

1. In general, techniques that would be successful in high poker will not necessarily turn out well at lowball;

2. In lowball, the action is faster (stakes usually signify double amounts); the edge to the leading hand — and, in fact, to the better players — is minimal compared with similar advantages in a high game; and you must risk comparatively large amounts

on "unmade hands" (hands requiring a favorable draw to become strong).

In short, lowball is a gamble—and one that must be made quickly to boot. To be a successful lowball player you must size up your opponent(s) in a few seconds, become familiar with their habits within a few hands, and generally be on top of all the action. For lowball is certainly where the action is—if it is the kind of action you want. The more conservative, calculating players prefer to play for high.

SPECIFIC REQUIREMENTS FOR ACTIONS AT LOWBALL

I will spend somewhat less time discussing the values you should have for the various actions in lowball than I devoted to the high games. In lowball, with the enlarged chance that hands have been made worse (or, at least, not made significantly good) by the draw, much of betting tactics after the draw is a matter of semi-bluff and position. Before the draw, certain principles can be adhered to profitably, but these can be covered briefly. After the draw, while hand-values, as always, play a part, so much more depends on the psychology of the situation and the odds offered by the pot that a table of values would have little practical meaning.

Therefore, I will restrict the discussion of hand-values to opening, staying, raising and reraising before the draw. (Once again, action before the draw, following a reraise, must in great part be a function of the individuals involved.)

1. *Opening requirements.* The first man to speak is the player after the last straddler (or, when no straddles are allowed, the player to the left of the dealer). Lowball being pass and cut before the draw, it is impossible to sandbag, as is often done profitably in draw poker for high. However, as position is as important in lowball as elsewhere, opening requirements may be reduced,

since the potential opener has fewer players behind him still to speak.

After an opening in an early position (and, to a great degree, even at other times) most lowball pots are raised before the draw. So it does not make sense to open unless you are willing to stand a raise. Furthermore, on close hands, tend not to open unless you have a hand with a choice of plays—and which can be treated differently depending on the number of players in the pot. Thus, 8-7-6-5-3, a rough eight, is simply a pat eight—it cannot be played in any other way. On the other hand, 9-5-3-2-A, a smooth nine, can, at the player's option, be treated as a one-card draw to a wheel. Since the action following the opening bet may indicate that one method of drawing (pat or one card) will be more advantageous than the other, it is dangerous to open, especially in an early position, with a rough hand. Thus, a smooth nine (or, more to the point, four cards to a very good low) is a better opening than a rough eight. Remember that if you keep your eight-low, and several people draw against you, it is not to be expected that they will *all* bust!

Note that if you go into a pot of draw poker for high with a similar "advantage" (e.g., you have a pair of aces, and all the other players draw three cards), you are much better placed; for whereas it is true that one of the several other players may outdraw your aces, you yourself have a chance to improve! (In fact, this type of reasoning will indicate why a holding of two low pairs is deceptive at draw poker for high: if several other players are in, you figure to be outdrawn by one of them, and you have little chance for improvement yourself. Thus, if you hold two low pairs, and a hand of draw for high is opened in front of you, it is usually best to fold unless you have very good position, in which case a raise may be indicated. Whatever you do, you are trying to avoid playing two low pairs with many players in the pot. For a more complete discussion, see Chapter 4.)

Open in an early position with a smooth nine (or better)—one which can, if necessary, be broken down to a one-card draw to a wheel or six (or, in a pinch, a seven)—or any pat eight or better, or any hand which will give a one-card draw to a wheel, six, or possibly a good seven (or a seven if the bug is held). These requirements can be loosened as your position becomes more favorable. Avoid opening when you must draw two cards, even with Bug-2-A, unless there are just one or two other players remaining.

Remember that when you open it is on the assumption that (at least most of the time—the variety being so that you do not become stereotyped) you will stand a raise. This will usually be to stand pat with a good eight or better or, unless there are few opponents, to break a smooth nine (if you should have that to start with) and draw to a wheel, a six, or possibly a smooth seven.

The power of the bug is very similar to that at draw poker, except that it is somewhat more advantageous to hold the bug in lowball, as it can simply be used as a joker. (In high it can only be an ace, or part of a straight or flush.) Any hand with the bug is much better than without the bug: not only does it open up another rank which can be drawn favorably—if you intend to draw—but, equally important, even if you do not draw a card, none of your opponents can have it!

2. *When to stay; when to raise.* When the pot has been opened but not raised, the chance of a raise is still very high. If you are considering calling very close to the opener (i.e., there are still a significant number of players to be heard from) the chance of a raise is virtually what it was from the opener's point of view. Of course if there are only a few players still to speak, the chance of a raise is diminished.

However, even when the chance of a raise is only slightly diminished, it must be remembered that because of the peculiar positional rule whereby betting after the draw again starts at the left of the dealer (i.e., with the opener if he is still in the hand), you may be sandwiched between the opener and a raiser if you come in. Therefore, even when the chance of a raise is diminished, you must have sound values to call. You should certainly not call with less than you would require to open in a similar position, and you should depend less on pat nines and eights. These hands will feel the pressure if placed under the raiser and if faced with a bet after the draw. Far better possibilities are one-card draws to a wheel or a six. Here, at least, you are drawing to a hand which, if made, can stand you in good stead if action develops after the draw, and can win you a potentially fat pot. In other words, do not play on a hand you will keep (or a potential one you will try to make), if that hand will not be strong enough to overcome your potential positional disadvantage after the draw. A raise, remember, is quite likely. Thus, while 8-6-4-3-2 might be a suitable opening hand (you are intending, in the absence of unusual circumstances, to stand a raise and remain pat), it is losing strategy to call on this hand (compare again with two pairs at draw for high, pages 89 to 91). If there is a raise behind you, you will be forced to drop. You cannot logically draw to this hand, and your position after the draw — with a raise behind you — is likely to be untenable.

Just as you don't open the pot if you will be forced to drop out after a raise, do not *call* an opening bet if you will be forced to drop a raise. Note that here, because of the different natures of the games, the principle is *different* from high poker. The reason for this difference is that in the case of similarity — having two pairs at high or an eight at low in front of a potential raise — *position* is the most important factor.

When we come to raising, the matter of psychology enters the picture full force because you yourself are creating the "situation." Thus, a raise can be made on any pat hand — from a smooth nine (somewhat aggressive), intending to try to run the pot, to a pat six or wheel, simply trying to get in as much money as possible. Another good hand with which to raise is one with a high percentage chance to become a very good hand. Thus, I recommend raising if you have a one-card draw to a wheel or a smooth six with the bug. Possession of the bug gives you a better chance to draw the really fine hand, and the fact that you are drawing at all increases you chance for action after the draw. Remember that with a lot of semi-bluffing going on in lowball, you will almost automatically get at least one call after the draw, and you may even get a bet into you.

3. *Reraising.* The reraise by opener (or some other player who speaks after the raiser) should be considered within the same framework as the initial raise. However, you should step up (or, perhaps, this should be written "step down" for low poker) the requirements for each type of hand. For example, as opener it does not make too much sense to reraise the same "made" nine, except as a bluff. A fold would be more sensible. If the raiser has a pat hand he probably has you beaten; if he elects to draw one card, he does so after seeing your draw, *and you must speak first afterwards.* You will win additional chips from him only if he suspects a bluff.

Once again, however, reraising (and continued action) makes good sense on potentially excellent hands, and here the wheel (may you be dealt many!) has turned full circle and we have arrived at the "risk strategy" which I recommended under special pointers (pages 128 to 130).

AFTER THE DRAW

As you are already familiar with positional considerations from previous sections of this book, there is little that could profitably be said about the play after the draw. Undoubtedly, a list of a great many situations could be given, with recommendations for each, but these all boil down to the fact that psychological considerations are paramount. There are, however, three things worthy of special mention.

First, it is important to understand *why* the situations become so predominantly psychological at this form of poker more than at any other. Once again it is because of the high probability of "busting" a hand when a card is drawn. Since the frequency of bluffing which can be done profitably is much higher at lowball than at, say, high draw, it is easily seen that psychology rather than analysis of a mathematical nature becomes paramount.

However, one piece of advice may prove helpful. It is often easy to slide over the important fact that the size of the pot is crucial in gauging whether or not it is profitable to call, especially against a potential bluff. Particularly in view of the fact that the lowball player is expected to act relatively quickly, I recommend keeping track of the amount in the pot at all times. This will let you reckon the risk vs. gain ratio immediately, and help you make intelligent decisions without delaying the game.

Second, remember that lowball is more of a gamble than other forms of poker. Whereas especially in pot-limit or table-stakes competition a player has the opportunity of making a "brilliant fold" when he realizes he is defeated, this situation rarely arises in lowball. For one thing, the odds offered by the pot are usually too great to permit such plays to be made with profit in the long run—unless, of course, you don't like money but derive great enjoyment out of "being right," no matter what the cost is in the over-all picture. Thus, if one player has a 6-4 and the other has a wheel, the man with the 6-4 is going to lose a lot of chips (possibly his entire stack), and that is all there is to it. As I mentioned at the beginning of the discussion of lowball, if you cannot steel yourself to having this happen to you once in a while, you will never be a winning lowball player. The reason is that you will never get enough mileage out of your good hands, for you will stop raising when even riper fruit was available for the picking. Remember that the pot offers your opponent good odds for *his* call, too!

Finally, of the many situations that might be discussed, I have chosen one, the positional bluff, which should give you the flavor of lowball after the draw, and introduce some of the principles which can be applied to other situations.

POSITIONAL BLUFFING IN LOWBALL

Because lowball admits the "semi-bluff" technique as a matter of basic strategy, it paves the way for an unusual form of positional bluff. A positional bluff may be made when you are the last person to speak after the draw. That is, the hand has been opened on your left and you are the last caller.

In such a position you may be able to trap a player (particularly the opener) between your own hand and a semi-bluffer, and then win the pot from the remaining players because of the weakness of their hands.

For example, A opens; B, C and D call; all other players drop, and you call. Everyone draws one card. After the draw A checks, B bets, C and D drop. This is a perfect position for you to bluff in. If A has only a moderate hand, he will be forced to drop for fear of a reraise from B. Because of the nature of lowball, B will be only half-serious with his bet a larger percentage of the time than he would be (in his position) in a different form of poker. There is a good chance that B will drop out even if he suspects your raise, simply because he may fear your fair hand is better than his fair hand.

In high draw poker, in a similar betting position, B will call your raise more often than not. A player lacking good position usually does not bet unless he is willing to call a raise. In lowball there is a strong chance that B was trying to steal the pot with a fairly good hand, but one that does not measure up to the call of a raise.

For such positional bluffs to succeed, it is important that you establish yourself as a *relatively* tight player. As most lowball players bet freely on hopeful hands, a few conservative plays on your part will stick out like the proverbial sore thumb. If, for example, you merely call a raise after the draw with a rough seven, your opponents are bound to mark you as a conservative player (through reasoning of what they would do themselves). Thus, the loose nature of lowball provides a strong incentive to become known as a mildly conservative player. There is little to be gained by the reverse strategy—trying to become known as a loose player in order to get calls on your good hands—because your efforts will go unnoticed in the general aura of loose play. To stamp you as a loose player, your play would have to be virtually foolhardy. No potential gain through "advertising" is worth the cost of such a strategy.

THE ODDS AT LOWBALL

For reasons which will be described below, calculation of the odds at lowball involves some interesting mathematical problems. Fortunately, the results of investigations into lowball probabilities can be summarized very briefly insofar as they can be of value to the lowball player.

However, it is still important to understand the factors which go into the makeup of lowball odds.

The odds we are interested in for purposes of practical play are those dealing with the chances of improving a hand—our own and/or an opponent's.

We can restrict our attention primarily to one-card draws. Except in those rare situations in which the pot offers you tremendous odds—greater than 8 to 1 for your money—a two-card draw is so unlikely to produce a suitable hand that for practical purposes it need not be considered. In fact, avoiding two-card draws (even to such tempting combinations as Bug-2-A) will save you a lot of money in the long run. Virtually the only time a two-card draw is likely to be profitable is when you are the next-to-last straddler and everyone except the last straddler has dropped out. (Compare with pages 102 and 103 in Chapter 4.)

With regard to one-card draws, the basic result can be summarized briefly:

Under "normal" conditions, the odds against completing a seven-low or better by drawing one card (the bug not being held) are approximately $3\frac{1}{2}$ to 1. (If the bug is held, the odds are only about 3 to 1 against.)

The fly in the simplicity of this ointment is the phrase "under normal conditions." We know that, paradoxically—and most features of lowball will seem paradoxical to high players — although in high draw the number of players in the pot usually increases the money odds offered by the pot without necessarily reducing the odds against a player's filling his hand, *in lowball, the greater the number of players "in," the less the chance of improving a good hand with a one-card draw*. The reason behind this phenomenon is simple: The more players in the pot, the more low cards are known not to be in the pack (since, presumably, those playing have at least four low cards each). Thus, the chance of drawing a low card is decreased.

Many complicated tables have been drawn up which attempt to take into account the number of players in the pot. None I know of, however, takes into account the fact that when there are more players *out* of the pot, the chances of drawing a good low card are *increased*. There is a good reason for this. It is difficult to calculate the number of low cards held by players who do not stay for the draw. After all, K-Q-4-3-2 is, in effect, just as bad a hand as K-K-Q-Q-J. Virtually no lowball players (except the uninitiated) would stay for the draw with either hand. Thus, the number of low cards held by a player who does not stay for the draw is an imponderable. Conversely, if a player stays in, he can be assumed (with the loss of very little accuracy) to hold four low cards. Since the low cards held by dropping players can be determined only on a percentage or "average" basis, the entire affair becomes unimaginably complicated and is shunned by even the heartiest mathematicians — certainly by all those who might ever play lowball!

In addition, there is the reassuring fact that these calculations are unnecessary for the practical player. As long as you remember that your drawing chances are decreased somewhat when more players are drawing cards and increased somewhat when fewer players are drawing, you will be able to make any necessary calculations without resorting to the memorization of complex tables. True, you may be off a decimal point or two, but not enough to make any realistic difference. Remember also that lowball players are expected to act quickly, or at least without unusual delay, at all times.

The figure of 3½ to 1 against a draw to a seven-low (the bug not being held) applies almost exactly to a game with seven or eight players and a deal in which two or three others besides yourself remain for the draw. Bear this figure in mind, remembering to make slight modifications when the conditions change, and you will know all you need to know about the odds for drawing at lowball.

As for how to make use of this knowledge, the considerations are exactly the same as in other games. What odds does the pot offer? How much do you stand to gain or to lose in each instance? What is the chance of success? (If you do not feel confident about how to make use of the knowledge of the odds against completing your hand, review pages 57 to 61.)

ADVANCED STRATEGY AT LOWBALL

For those players who may take a serious interest in lowball, I will discuss the two points of advanced strategy which I feel are the most important. One of these, the "automatic bluff," is a special strategy which applies only to low games, and especially (and *almost* solely) to lowball. The other, dealing with cards flashed in "the window," is applicable to the many lowball games which—owing to the habits of the players, as opposed to the rules of the game—include this feature.

THE AUTOMATIC BLUFF

The technique which I call the automatic bluff can best be explained by an example. In a seven-handed game of lowball, stakes $1 and $2, you are first to speak with Q-5-3-2-Bug. You open, player A calls, player B raises (to $2), player C calls, players E, F and G (the dealer) all drop. You reraise to $3, A drops, B calls, C drops. Including the $1 ante, there is now a total of $10 in the pot. You draw one card, and so does player B. You draw a five, giving you a pair of fives. It is now your turn to speak. *Although you have a hand which can win only if player B has paired on fives or a higher card—* and he may not even have started with such a card!*—you must bet* ($2).

To understand why this bet is essential, let us make the simplifying assumption that in a showdown you will always lose. (This is so close to being the case that virtually no accuracy will be lost if we assume it.) Therefore, if you check, whatever B does you will neither win nor lose any money from this point on. Remember that any money you may have put into the pot is no longer of any importance. (If this is not completely clear, reread pages 57 to 61.) On the other hand, if you bet $2, B may fold, call or raise. If B calls or raises (you will drop if he raises, of course), you will lose $2 for your trouble. However, if B drops, you will win $10.

Thus, if this situation arises six times, even if B calls or raises *five times out of the six,* you will break even.

Now let us consider how often B will actually call. While it is true that he is getting good odds for his money, remember that because of the nature of lowball *there is a very strong chance he has made a relatively poor hand—* one that will certainly lose if you have the strength you have represented, and would lose even if you have a "semi-bluff." Also, much of the time B will have a hand in the semi-bluff category, and he will not call *every time* on such hands, even though the pot offers good odds. Nor can he afford to raise without suitable values, for he must be wary of a reraise!

In other words, while it is certainly true that B will call you more than half the time—including a certain portion when he calls with only moderate values—because of the odds the pot offers *him,* you will still be a big winner in the long run.

Furthermore, by making plays such as this, you will *greatly increase your winnings on your big hands.* Many players, not realizing the essential soundness of your play, will mark you as a big bluffer when you expose a hand like this in the showdown in one of your losing automatic bluffs. They may even raise after the draw on some later hand, holding only moderate values themselves! Or, at the very least, they will tend to call you after the draw when you have made your hand and they have only moderate values.

It is important to understand the basic principles behind this automatic bluff, so that you do not apply the technique improperly. There are two crucial factors which lead to an automatic bluff situation. The first is that your hand after the draw must be *essentially hopeless!* It is a paradoxical part of lowball — probably the strangest of all poker games, anyway — that after the draw you must bet with either a very good hand or a very bad hand! The reason is that if your hand is not a sure loser you can always hope to win on a check out after the draw. Thus, if you had drawn a jack in the example hand, there would be about a 50% chance that your hand would then be better than your opponent's! The second factor is that the pot must offer suitable odds. If there is little money in the pot, say only two or three times the amount you risk with the automatic bluff, then the play will be a big loser in the long run. For now your opponent need call you only about two times in three to hold you even, and he may well do that even though his own odds are correspondingly shorter. Using the amount in the pot as a basis for calculation has been described in great detail previously, so nothing more need be said on this subject.

A final word of advice on the automatic bluff. In the long run it will not pay to try to run this bluff against more than one opponent unless the odds offered by the pot are enormous. With two opponents, for example, there is quite a good chance that one of them will have made a hand which warrants a call on its merits. When you add to this the number of calls you will get in lowball "on suspicion" — and these will occur more often than in any other game since the pot offers good odds for such a call — your chances of running the pot are slim indeed.

"THE WINDOW"

It may prove surprising to many that some lowball players have a habit of holding their cards in such a way that the card on the outside is exposed to the other players. In fact, in many games this is virtually standard procedure. Holding a card exposed in this way is called "holding it in the window." Most of the time, the window plays a meaningless part in the game. You will simply see everyone flashing a low card so as not to give away any information. If you find yourself in a lowball game where this is the accepted practice, you must only take care never to expose a bad card in your hand. To guard against this, it is wise practice to place the card you draw in the center of your hand. This will enable you to hold your cards in such a way that no one else can catch a glimpse of your draw.

There is one situation on which experienced players have learned to capitalize. When a player flashes a six-spot in his window after the draw, it is very likely to be a bluff! After all, it would be silly for him to advertise that he held a six-low—a hand he could expect big profits from after the draw. Thus, when you see a six flashed in the window, you should suspect that the player has not made his hand.

HIGH-LOW
POKER

HIGH-LOW POKER differs from other forms of the game only in that the high and low hands split the pot. This one variation in the rules has such a great effect on the play of a hand, and produces so many interesting situations and strategies, that it is rapidly replacing all other forms of "serious" poker. (The only exceptions are those few games which permit only one-winner forms of poker.)

The main effect of the high-low division of the pot is to increase the number of potential winning hands. This augments a player's interest in the game, as well as the "action" (number of bets and the amount bet at each turn). The average player enjoys high-low because it is more exciting than any other form of poker, and he feels (erroneously) that the larger number of potential winning hands will enable him to overcome the luck of the deal.

The expert player prefers high-low, both because of the increase in betting and because it gives him a greater chance to take advantage of his skill. In general, the more complicated the game, the greater the advantage of the superior player. Further, since the theory of high-low poker is not as highly developed at the present time as that of other forms of the game, the expert

143

has the additional opportunity of cashing in on his opponents' lack of sophistication.

High-low poker is a game of fairly recent vintage, and little has been said about it in the standard poker texts. To rectify this situation, I will discuss this form of poker in detail in the present chapter.

Because high-low poker is comparatively young, there has been little standardization of the rules. Most high-low games rely mainly on house rules to cover vague situations. In the next few pages, I will cover the most popular sets of rules and make some clarifications which may lead to a standard code among high-low players.

RANK OF HANDS

High-low poker is played with many variations in the ranking of certain hands. The two most important clarifications which must be made in a high-low game are the treatment of aces and of high hands (straights and flushes).

The ace may be treated only as a high card, or as *either* a high card or a low card (at the player's option). Under the latter rule, if the game is being played with more than five cards, a player may use an ace as a high card in designating his hand for high, *and* as a low card for low.

A straight or a flush may or may not be allowed to stand for its value as a low hand. Assuming the ace is either high or low, the lowest hand is 5-4-3-2-A, unless this is deemed to be a straight. In that case the lowest hand is 6-4-3-2-A.

The treatment of straights and flushes as *only* high hands or low hands carries over from lowball. If straights and flushes are allowed to have value as low hands as well as high, the number of potential two-way hands is greatly increased. This tends to stimulate betting and heighten interest. Thus, most high-low games accept straights and flushes as high *or* low, as well as allowing an ace as high *or* low. The calculations in this chapter assume that aces, straights and flushes "swing" — that is, are high or low.

THE SHOWDOWN AT HIGH-LOW

There are three different ways in which the showdown can be effected at high-low poker. In one method, sometimes called "cards speak" (a shortening of "the cards speak for themselves"), the players simply expose their hands just as in the other forms of poker. The players with the lowest and highest hands then divide the pot equally. If the same player has *both,* he wins the entire pot.

The other showdown methods involve "declaration." Under these methods a player must declare his intention to try for the high or low half of the pot, and he is then eligible to win only the portion of the pot for which he declared (with certain rare exceptions; see "Dividing the Pot"). It is also possible to attempt to win the entire pot by calling "high-low" (sometimes called "swinging" or "scooping").

Declaration may be either simultaneous or consecutive. Simultaneous declaration is achieved by having each player involved in the showdown hold chips, coins or other tokens concealed in his closed fist. Different chips or tokens indicate the three different declarations: high, low, and high-low. When all the players have made a decision, the fists are opened and the pot divided accordingly. Should one direction remain undeclared, the entire pot is awarded to the winner of the other direction.

In consecutive declaration, the players declare their intentions *in order.* This gives great advantage to the players who have good position and can speak last, or near the end. Usually, the player who made the last bet or raise (of, if there was no bet made on the last round, the highest or eldest hand) is required to declare first, declaration then following in clockwise rotation.

DIVIDING THE POT

In "cards speak" there is no problem dividing the pot. If two (or more) players tie for either high or low, they share equally in that half of the pot. When the pot contains an extra chip and thus cannot be divided exactly equally, it is customary to give the extra chip to the winner of the high half.

Certain complications may arise when declarations are being used. If there are no declarations in a given direction, the entire pot is awarded to the winner of the other direction. *If there are no high-low calls,* the pot is considered as two separate entities. One half is contested by the players declaring high, the other half by those declaring low.

There is a general rule, however, that when a player declares high-low, if he is defeated in one direction he also loses his chance in the other direction. This rule is abandoned only under exceptional circumstances (as described below).

Division of the pot when (exactly) one player calls high-low. If just one player calls high-low, he is awarded the entire pot if he wins in both directions. If he is tied in one direction (but wins the other), or in both directions, he takes either half he has won outright and shares equally in the portion(s) of the pot for which he tied, along with others in the tie. If the high-low declarant loses in one direction but wins in the other, the player defeating him is awarded the entire pot.* If the high-low declarant loses in both directions, the pot is divided between or (in the case of a tie) among the rightful winners.

Division of the pot when more than one player calls high-low. If two or more players call high-low, the division of the pot may be complex. *This is the only case in which a high-low declarant can share in the pot even if he loses in one direction.*

* This rule is not universal, but I strongly recommend it.

1. If one of the high-low declarants wins in both directions, or wins in one direction and ties in the other, or ties in both directions, the pot is divided as if his were the only high-low declaration (see previous section) *except* that another player who called high-low and lost in one direction may not share in the pot.

2. If each high-low declarant loses in at least one direction, and one or both directions are won by one-way declarants, none of the high-low declarants shares in the pot. *However, a player who called one direction and lost to a high-low declarant in that direction may not share in the pot either.*

Example: A and B call high-low; C calls high; D calls low. C has the highest hand, B has the lowest hand. C wins the entire pot.

3. If each of the high-low declarants loses in at least one direction, but neither direction is won by a one-way declarant, the pot is divided as in "cards speak."

Example: A and B call high-low; C calls high; D calls low. A has the highest hand, B has the lowest hand. A and B share equally in the pot.

Side Pots. Side pots are settled separately among the players with equity in the side money. However, unless the game decides otherwise (and provides special equipment), a player may make only one declaration, and that declaration holds for both the main pot and any side pots in which he may be involved.

FORMS OF HIGH-LOW

High-low poker may be played in any of the standard forms. Draw poker with five cards, and stud poker with five or seven cards are the most popular forms. Six-card high-low stud is gaining limited popularity. Wild cards are not usual in high-low games.

VARIATIONS

1. *Option (sometimes called English Stud).* This form of high-low is usually applied to five-card stud and is sometimes played Canadian style (using four-card straights and flushes).

After the betting round following receipt of the final card, each player has the option of exchanging any one of his cards for a new card. If an upcard is replaced, the new card is dealt face up; if the hole card is replaced, the new card is dealt face down. The options are elected consecutively (last bettor or raiser, or high or low hand electing first at the discretion of the players) and are usually revealed before the next option is taken. Some games (wisely) allow the players to conceal the new cards until all options have been elected.

Another round of betting now precedes the declaration.

2. *Selection.* At the beginning of a hand, each player is dealt a number of cards (usually four cards in five-card games and five cards in seven-card games) from which to select his original hand. The purpose of this variation is to add interest in trying to determine the unseen cards as well as to increase the number of good hands in play.

RESTRICTION ON RAISES

In limit and pot-limit high-low games, a restriction is usually placed on the number of raises which may be made on a given round. The purpose of such a rule is to avoid a situation in which a player must pay an unlimited amount of money to call a potential "immortal" hand.

Example: A, B and C remain in the pot. A has an immortal high and B has a potential immortal low. Player A will, of course, raise at every opportunity. If the number of raises is unlimited, B can also continue raising. There is thus no limit on the amount C must call to reach the showdown.

The situation is different from one-way poker, for in such a game C could stop the raising by refusing to raise on his own. If, in a one-way game, A and B continue raising each other, C has no right to see the hand through unless he is willing to meet the stake. (A and B cannot profitably continue this policy if C may have the best hand.)

SEVEN-CARD HIGH-LOW STUD

This game has gained great popularity in recent years and is still on the upswing. Since it is becoming *the* modern form of poker, it will be considered here in great detail.

In the next two sections, I will describe the strategy for playing the two major forms of seven-card high-low stud: cards speak, and declaration. These two forms are considered separately because they are essentially different games and they require different techniques for successful play.

In the games under discussion, an ace, a straight, and a flush may be considered as either high or low (possibly serving different functions in the selection of high and low hands), at the player's option. Thus, a "wheel" (5-4-3-2-A) is the best low hand as well as a good high hand (the lowest straight).

Except when specified to the contrary, betting will be by the limit method. The dealer antes one chip, and all bets and raises are one chip until each player has six cards, after which they are two chips. This method is most common in limit games, although a gradual increase in the maximum bet (with each round) has more to recommend it.

Modifications of strategy and money-management when these basic rules are varied will be covered separately. I recommend that a poker player eager to learn how to cope with each of the various forms of seven-card high-low stud begin by learning these two basic (and most popular) games in the following pages, then go on to the differences in technique necessitated by possible variations in the rules of any one particular game.

CARDS SPEAK

Opening and middle-game tactics at cards speak can be summarized in one short sentence: *Always* play for low. When there is no declaration, it is wildly unlikely that a hand which is essentially high can be turned into a winner for low. (In a declaration game, a high hand can be maneuvered into a full-pot winner if the other players can be induced to call high.) Therefore, the high player never has any expectation of winning more than half the pot. The low player, on the other hand, retains the chance of turning his low hand into a straight (or occasionally a flush) and winning high.

There is a great temptation to stay too long on a good high hand because habits from high seven-card stud and other straight-high games tend to carry over into high-low. For example, the holding of triplets on the deal (of three cards) is so unusual, and such a good hand for seven-card stud *high,* that the high-low player is often tempted to play this hand. He knows it is a good hand for high, and he thinks that his excellent chance to win the high half of the pot justifies playing this combination — in many cases to the bitter end.

To demonstrate the fallacy of playing high hands in high-low seven-card stud, cards speak, I will illustrate some of the situations a typical player, starting with triplets, might encounter.

In these examples, player A is dealt three queens.

Example 1: At the sixth and seventh cards, when the size of the bet is increased, only A and B remain in the pot. A has triplets; B has an obvious low hand. In this situation A has the worst of it. Regardless of the cards drawn, B will win the low half of the pot. More often than not, A will win the high. Unless B improves (say to a straight) and A does not, A does win the high. However, on those occasions when B does improve and

A does not, B wins the entire pot. On hands of this type there will be very little money in the pot besides that bet by A and B.

In other words, when A is lucky he gets his money back. Part of the time, A loses everything. The situation is worse for A at pot limit or table stakes: B can bet increasing amounts with no fear of loss!

Example 2: A, who has triplets, is in the pot along with more than one other person, near the end. Each of these other players has a low hand. A now has an equity in the pot; he stands to win an amount depending on the number of other players. However, as A's potential win increases, so the chance that he will win *at all* decreases. With more than one player having a potential low, there is considerable danger that one of them will draw a straight (or, rarely, a flush). A's position is better than in the two-handed case (in which he could only lose) but is not a profitable situation.

Example 3: A is involved in a pot with other players, some of whom are going for high also. This case cannot be more advantageous to A than that of Example 2, for now A may not even have the best hand for high! (In a limit game, you can expect quite a few players at the showdown.) Furthermore, he is at a disadvantage versus the low players who have a chance at *each* half of the pot if they fill their hands.

In other words, triplets (especially high ones, which give their owner no chance to convert his hand to a low one) on the deal is *not* a good hand in seven-card high-low, cards speak, *and should generally be dropped on the first round.* The great temptation to play this excellent high hand should be resisted. Some players prefer to stay on triplets in the hope that they will "fill up" early and find themselves in a favorable position if several other players have good hands for low. However, when such a hand is played at the early stages, the holder must have enough discipline to drop out as soon as his chances of making a full house are the least bit diminished (as by other cards of the same rank as his odd cards appearing around the table).

This extreme example is an illustration of the basic strategy at cards speak: At the early stages, forget about high. Don't play unless you have a chance for low.

As even three-of-a-kind is not an especially good hand, it is clear that playing on a high pair, or any collection of high cards, is the height of folly. The only hands with prospects for high that should be played are those which may later be converted into low hands.

WHEN TO STAY

The following are the basic minimum "stays" on the first round in a seven-card high-low cards speak game:

(a) Any three to a seven.

(b) Three to an eight under the following circumstances:
1. with an ace and another card five or lower;
2. with an ace and two to an ace-flush;
3. with three to a flush.

(c) Three to a nine with either:
1. an ace, the third card five or lower, and two to an ace-flush;
2. three to a flush.
(In a conservative game the hands in category (c) should be folded.)

(d) Any three to a flush, with two cards six or lower.

(e) A pair of aces and a low card.

(f) Three aces. (*Note:* This three-of-a-kind has a special position because of its extra advantage as a high hand, because some chance for low is maintained, and because it is defensive against other players making especially good low hands. However, be prepared to fold quickly if the possibilities of straights against you develop.)

These requirements should be relaxed only if it becomes clear that the game is a loose one. In general, the winning strategy at cards speak is to be one notch more conservative (in hands played at the early stages) than the rest of the game. Thus, in a tight game, stick to the (mathematically sound) standards set down above. If it becomes obvious that almost all of the players are *two* steps removed from these standards (e.g., they play on three to a nine) then you may move your own standards one step in that direction (e.g., play with three to an eight).

CARDS SPEAK (MIDDLE GAME)

In general, there will be only moderate betting (no raise or one raise) on the third card (first betting round). After the fourth card has been dealt, the first significant threat of a raise appears. (In pot limit or table stakes, this is the usual time for the first sizable bet.)

A very important decision of the middle game, therefore, is whether or not the first four cards justify a stay or a raise, or should be dropped. From this point on, any *close decision* should be resolved as follows: *Don't play unless you have an ace.* (The significance of the ace will become more apparent when I discuss the six-card game.)

The fourth card. Assuming there is a bet made on the fourth card (second betting round), you should stay in the pot *only if* *you drew a satisfactory card,* that is, one which improved your hand. Most often, you will have begun play with three low cards. Therefore, call a bet on the fourth card only if you drew another usable low card. At this stage, if you hit a low pair or a high card (called a "bust"), you should generally fold. You are not in a favorable position for low, and although your low pair (or one high card) may be the highest hand at the present time, you will not remain high often enough to risk money in the hope of winning only half the pot (see opening strategy).

Similarly, if you started with a three-flush, drop against a bet on the fourth card unless you made a four-flush, or you now have three cards towards a good low. If you started with a pair of aces and a low card, drop unless you made triplets, or aces up (with no pair on board), or hit another low card. Similar considerations apply if you started with a middling three-straight (such as 5-6-7). Drop unless you hit an open-end four-straight or a good low card.

You should bet (or raise) when you have a hand which gives you a good chance to improve in either direction. Four low cards without a bust should be bet; you have improved your low, have a chance to make a straight for high, and are very likely to have at least as good a hand as anyone else. Even if someone else has four low cards with a better low, his edge over you for low will be minimal (see Low Poker). Because you have the opportunity to win in each direction, even if you bet into a stronger hand you have a good chance to come out alive by splitting the pot.

With a three-flush, or an open-end three-straight, and a moderately good start toward a low, you should also bet. A four-flush should be bet even with a moderate low; this is justified by the enormous chance that a flush will win the high, overcoming a straight made by a player with several low cards.

In deciding how good your hand is for low, it is no longer solely a question of how low your actual cards are. You should note carefully the low cards you are lacking, and calculate how many of these cards are yet to appear. Thus, if you hold 2-3-4-6, you should be wary of betting strongly if several aces and (especially) fives have shown. You have a less than normal chance of hitting the cards you need, while the other players (who have the aces and fives) do not have correspondingly diminished chances—for their cards are still "alive." Similarly, if several cards of a rank you hold have been folded, you have a great advantage over the remaining players in the pot—you have one of the crucial low cards and it will be difficult for them to draw this card. You can value your hand higher and bet accordingly. The two examples shown on the following pages illustrate such calculations.

Doors Open (Cards Speak)

YOUR HAND	HANDS OF OTHER PLAYERS *(read down for order of upcards)*						
	A	B	C	D	E	F	G
◇ 4 ♣ 3 (concealed)	?	?	?	?	?	?	?
♡ 6	♠ A	♣ 2	♠ 10	♣ 6	♡ J	♣ Q	◇ 3
♠ 7	♠ 6	◇ 7	×	♡ K	×	×	♡ 7
◇ 2	♣ 9	♡ 3	×	×	×	×	♠ J

You are in a strong position. No fives have shown, and only one ace. Further, it will be difficult for A to get a three or a seven, and for B to get a six.

Doors Shut (Cards Speak)

YOUR HAND	HANDS OF OTHER PLAYERS *(read down for order of upcards)*						
	A	B	C	D	E	F	G
◇ 4 ♣ 3 (concealed)	?	?	?	?	?	?	?
♡ 6	♠ A	♣ 2	♣ A	♠ 2	♡ J	♡ 5	◇ 5
♠ 7	♠ 6	◇ 7	×	♡ K	×	♣ Q	♡ 2
◇ 2	♣ 9	♡ 3	×	×	×	×	♠ J

Here your competitors (A and B) have the same cards, yet your chances are slim. Two fives are already accounted for (as well as two aces).

The fifth card. After the fifth card, to justify playing on you should have a strong possibility for one direction or the other. You must now consider your strength in relation to that of the other players. In calculating your chances, it is often useful to use as a basis *the number of working low cards* that each player is likely to hold. Suppose that you had four to a seven after the fourth card; other players had good low cards exposed. On the fifth card you hit an open (low) pair while the other players "bust" — hitting picture cards. Although you do not now have the lowest hand (in fact, you probably have the highest!), your position for low has not been damaged to any great extent. In almost all cases the picture cards will not be used in making the best low hand for the other players. You are still competing for low on the basis of the first four cards. However, while maintaining your position for low, you now have a big edge in the high direction because of your chance to make three-of-a-kind or two pairs. In other words, you have a chance to win in each direction and probably have the best hand at the table. This is a most favorable situation, and you should bet strongly.

On the other hand, suppose that after five cards you have 2-5 (concealed) 7-4-10 (exposed) and other players have lower boards exposed. It is unlikely that all the other players have busted (that is, made a low pair on the fifth card). You are now in an inferior position in the fight for low because you are essentially one card behind. In fact, even if your opponents have made low pairs, they are in the strong position described in the previous paragraph. In this situation you should *not* call a bet. In high-low (especially at pot limit or table stakes) the most important factor for a winning player is the self-discipline to drop when he realizes that his position has *suddenly* become unfavorable.

It is tempting to play on in such situations because there are still two cards to come and there is always the hope that a good low hand can be made. But it must be remembered that the other players are in stronger positions at present, and they also have two cards coming. If you can improve, so can they; the odds are just as much against "chasing" the best hand in high-low poker as in straight high poker.

END-GAME STRATEGY

The sixth card. Assuming you stay in to see your sixth card (which will be turned up), you are now reaching the closing stages of the hand. At this point, there will usually be no more than three players remaining in the pot (except in a low-limit game), and the amount of the bet is increased. In a contested high-low hand,

Favorable Situation with a Low Pair (Cards Speak)

YOUR HAND	HANDS OF REMAINING PLAYERS (read down for order of upcards)			
	A	B	C	D
◇ A ♣ 6 (concealed)	?	?	?	?
♡ 5	♣ 8	♠ 2	♣ A	♠ 9
♠ 7	♡ 6	♡ 3	♠ 4	◇ 4
◇ 5	♣ 10	♡ Q	◇ J	♡ 8

You are in a strong position at this stage and should bet. (But be wary of D. If he stays in, he may have three nines!)

Unfavorable Situation Against a Low Pair (Cards Speak)

YOUR HAND	HANDS OF REMAINING PLAYERS (read down for order of upcards)			
	A	B	C	D
♠ 8 ♠ A (concealed)	?	?	?	?
♡ 3	♣ 2	♣ 7	♡ A	♠ 2
♠ 4	♡ 6	♠ 5	♣ 5	◇ 7
♣ 10	◇ 2	♡ 9	◇ J	◇ Q

There is no advantage to continuing in this position. A and B quite likely have better hands than yours, and D has a potential (ace-queen) flush.

the typical result is that three players stay to the end, two of them splitting the pot. You don't want to be that third man—the man in the middle—and great pains should be taken to avoid being caught in this trap. The best way to avoid it is to follow the general rule that (barring very exceptional cases) you should not call a bet after the sixth card unless you have a "made" hand —one that figures to give you a good chance to win one half of the pot without improvement. More money is lost at high-low on the hope of drawing a perfect or at least favorable seventh card than in any other way. Stating this another way, don't call on the sixth card unless you are prepared to call on the seventh card!

When you have what appears to be the best hand in one direction, *plus* a draw to make a hand in the opposite direction, you are in raising position. In other words, while you are anxious to protect one half of the pot when you *hope* to win one way, there is no advantage to putting in more money. (Of course if you are *certain* to win one direction, you also raise, but these situations are, alas, rare.) When you have a chance to win both directions (but have a good enough hand to protect yourself in one direction), it is in your interest to get as much money into the pot as possible.

When you have a draw to a good hand in each direction, but no hand actually made either way after the sixth card, *it is to your advantage to drop out*. Remember that the other players probably have good hands, and that even though you have a chance to win both the high and low, you are still playing an inferior hand. You can draw only one way, and if you do so, you get only half the pot. Since the opponent started with a better hand, he can outdraw you as easily as you can outdraw him. It's not worth it.

The last round. There is little that need be said about the final round. In almost all cases you have reached this stage because you already had a good chance of success with a hand completed after the sixth card. In a limit game if often pays to call on the last round with a possibly inferior hand because of the odds offered by the pot. Bear in mind, however, that if two opponents hold outstanding hands, and they are headed in opposite directions, you will be required to call the maximum number of raises to reach the showdown. Therefore, in situations of this kind it is best not to call any bet (or raise) on the final betting round unless you are prepared to see the hand all the way through.

SIX-CARD HIGH-LOW STUD, CARDS SPEAK

When only six cards are dealt, the chance of making a straight or a flush is greatly diminished. Because of this, the only hands that are *likely* to win the entire pot are hands which include aces.

An ace therefore assumes great significance, and very few hands without an ace should be played at all!

Why is an ace so valuable? First of all, a low hand which includes an ace *that does not stand up for low* may win the high solely on the strength of the ace. After all, if you are beaten for low, your opponent has only one spare card with which to turn his hand into a higher one than yours. It is true that an opponent may make a good low hand and also win high with a *low pair*, but he must make this specific hand (unless he has an unlikely straight or flush) to defeat you in both directions when you have an ace (unless he also has one). Second, if you can make a pair of aces, you will probably lose high only to a very unusual hand—a straight or a flush in six cards. Furthermore, you still have a chance to win the low! If your opponents "pair up," it will be a matter of who has the highest (i.e., worst) of the odd cards—almost a random factor. If you should draw badly to your low and make two pairs, you win *both ways* if your opponent draws two pairs (remember that aces can be high *or* low).

Since it is every advantage to have an ace, and every disadvantage not to have one, possession or lack of an ace should almost always determine your play in the opening stages. (The ace is not magic, however. If you hit high cards, do not bank on winning high if your opponents' boards—i.e., upcards—indicate straight possibilities.)

WHEN TO STAY

Stay in a pot of six-card high-low stud, cards speak, with any of the following:

> an ace and a low card;
> two to a five low;
> a pair of aces (the best hand).

The reason a pair of aces is such a good hand in this game is that it is enough to give you a good chance to win high *without improvement,* yet maintains a reasonable chance for low.

STRATEGY

Needless to say, you do not stay unless you are in strong contention for low (or have one or more aces). However, after five cards have been dealt you should give some consideration to your chances of winning high. The situation after five cards is not identical to that in seven-card stud after six cards, because it is unlikely that anyone has a good hand made after five cards. Other players will now be in the pot on possibilities, and the rule about having a "made" hand, with one card to be dealt, does not apply.

Otherwise, the basic strategic considerations carry over from seven-card high-low, as well as the tactics.

HIGH-LOW WITH DECLARATIONS

High-low with declarations is so different from cards speak that it might well be considered a completely new poker form. However, it is valuable to analyze this game from the point of view of its differences from cards speak. An understanding of these differences will lead to a fuller grasp of the strategy of declaration.

In general, a declaration game is more complicated than cards speak, therefore more difficult to play. There are more factors to take into account: not only must you decide your own declaration, but for successful play you must analyze the probable declarations of your opponents as well. Better players tend to call declaration (in dealer's choice games) because it increases opportunities to exploit their poker skills.

There are two popular forms of declaration high-low poker. In *simultaneous declaration*, after the pot has been evened at the showdown stage, each player conceals a chip (or some other token) in his closed fist. Different chips (or tokens) are used to indicate the three different calls—high, low, and high-low. When each of the participants has made a decision, and has his closed fist on the table, all reveal the declarations simultaneously. The pot is then divided accordingly (see pages 146 to 147). This form of play is sometimes referred to as high-low "with fists."

I consider simultaneous declaration a superior form of poker to *consecutive declaration*. In consecutive declaration, one player is designated as the first to declare. This is usually the player who made the last aggressive move (raise or bet) on the final betting round. If there was no bet on the final round, the high hand is usually required to declare first. Declaration then proceeds in clockwise rotation.

It is clearly a great advantage to call last, or near the end of the declaration, if consecutive calling is being employed. Very often, a player with good position is able to secure half of the pot without good values because all others have declared in one direction. Such a position is called being "in the catbird's seat."

Because of this enormous positional advantage, a great deal of maneuvering goes on to avoid betting or raising on the final round. Like the men riding a race to see whose horse was the *slower*, high-low players using consecutive declaration do a lot of backing off and stalling. The riders solved their problem simply enough: they switched horses and took off in a flash. Unfortunately, a poker game will only become stultified if consecutive declaration is used. The final betting round should be the most important and exciting phase of the hand—not a playing field of retreat, cowardice and conservatism.

Therefore, I recommend that you use simultaneous declaration (presently *not* the more popular form), and this section will temporarily assume that method to be in use in the declaration high-low games. Techniques for consecutive declaration will be given following the general discussion of high-low with declarations.

WHY DECLARATION IS DIFFERENT

What is it that makes declaration poker different from cards speak? Perhaps the best way to answer this is with an example. When we discussed cards speak, we indicated that an original holding of high triplets was *not* a satisfactory hand for your first three cards. Why not? Because in a basic situation you would wind up competing with a player who had a low hand. This player will generally have a draw to a straight, sometimes to a flush. If he does not make his straight, the pot is split. If he fills a straight or flush, and you do not fill, he wins the pot. If you both fill, the pot is split. In other words, the low player has a free shot to try for the entire pot. He has every advantage, for he is safe to recover half the pot under any circumstances.

Now consider the same situation in a declaration game. The low player can secure half the pot if he wishes. Suppose, however, that he is interested in more. If he fills his straight, *he must declare for high* (as well as low), and by so doing he runs the risk of losing the entire pot when the high player (who started with triplets, say) makes a full house. In cards speak, the low player merely exposes his straight and tries to win the entire pot. In declaration, the low player who makes a straight must run the risk of losing the entire pot to try to win the entire pot. Quite a difference!

Obviously, three-of-a-kind is not still the terrible hand it was at cards speak. In fact, it is quite a good hand, because the basic nature of the game has changed. A one-way hand may now win the entire pot because of the declarations. It is clear, therefore, that your strategy must be quite different at declaration from what it is at cards speak.

WHEN TO PLAY

In addition to the hands suitable for play at cards speak, the following holdings should be played on the first round at declaration:

(a) Any three-flush including the ace and a low card;

(b) Any *concealed* two-flush to the ace, with a low card on board;

(c) A low card on board with a concealed pair from sixes to nines;

(d) A pair of aces and a low card;

(e) Any three-of-a-kind (the best hand is three aces; three-of-a-kind is a *good* hand—one of the best—in *this* game!).

TREATMENT OF PAIRS

I recommend that a low pair which is *not completely concealed* be dropped. A holding of ♠ 2 ♡ 6 concealed, with ♢ 6 upcard is not nearly as good as ♡ 6 ♢ 6 concealed, with ♠ 2 upcard. The latter hand is much stronger because of the possibility of representing a low hand on board at the time the third six is obtained (if ever). The concealed pair should be at least as high as the six, to provide a good chance to win high against "busted" low hands which make pairs or triplets, but not higher than the nine, to provide a good chance to convert into a suitable low.

Some players recommend playing on any three working cards. They play on a hand such as ♠ 2 ♡ 6 concealed, with ♢ 6 upcard. This is a slightly loose style of play and should be adopted only when the other players in the game are staying on even worse hands. Again, you should try to be one notch more conservative than your opposition.

The idea behind playing with a pair is to win at least half of the pot when you make triplets. To give yourself a good chance to win the entire pot, you should hope to represent a low hand on the board when you catch the triplets.

The fourth card. While there are more hands justifying an initial stay at declaration (compared with cards speak), so must a higher percentage of these be folded after the fourth card is drawn.

Suppose you start with ♡ A ♡ J concealed and ♠ 3 upcard. This hand is worth a stay on the first betting round because it offers a good chance to go in either direction, plus the fact that you can draw good cards (such as low hearts) which will allow your board to misrepresent the essential nature of your hand.

However, you must be wary of carrying these "possible" big winning hands too far. First of all, if you don't hit a working card on the second round (fourth card), forget the whole thing, regardless of the over-all situation. Your jack of hearts was only a half-working card to begin with, and your hand was played mainly because of the concealed flush possibility. If you hit a card which gives you a possible hand *one way* (such as a middle heart, or a good low card that is not a heart), you should play *only* if there are no good boards going in your direction. Be especially conservative about continuing to play when you have only a one-way chance, unless you can hope to have your board misrepresent your hand. Of course, if you hit a two-way card (a low heart), you have good possibilities almost regardless of the other boards, and you should drop out only in rare circumstances. If the other boards are only moderate, you may raise. Note that the strength of a hand depends both on its value *and how well it is concealed.* This is consistent with your representation of a low hand. If your low fails, you hope to win the high (and possibily the whole pot thereby) with a flush.

General middle-game strategy. Your middle-game strategy should be guided by two considerations: (1) Whether or not you have the best hand (varying from a lead to a sure winner) in one direction, and (2) whether or not your board represents your hand accurately or not. You should play when you are satisfied that you have a good winning chance based on either or both of these considerations. If there is no chance for a representation, but you feel nearly sure of winning one direction, you should simply raise in order to build up your equity in the pot. The more people you can entice into the pot, the more money you will win. If you hope to win by means of a representation, you should bet and raise consistently in the manner you would follow if you had a nearly certain or sure winner *in the direction you are representing.*

Declaration is a dangerous game. There is one danger inherent in a declaration game which is not present at cards speak. At cards speak, if you have a good hand you can be fairly certain that any given opponent cannot defeat you in both directions (or, in the middle-game stage, that it is wildly unlikely that he can outdraw you in both directions). At declaration, however, if you cannot read the holding of an opponent who may have a strong hand and is betting strongly, *you are in a dangerous situation even if you are certain you cannot be defeated both ways.* If an opponent may have you beaten in either direction, even though he cannot beat you both ways, drop out unless you have a very large equity in the pot. At cards speak you could afford to play, and simply hope to split the pot. At declaration, if you cannot read your opponent's hand accurately, you will be forced to guess which way to declare. Your opponent, on the other hand, is in a safe situation with a one-way lock. He will keep betting, and you must guess which immortal hand he has. This situation is extremely dangerous (more so in a pot limit or table stakes game than in a limit game) and should be avoided whenever possible. If the betting gets stiff and you don't have a good "reading" or a sure thing, drop out as soon as possible.

When you and one other player remain near the end of the hand and several other players have been calling bets in the middle rounds, the equity in the pot may be sufficient for you to call in the hope that you will guess correctly. (This usually applies only in a limit game.) For example, you and one opponent remain on the sixth card. Your opponent, who may have you locked out

either way (but not both ways), bets two chips. It will cost you
four chips to see the hand through (two on this round and two
on the next), so your potential loss is four chips. If there were
several other players in the hand, there may be about 15 or 16
chips in the pot. Your potential win is about eight chips, and the
pot therefore offers you two-to-one odds. You should be able to
escape with half the pot more often than one time in three (either
by hitting a very good hand or by guessing the correct call), so
you should stay in.

Conversely, in a similar situation, if the pot has seen little
action and it contains only nine or ten chips, it is not worthwhile
to pay four chips in an attempt to win five. You will have to be
right almost half the time for such a maneuver to pay off. Con-
cede the pot to your opponent! After all, why play a guessing
game at even money when you can get better odds by exploiting
your superior skill on succeeding deals?

REPRESENTATION

High-low with declarations gives a good player additional
scope to display his talents. The most significant way in which
this can be done is by turning a one-way winning hand into a
winner of the entire pot. For this, it is obviously essential to
misrepresent the hand so that any opponents remaining at the
showdown will believe either that:

(1) They can defeat you in the direction they anticipate you
will declare;

(2) They can defeat you in both directions;

(3) They can play safe by calling opposite to the direction they
anticipate your declaring.

In each case your objective is to make a very strong hand in
one direction, while representing an attempt to win in the
opposite direction (or in some other way concealing your true
strength). In many instances this cannot be done effectively
unless certain cards appear on your board (your collection of

upcards). Unless your board runs opposite to the true nature of your hand, your representation of a hand different from the one you hold cannot succeed.

On the other hand, in those instances when you are lucky enough to have your over-all holding misrepresented by the upcards, you must adjust your betting cleverly so as to appear to be attempting to win the reverse direction.

The basic strategy is to bet, raise or call in a straightforward manner, *just as you might with a hand of opposite orientation.*

Example: Your original hand:

♠ A ♦ 6 concealed;

♠ 6 upcard.

Good players usually welcome a hand of this type at declaration because it gives them ample possibilities for misrepresenting and winning a big pot against weaker opposition.

On the first round you call the minimum bet. Your next upcard is the ♡ 7. This would normally give you an adequate low, but not a raising hand (not enough near cards for a straight), so you simply call the bet on this round.

Your fifth card (open), is the ♣ 6. This is just the opportunity you have been waiting for! You have represented a low hand thus far. With the exposed pair of sixes you will probably be the high hand. You therefore continue what your natural reaction would be if you had started with a low hand. You check. Even if all the other players appear to be going for low, and do not have straight or flush possibilities, you do not raise on this round; you simply call if another player bets.

What you hope to gain from this strategy is simple enough. You are trying to create a fixed impression in the minds of the other players that you have a low hand, or are trying to make a low. You may gain nothing from this, but it may well bring you the entire pot. At the showdown, players with broken lows (especially those who have paired up at or near the end) may believe you have a better low hand, and either nothing for high or that you have no intention of calling high. They will therefore call high against you—and slam up against your three sixes (or more). (Needless to say, when this occurs and you have to show your hand, you announce that you were lucky to have caught a six on the last card — assuming the game permits such coffeehousing.)

Of course, such an obvious strategy will not work against experienced players. If your opponents are likely to see through such blunt (yet, surprisingly, little-known) tactics, you must vary your plays. Remember that you can bluff a representation just as you can bluff having a particular type of hand. If you can gauge your opponents' tendencies well enough to know when a "straight representation" will be successful, and when to "mix them up" — this usually depends on the relative skill of the particular opponents in a given pot — you will find yourself stealing many pots in the middle stage because your opponents don't want to guess what you are trying to do to them.

SPECIAL END-GAME STRATEGIES AT DECLARATION

High-low with declaration lends itself to several "end strategies" which were not present at cards speak. The factor that adds these new considerations is that *the last round of betting may influence the declarations.*

Before proceeding, it is wise to observe that each of these strategies has a counterpart, namely, reversing the strategy in the hope that your opponent will read you for having used the opposite strategy. Just as in the discussion of representing hands, we will present the basic methods which may be employed, especially against opponents you consider weaker than yourself (and also against those who consider themselves stronger than you). The quality of the particular opposition on a particular hand (plus the history, if any, of this situation against this particular player or players) must always be a better guide than any recommendation of a special form of play.

1. *Betting to avoid a high-low call.* Suppose you have reached the last card, with only one opponent. Your play has been based on a strong hand in one direction, while your opponent obviously

has a cinch for the opposite half of the pot. (Your play up to this point may have been quite proper; for example, you may have built an equity in the pot from several players who dropped out during the middle rounds.)

Either you or your opponent could win both directions by hitting a perfect card at the end, but neither could be certain of victory over the other's best hand in one direction. You are worried that your opponent may have hit a two-way hand and may risk calling both ways. Your best strategy to avoid this may be to bet into him on the last round. (This play should not be made too often, as it will be noticed.)

Observe that such a play does not make sense unless there is some possibility that you yourself might win the entire pot, either with a two-way hand, or by your having an immortal in one direction and tempting your opponent into a high-low call.

In this situation your opponent may be cowed even with his perfect card drawn. He may reason that unless you made your immortal, you would not risk increasing the pot (which you might lose completely).

2. *Checking to determine a high-low call.* Similarly, if you are in the situation where you are wondering whether or not to risk a sure half of the pot by calling high-low into a possible but unlikely strong hand in one direction, it is sometimes good strategy to check and observe the reaction of your opponent. (This reaction need not be solely in terms of whether or not he bets.) Depending on his action and/or betting, you may have some good clues as to whether or not you can win in both directions. This is often worth more than the two additional chips you might win (in a limit game) by betting on the last round.

BASIC END-GAME PLAY AT CONSECUTIVE DECLARATION

There are three basic end-game strategies you can employ when you are involved in a consecutive declaration pot:

1. *Build the pot.* You have a good hand and expect to win in

one direction. You should bet strongly in the hope of building the pot. This can be done in two ways. First, you may trap a player going your way. He will lose to you and become the man in the middle. Second, you may catch two other players going the opposite direction. They will fight against each other and you will walk off with half the pot.

Needless to say, a combination of these situations is most desirable, but it is almost too much to hope for.

Since there is no attempt to fool anyone about your declaration, you should simply try to build the pot. This may involve betting or raising on the last round. You should be willing to do this, since it should involve no disadvantage to you to have to make the first declaration.

2. *Positional advantage.* You have a possible hand in each direction but you are not sure whom you can beat for which direction. In this case you should forget about building the pot and concentrate on making sure you don't get wiped out completely. The best way to do this is to ensure that you can declare last (or as near the end as possible). Therefore, do not bet or raise on the last round even though your chances may seem good. You may guess wrong and bet the direction in which one player has an immortal. If you check, this player may reveal his strength on the last round. Alternately, after you see the other declarations, you may be in a better position to give yourself the optimum chance for half the pot.

If you are in a doubtful situation of this type and realize that you would greatly prefer to call last, and, if you see that you cannot arrange this satisfactorily, *go out as early as possible.* This is similar to the situation in simultaneous declaration where you drop out quickly if you are sure you cannot be defeated both ways but cannot be certain of winning either way. Don't chance it; the odds are all against you.

3. *Aggressive betting to force a decision.* If you are worried about a particular direction, you may make a bet or raise at the end to feign strength. This can be applied to two situations. First, you will declare in a certain direction, and you wish to

drive out a player who may have you beaten. If you take the action on the last round, thereby committing yourself to the first declaration, this opponent may play you for a strong hand and drop out. He cannot be sure of your intentions, since you may well be using strategy No. 1 (to build the pot) with a locked hand. Second, you wish to avoid a call against you by a player who you know will not be driven out by your bet or raise. This may be a player contemplating a high-low call (e.g., he has a low and a straight but you may have a flush—if you bet out and call high he may settle for low), or a player uncertain whether to go against you or another player. If you bet, he may contest for the other half of the pot instead.

It is useful to know the likely occurrence of events in a high-low consecutive declaration game. In most endings there will be three players remaining. If there is a bet on the last round, *the bettor will usually not be opposed by either of the other players*. About 60 per cent of the time it will go: low, high, high; or high, low, low.

SPECIAL LAST-ROUND TACTICS AT CONSECUTIVE DECLARATION: SANDBAGGING

Whenever possible, you will maneuver to be able to call as near to the end as possible. When you are the high hand, or to the left of the high hand, you must play conservatively because of the strong possibility that you must make an early declaration. If you are on the right of the high hand, you can play more aggressively.

When the final betting round arrives, the necessity for the last raiser (or last bettor if there is no raise) to declare first becomes important. It is usually not worth the extra few chips you might get into the pot to bet or raise if it will put you at a disadvantage in the calling. This does not apply, of course, where your declaration will be obvious to the other players in any event. In that case, if you have the best hand, just raise!

Here are several specific tactical maneuvers in the form of sandbagging (holding back with a good hand) which may be employed on the final round of betting:

1. *Checking to see the action.* If you are the high board, and are contemplating a high-low call but are uncertain of its probability of success, you should check to see if any player with a potentially strong hand takes action. Your objective is not so much to avoid calling first, but to determine what your call should be. A typical hand for this maneuver would be: ♠ A ♡ 7 ◇ 4 ◇ 7 (exposed) ♡ A ♡ 6 ♣ 2 (concealed).

You have a seven-low and aces-up — possibly a winning hand in both directions. However, if a potentially strong hand bets on the last round you may decide against calling the direction he declares. (He must now declare ahead of you, as the last bettor.)

2. *Avoiding a raise to call last.* When you have a sure winner in one direction, you should sometimes avoid a raise at the end in order to call last, thereby having a chance to win the entire pot. Suppose the high board (an ace) is to your left (player A), with several low cards. A second player, C, made a pair of sevens on a low board at the sixth card. You started with a pair of eights concealed and your upcards are 6-4-8-2. On the last card you draw a six, giving you eights full.

Player A, who will have the high board anyway, bets. Player B, also in the pot, who was apparently drawing to a flush or a low (he probably should have gone out earlier), drops. Player C calls. You have a cinch for high, but your hand has been well concealed, and as there is no straight possibility on your board, the opponents may assume you are playing for low.

Player A obviously has a good low and may have drawn a straight on the last card. If you raise, you must declare first. When you declare high, A may reconsider and call low. Even if he calls high-low anyway (on the assumption that you have only triplets), C will almost certainly call low. You will split the pot in either event.

But if you merely call A's bet, A will call high-low if he has his straight (if he doesn't have a straight, you have no chance for the whole pot anyway), and C will probably call high, hoping against hope that A has no better than a pair of aces. You will then call high and win the *entire pot*.

3. *Refusing to bet or raise, to imply weakness.* This is a basic technique which applies even when you will be forced to call first anyway. Suppose you have obviously started with a high hand—no chance for the opponents to misread your cards. An opponent has a good low and is obviously thinking about calling high-low (possibly with aces up, or three aces, or a straight or a flush). You will have to call first anyway, but you do not bet. When you call high without having bet—you might bet with a sure high to get money from a third player in the pot—you may find your opponent calling high-low. The third player now must beat the high-low caller for low to share the pot with you. Needless to say, you have a full house (or possibly an ace-king flush). Surprise!—you win the entire pot!

ADVANCED STRATEGY: THE DECLARATION

At consecutive declaration there are many bluffs and counter-plays that can be produced in the declarations themselves. Suppose A and B are the only players remaining. B has had an obvious flush possibility throughout the hand; A has four good low cards on board. Player A now may bet out and call high-low into the obvious flush possibility. His objective is to force B to guess whether or not A has made a full house. If A has a full house, B must call low (B will then win the entire pot, since A can have no better than a pair for low). If B thinks A is bluffing, he can call high.

Gambits of this sort are often offered by stronger players against less-experienced opposition. The weaker player will usually call his best direction, and will usually lose. The safe course for B is to call high-low right back (if he has a flush and better than a pair for low). This insures B a split of the pot (at least). B cannot hope to win the entire pot unless A (with three pairs) has suddenly become irrational.

The supreme expert gambit is for A to call high-low with nothing but a low hand! His hope now is that B will read him for original triplets and a full house, and therefore call low. This is a very high-level play, and is not recommended unless you are sure of your customer — and the customer must be a good enough player to recognize the situation.

EFFECT OF THE FORM OF BETTING: REPRESENTATIONS

In a limit game the main objective of a representation is to drive out all the players trying for the direction which you are representing, then to beat the others in the direction you really have. In this way you garner the entire pot.

In a pot limit or table stakes game the idea is to misrepresent your hand in such a way that you trap one player for a big bet at the end, then to go against him.

The plan of campaign of a representation should be based on these considerations. There is little to be gained if you play to trap one player in a limit game — and you may be trapped yourself if you do not draw a suitable hand in time. In a limit game a sizable pot can be won only if several players stay for the ride, and the ones not going your way fold near the end because of the strength of your representation. In a pot limit or table stakes game you are content merely to trap one player when you are representing.

THE ART OF DROPPING OUT

It is always painful for a player to drop out of a pot, especially when he has a good hand. This is particularly true in high-low because it is sometimes necessary to leave the field of action with a good hand *in each direction*.

As the end-game approaches (and the bet is about to be increased), you must value your hand *in relation to the others*.

What may be a good hand when viewed alone—even a potential two-way winner in normal circumstances—may be a clear-cut "man-in-the-middle" hand.

If there is one factor which determines a good high-low player, it is the discipline to drop out *as soon as one of two things happens*:

(1) His own hand is *suddenly* ruined;

(2) His own hand is good, but the other hands have *suddenly* become better.

This discipline is hard to come by *because a hand may go from best to worst in a single round!* A player who may have had the lead all the while may be placed in an inferior position after receiving a particular card *even when he has filled his hand!*

Careful study of the advanced example on the next two pages will yield big dividends in your high-low game.

In this example, the game is seven-card high-low stud (pot-limit table stakes) with simultaneous declarations. (The considerations in this case would be the same for consecutive declaring.) There are eight players. A, B and C are conservative; D, E, F and G are somewhat loose. *Your play, round by round*:

Third card. You are dealt ◊ A ◊ 5 (concealed) and ♣ 4 (up-card). Your first impression should be that this is an excellent hand. You have an ace, a concealed two-flush, and three cards to a perfect low. F, who has an ace up, bets. G drops, and all others call. This is an unusually high number of callers on the first round, and you expect to find several fine hands around the table. Your attention should immediately be drawn to the fact that player A called with the ♡ K for his upcard—an exceptional circumstance, especially as you know A to be a tight player.

Fourth card. You draw ◊ 3. This, of course, is a perfect card: it gives you a three-flush, a four-straight, and four to a perfect low. F, who is still high, checks. You have a good chance to win the entire pot, so you bet. (You have no hope of misrepresenting your hand since your board is beginning to look like a possible straight.) To your surprise, you get four callers. B and C appear to have possible lows; A stayed with a king originally, which is

High-Low Simultaneous Declarations

		YOUR HAND		CARDS HELD BY OPPONENTS (read down to see open holdings)						
				A	B	C	D	E	F	G
Concealed ⟶		◇ A	◇ 5	?	?	?	?	?	?	?
Upcards	Betting round 1.	♣ 4		♡ K	♡ 6	♣ 7	♣ 6	♡ 7	♠ A	♠ 10
	2.	◇ 3		♠ 7	♣ 2	♣ 5	♡ Q	♠ J	♣ Q	X
	3.	◇ 7		♣ 3	♣ J	♠ Q	♣ 9	X	X	X
	4.	◇ 10		♡ 3	♠ 3	X	X	X	X	X
Final card (closed)	5.	X		?	?	X	X	X	X	X
Declarations				H	L ·					
Hole cards				◇ K ♣ K ♣ 10	♡ A ♡ 4 ◇ 9					

A and B split the pot.

still the key factor in determining his hand. You should find it hard to understand why D is playing. E and F, having busted, drop out.

Fifth card. You now draw the ◇ 7. (This must be your lucky day. You already have a seven-low, and a four-flush with two openings to make a straight!) A is now high with his king, and the bet is checked around to you. You bet, and A and B call. C and D, each now with "garbage on board," drop out.

At this stage you should be trying to analyze your opponents' possible hands. You should credit player A with three kings. A loose player might be in with ♡ A and another low heart in the

High-Low Simultaneous Declarations

	A	B	C	D Dealer	E	F	G	AMOUNT IN POT AFTER EACH ROUND (pot-limit table stakes)
BETTING BY ROUNDS (*read across*)								
You	A	B	C	D Dealer	E	F	G	
								1
Call	Call	Call	Call	Call	Call	*Bet(1)	Drop	8
Bet(5)	Call	Call	Call	Call	Drop	*Check		33
Bet(20)	*Check Call	Check Call	Check Drop	Check Drop				93
Drop	*Check Call	Bet (80)						253
	*Check Call	Bet (tap)						253 + tap
RESULT OF EACH PLAYER								
−26	+21	+20	−6	−7	−1	−1	0	

Your drop avoids a loss of (at least) 80 chips.
*indicates high hand

hole, but A is conservative. He would not have stayed in on the fourth card with three low boards (yours, B's and C's) facing him. You might be somewhat suspicious of B's ♣ J. Perhaps he has ♣ A and a low club in the hole and has a possible ace-jack flush; maybe he has only a draw to a good low.

Sixth card. You now draw ◇ 10, giving you an ace-ten flush to go with your seven-low. A, who hits an open pair of threes, checks. B, who has also drawn a three, bets. You have an ace-ten flush for high and a seven-low, with a draw to a five-low. This is a strong hand and would often win the pot in both directions. Should you raise?

Not only should you *not* raise—*you should drop out!*

While it is true that you have a powerful hand, the upcards just drawn by your opponents are crushing blows to you. You have already strongly suspected that A started with three kings; you have, in fact, all but *credited* him with three kings. He has now hit an open pair. B is obviously playing for low, and he has just hit the "case" (last remaining) three! All four sevens have shown (naturally, you have been watching the cards carefully and know this), so B cannot have a seven-low—he must have a *six*-low. Your only hope is that you might draw a deuce on the last card and defeat B for low.

Clearly, it is not worthwhile for you to call at this point. A, with a lock (sure thing) for high, will surely raise. B, who wants to make it as expensive as possible for you to try to draw your perfect low, will reraise. You might be forced to put in your entire stack (or, in a limit game, call the maximum number of raises, say, six chips) just to see your seventh card. There were only 93 chips in the pot prior to this round and you would have to pay at least 80 chips for the *chance* to draw a perfect card, after which you would win only 46 (from the present pot) plus 40 (half of B's chips on this round) plus possibly half of B's stack (from the final round). Your potential gain is perhaps 200 chips. The odds would be almost as unfavorable in a limit game. (There is also the possibility that B will tie you for low by also drawing a perfect card.)

Obviously, the odds are all against you. You have no better than a 15% chance to catch a deuce, even if you draw no inferences about the probability that some of the players who stayed on the first round held deuces (rather than other cards) because they stayed in originally.

Conclusion of the deal. After you fold, A calls. After the seventh card, A (high with a pair of threes) checks, B taps, A calls. A declares high and B declares low; A and B split the pot. A's hole cards are ◇ K, ♣ K, ♣ 10; B's hole cards are: ♡ A, ♡ 4, ◇ 9. You can use your imagination to determine which were the original hole cards. Your reading of the hand has been justified:

at the point you dropped out you were beaten in both directions!

Analysis of the other plays. Let us gain further insight of this important example by examining how the other players handled their cards.

Player A. A's original hole cards were ◇ K ♣ K. Three kings is a good original hand (A probably would have dropped out at cards speak), so A stayed along. During the middle stages, even though there were no other *apparent* high hands, A did not force the betting because his first upcard (♠ 7) was matched on the board (C and E each had a seven as their original upcard), and his ♣ 3 also had a mate upturned. Had A not caught a pair on the sixth card, he probably would have dropped out, because his chance of catching a full house was greatly diminished and your board suggested straight and flush possibilities, as did the upcards of B.

In the ending, A's check with a full house was a clever stroke, designed to trap you into the pot if you had misread the hands. From the appearance of the sixth cards, he knew that at least one of his opponents had a good hand for at least low. There was no chance A could win more money by betting out, because it was almost impossible that he would get two calls. A's best chance was to hope that he could feign weakness by checking, and trap you into the pot when B bet. If you called, A would raise and thereby build up the pot (your call would probably commit you for at least the remainder of the round).

After you dropped, A refused to raise with a lock for high in the hope that B would be tempted to call high-low if he had a straight. (A could not hope for more than half the pot unless B had a straight.)

Player B. B's original hole cards were ♡ A ♡ 4. His plays were fairly obvious all along the line, except that his stay after drawing the jack of clubs was slightly speculative (two threes and one five had already shown on the board). B could be pretty sure that both C and D were about to drop behind him (on the third betting round) and since this would reduce his equity in the pot, his call on that round was a close question. Perhaps he felt you were trying to drive him out (although the seven could not have given you a pair). Perhaps B's play was slightly inaccurate and it simply turned out to be lucky. This should have no effect on *your* final decision to drop out on the sixth card with a good two-way hand.

B was not taken in by A's end-game strategy — B would not have called high-low even if he had drawn a five for a straight.

Player C. C's original hole cards were ♠ 8 ♠ 4. His play on the first round was marginal. (*You* would not stay on this hand: you are trying to be more conservative than "the field.") Even though the ♣ 5 improved C's hand, C might have dropped on the fourth card because there were two sixes showing. His stay at this stage was somewhat of a gamble and it cost him five chips.

Player D. D started with ♡ 5 ♡ 8 concealed. He contributed generously to the pot. His stay on the first round was about equivalent to C's. His stay on the second round was a serious error. The ♡ Q gave him a virtually useless three-flush (quite a few hearts were out and he probably would not be able to see his flush chance through in any event). Also, with 5-6-8, a seven was a crucial card for D to draw; and three sevens had already been turned up! (Playing on hands such as this will make D a big loser in the long run.)

Player E. E, with ◇ 8 ♣ 8 concealed, made a reasonable call on the first round. As soon as he drew a bust for his fourth card (♠ J) he folded — quite properly, of course.

Player F. F, with hole cards ♣ A ♠ 2, started with an excellent hand. Even though he suspected that A might have three kings, F had a fair chance to draw three aces (no other aces showed). He also had a low possibility and a two-flush. But as soon as he received a useless card (♣ Q), he dropped out. This is typical of good high-low strategy, and is similar to the technique you employed on this hand (at a different stage), i.e., play with a good hand — even take the lead in the betting — but as soon as your hand turns sour, *drop.* Don't wait for another card.

Player G. G had ♡ 10 ◇ J for his hole cards. This gave him a near-worthless hand, and G did not even bother to call on the first round.

In general, this hand was well played. B, C, and D made questionable plays at different points and D made a serious error by calling on the second betting round. It may seem that this error should not be called serious—it cost D "only" five chips. However, this *type* of error will sneak into the more significant money situations if a player allows his game to remain loose. D is probably the game's big loser.

Any way, in a limit game every chip counts. The more correct decisions you make *at every stage*, the more you will win.

HIGH-LOW DRAW POKER

Draw poker played high-low has some unusual twists which may catch the unwary player. In this section I will describe some of the features of this game which are not widely understood and are therefore worthy of study.

The rules are quite simple. Draw poker is played, but at the showdown there are declarations—almost always simultaneous at this form of high-low (see page 145), and the pot is divided as described on pages 146-147. This game is favored by groups preferring closed poker (in which a player gets to see five cards for his original ante), but wishing to vary the steady cautiousness of high draw and the wildness of lowball.

The most important thing to remember is that it does *not* suffice to know the hand-values for both high and low draw. Although it might seem that you are battling half the players (on the average) for half the pot, and therefore the same values would suffice, this is a fallacy. The reason these values do not suffice is because of the possible turns the betting may take.

Let us suppose you have a hand which is a potential high and would ordinarily justify a certain bet, call or raise at high draw. If you become involved in betting during the progress of the hand, you will have little or no idea whether your opponents are trying for low or high. Thus, you have no idea how to compare your values to theirs. Suppose you have a pair of aces. The pot is opened, two players drop; there are three players yet to be heard from. In an ordinary high game, you would call. In a high-low game, you should drop! The reason is that if there is a raise behind you, you have no idea what action to take. You may be tempted to stay in the hope that your opponents are playing for low, only to find that the raise was based on three-of-a-kind (or better) and you had no business being in the pot at all.

In short, you should not take actions in high-low draw unless you have considerably better than the values required for these actions at straight high or straight low (depending on whether you are trying for high or low). In a game of normal standards, wait for aces-up or three-of-a-kind to stay in to try for high, and four to a wheel, or a low open-end four-straight or low four-flush or possibly a pat seven-low to try for low.

Concealment is another important factor at high-low draw. Most draws will be one card (or no cards!). This is because there will be no two-card draws to low hands. (Do not be tempted by holdings such as ♠4-♠3-♠2. The odds against improving to a significant degree in either direction are so high that the pot—that is, *half* the pot—will almost never offer you enough of a run for your money.) And a player with three-of-a-kind is best advised to draw one card to avoid tipping his hand. The only point to remember here is that it should not be assumed that a man is going for low if he draws one card—it is the usual play even with a hand trying for high.

If a player remains pat, of course, the odds favor that his pat hand is a pat low. However, this opens up the field for bluffs, such as standing pat with three aces and similar hands. A good high-low draw player will mix up his draws in these situations to keep his opponents guessing. The most important phase is determining how your opponents will declare, for then and only then can you gauge the relative strength of your hand. The less accurately your opponents can read your intentions, therefore, the better off you will be. Also, in the same vein, it is most important to study your opponents' drawing tendencies with various hands so that you can judge the probability that they will be calling in one direction or the other.

In high-low draw, the only hands likely to win in both directions are low straights and low flushes. Because you get better odds for your money when you have a chance to win the entire pot, play aggressively with holdings such as 6-5-4-3. If you draw an ace, you have a good low. If you draw a deuce or a seven you may have a chance at the entire pot. Even the drawing of an eight may give you a chance for low (although you probably will not be able to stand a raise after the draw). Since it is only 3 to 1 against drawing a suitable card (even if the eight is discounted), the pot will usually offer good enough odds for you to stay in, and even to raise if you have good position. A low four-flush can be treated similarly.

In the other forms of high-low I recommended that you should be conservative with your original stays, etc., unless it became clear that you were *several* notches more conservative than most or all of the other players—in which case you could loosen up one notch. In high-low draw, however, with its fewer betting intervals, you should *not* use this tactic. In other words, no matter how loose the game is, keep to your strict standards. Becoming loose, even while staying more conservative than the game, will not profit in the long run because there will be too many good hands out in one direction or the other during the course of the game, and you will not be able to call a raise. Therefore, stay conservative, and relax in the knowledge that the more unsoundly the opponents play, the more you will win.

DEALER'S CHOICE GAMES AND HOW TO PLAY THEM

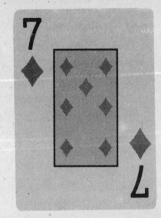

OLD-FASHIONED POKER was a game requiring patience and conservatism. Everyone got to know what was a poor hand and what was a good hand, and he would throw anything away if it did not fit the conventional requirements of a good hand. The effort to enliven the game introduced many wild cards, giving each player more than five cards to choose from, so that everyone would have what is a "good hand" under conventional standards. There are literally thousands of poker variants that have been created and are being created daily with this end in view. Many of them are born in "dealer's choice" games, in which each dealer can state the rules of the poker game that is to be played, which cards are wild, what will be the winning hand, etc. Nomenclature in this field is hopelessly confused because the dealer has the right to name as well as to define his game. Some of the principal variants are described in this chapter.

DEALER'S CHOICE

In most poker games, it is standard procedure for the dealer to determine the form of poker to be played for the hand he is dealing, or perhaps for one rotation of deals around the table.

In this way each player is assured of playing his own favorite form of poker his fair share of the time.

The only adjustment that need be made in a dealer's choice game is that if draw poker is mixed with stud, a marker should be used to indicate the "draw dealer." Since the dealer usually has a great positional advantage at draw poker, each player in rotation should be arbitrarily designated as draw dealer (for purposes of playing the hand) on each hand of draw poker. This player does not physically deal the cards, but the player to his left is the first to speak. In this way, no one can give himself an advantage by naming a draw poker game on his turn and thereby obtaining an immediate positional advantage.

Poker games often restrict the dealer's choice to some or all of the standard forms of poker (possibly with local variations) described in the three preceding chapters. Some groups, however, allow the dealer wide latitude, permitting him to name any of the variations of poker. None of these variations has wide popularity, but each enjoys a vogue in certain localities. (Occasionally the dealer is even permitted to remove the game from the field of poker and call such games as "put and take." We will not consider such games here, as they are not forms of poker.)

This chapter will deal with the sundry forms of poker most often selected in a dealer's-choice game (and not thus far covered). I will describe each such form played with any regularity, as well as its possible variations. Needless to say, I will not be able to cover every possible variation of each game, but most games that are likely to be called by your poker group should be very much like (if not identical to) one of the games described in this chapter.

Along with the rules for playing each of these games, I will gives pointers on strategy. These tips will necessarily be limited, for two reasons. First, I could not possibly give the complete strategy of each game without writing several books the size of this one. Second, some of the games are local in nature, and are therefore not played nearly as often as the major forms of poker. The theory of these games has not been developed fully, and in many cases it is difficult to speak with authority. Knowing the best techniques for a particular game is largely a matter of practical experience. It is difficult to gain such experience in games that are not called too often.

You should, of course, try to master the unusual games that are common to your own group or groups. By using the basic rules set down here, and studying the habits of the players in your own game(s), you will be able to devise your own methods for winning play.

HOW TO LOCATE A GAME IN THIS CHAPTER

I have divided the best-known dealer's-choice games into three categories: Games of draw (closed) poker, games of stud (open) poker, and miscellaneous games which cannot be strictly classified as either closed poker or open poker. Further subdivisions are indicated in the list below. Specific games can be located in the index. However, you may know certain games under other names. In this case, determine the *classification* of the game you are interested in and look through the relevant section. You should find either the game itself or a close relative.

CLASSIFICATION OF DEALER'S-CHOICE GAMES

I. Games of Closed Poker

  A. THE SPIT-IN-THE-OCEAN FAMILY
       (characterized by common cards which are potentially in the hand of every player, or the marking of the cards of a rank as wild through an upturned card).

  B. THE KNOCK-POKER FAMILY
       (characterized by the possibility of a player's improving his hand through discarding and adding cards discarded by another player, or adding cards from a fixed widow).

  C. OTHER FORMS OF CLOSED POKER.

II. Games of Stud Poker:

A. THE BASEBALL FAMILY

(characterized by two ranks of wild cards, the appearance of a card of one of these ranks forcing its holder into some serious action, and by a third rank, the appearance of a card of which entitles its holder to an extra card).

B. BASIC VARIATIONS OF STUD GAMES.

III. Miscellaneous Games:

A. GAMES COMBINING CLOSED POKER AND STUD POKER.

B. OTHER GAMES.

I. Dealer's-Choice Games of Closed Poker

A. THE SPIT-IN-THE-OCEAN FAMILY

The game now generally known as "Spit-in-the-Ocean" is actually a large family of games embracing a common essential feature: Each player combines the cards dealt to him with one or more cards exposed on the table and thus automatically made part of the hand of every player. This is not a new feature in games of the poker family; on the contrary, it is quite ancient, antedating the various games we know as "straight" poker. The old French games of Brelan and Ambigu (see Appendix) embraced this principle of play.

How to play: Playing a game of the Spit-in-the-Ocean family is similar to playing deuces-wild (see page 103). The primary consideration is the number of wild cards held. For each wild card you hold, the chances of the other players holding wild cards are reduced. A "natural" hand is therefore not as powerful as the same hand made up with wild cards, as there are more wild cards available for your opponents' use.

A principle which should be remembered when playing a game *with cards common to all hands* is that all hands must be valued with respect to those common cards. Although this is a secondary consideration in a game with many wild cards, it is of the utmost importance in a common-card game with no wild cards. Thus, if every hand has a king as the common card (nothing wild), a holding of a pair of queens is usually next to valueless; whereas in a similar situation a pair of kings might be a powerful holding if a queen is turned as the common card.

I will give pointers on the play of each particular form of game, but one essential principle applies to all games of this type: it is easier to overvalue your hand than to undervalue it. Poker players are used to thinking in terms of certain poker hands being strong hands because they are rare in a game without wild cards. In games with many wild cards, hands that would ordinarily be strong are often valueless. A straight, a flush, or even a full house may be useless in a game with many wild cards. In playing a game of this type, orient yourself to the usual winning hands. If, during a multiple-wild-card game, you find yourself wondering whether your hand is good or not—it isn't!

A good way to take this principle into account without paying too much attention to the precise values required for calls, raises, reraises, and so forth, is to adopt an extremely conservative strategy. It almost never pays to go "all out" on any hand in a game with many wild cards unless you have an unbeatable hand. The risk of running into an "immortal" is too great.

By weaving a conservative thread through your strategy, you will not only avoid the occasional huge loss to a not-as-unlikely-as-you-thought hand, but will pick up numerous gains from other players who are falling into the trap of overrating hands which would be strong in standard forms of poker but are worthless when wild cards enter the picture.

In the descriptions that follow, the games presented are the ones most frequent in the repertory of the particular form of poker being discussed.

Spit-in-the-Ocean. Four cards are dealt face down to each player, and one card is turned up in the center. The exposed card

and every other card of the same rank are wild. The exposed
card forms the fifth card of every active player's hand. There is
a betting interval; then each player may discard any number of
cards from his hand and draw cards from the dealer to replace
them, as in ordinary draw poker (except that a player may discard his entire hand if he wishes); then there is another betting
interval and a showdown.

How to play: Forget about trying for anything less than four-
of-a-kind! If your four cards are (for example) two pairs, you
should drop out unless one of your pairs is a high one and you
can try for four- (or five)-of-a-kind. Your full house is almost
valueless — the average winning hand is four-of-a-kind, running
from four eights to four jacks, depending on the looseness or
tightness of the game. Five-of-a-kind (which ranks above a
straight flush) is not at all uncommon.

The hands run even higher than in deuces-wild, because every
player has at least one wild card. As in deuces-wild, your main
consideration is the number of wild cards you have in your own
hand. Don't stay for the draw with less than a high three-of-a-
kind, and don't stay for a raise before the draw without three
aces (or a second wild card).

Variations of Spit-in-the-Ocean

Spit-in-the-Ocean is sometimes played with the center card
part of each player's hand, as described above, but not wild. It
is sometimes played with the center card not wild, but each card
of the same rank in a player's hand wild.

How to play: The first variation is very similar to ordinary
draw poker, except that the average winning hand is somewhat
lower because one card in each player's hand is fixed. Therefore, reduce your requirements for various actions by a few
notches. There is no special advantage to having the upcard
matched in your hand, except that it may give you a high pair. If
the upcard is a king or a queen, it may often pay to hold an ace
kicker when you have one card matching the upcard. It is likely
that another player also matches the upcard, and the odds favor

your winning if you draw two to that pair, plus an ace, while he draws three cards to the pair. The chance of improving the pair to triplets is obviously much lower in this case than in ordinary draw poker, because another player has one of the cards that will form triplets.

It is this variation of Spit-in-the-Ocean in which the comparison of the value of your hand with the value of the upcard is of the utmost significance. If the upcard is lower than a ten, you should simply value your hands slightly *higher* (an exception to the general rule of common-card games) than in ordinary draw poker. If the upcard is of a high rank (ace, king, queen, jack or ten) you should not play with a pair of a rank lower than that of the upcard. Conversely, the value of a pair of a rank *higher* than the upcard is increased, since each of the other players is "stuck" with the upcard as part of his hand.

The formation of two pairs must also be compared with the value of the upcard. If, with a king turned as the common card, you have kings and fours, your hand is not as powerful as you might believe. Kings-up will be far more common on this deal than in ordinary draw poker (while the other strong hands will be less common!). If another player has kings-up, your kings and fours are weak. Also, players with pairs of queens or jacks will probably drop out when a king is exposed as the upcard. If a player draws three cards, he probably has a pair of aces (or an ace and a king). In any event, if he improves his hand, you will be defeated.

The second variation (center card itself not wild) is only slightly different from deuces-wild. The hands run lower in this game because there are only three potential jokers, and because one card is fixed in each hand. A hand with a wild card in this game is therefore more powerful than a hand with a deuce in deuces-wild, and you should adjust your strategy accordingly. In general, value your hands several notches higher than in deuces-wild.

Wild Widow (sometimes called *Pig-in-the-Poke*). Four cards are dealt to each player, face down, and a fifth card is turned up on the table. All cards of the rank of this exposed card are wild.

There is a betting interval, then a fifth card is dealt, face down, to each active player. There is another betting interval, and a showdown. The exposed card in the center is not counted as part of any player's hand; it merely marks the rank of wild cards.

How to play: This game is nothing more than deuces-wild with only three wild cards, *plus* the fact that there is no draw! Thus, the wild cards notwithstanding, a pair of aces is a good hand (especially if a wild card is held). The strength of a hand at this game can be determined with reasonable accuracy from the table of possible hands with deuces-wild (see page 217). In its mechanics, it is quite similar to straight poker (no draw).

Stormy Weather. The dealer gives each player four cards, one at a time, face down; and after each of the first three rounds of cards, he deals one card face down to the center of the table, so that there is a widow of three cards. There is a betting interval, beginning with the player at the dealer's left, and with nothing required to open; then each active player may discard any part of his hand and draw cards to replace it, up to the full four cards. After the draw the dealer turns up one card in the center of the table, and there is a betting interval; a second card, and another betting interval; the third card, and the final betting interval. Each active player may select *one* of the three cards in the center to be his fifth card in the showdown.

How to play: If there were no draw, hand-values in this game would be slightly higher than in seven-card stud. However, *with* the draw before the center cards are exposed, the chances of very good hands being made are greatly increased. A flush should not be given too much faith as a winning hand, and for that reason an attempt to make a flush is usually a losing play. The best strategy is to keep high pairs in the hope of making high triplets. This holding can be turned into either four-of-a-kind or a high full house with the help of a favorable card in the widow.

Once again, it is important to compare the value of your hand with the ranks of the upcards. Suppose you hold ♠ A ♣ Q ◇ Q ◇ 8. You play before the draw and take two cards (keeping the pair of queens). After the draw you hold ♡ Q ◇ Q ♣ Q ♠ 6. You have a strong hand and should usually raise at this point. Suppose you raise and two other players call. The first card of the widow proves to be the ♠ K. You should now drop if another player makes a significant bet! The odds greatly favor that some other player will now hold a better hand.

This example illustrates the situation (very similar to one which may arise in a high-low game—see pages 174-178) in which the turn of a single card can change the entire complexion of a hand. It is especially important in common-card games to retain a flexible approach, and to remember that the turn of one common card may change the values of all hands! Just as in seven-card high-low stud, be prepared to drop out on an unfavorable card even when you were clearly leading on the previous card.

Cincinnati (also called *Utah* or *Lamebrains*). The dealer gives five cards to each player, face down, and an extra hand of five cards in the center of the table, face down. The cards in the center are turned up one at a time, with a betting interval following the turn of each card; the active player at dealer's left bets first in each betting interval. After the final betting interval there is a showdown in which each player may select any five cards from among his hand and the five cards in the center.

Tennessee. This is the same game as Cincinnati except that the five cards to be exposed on the table are not dealt as an extra hand but are turned up, one by one, from the top of the undealt portion of the pack.

How to play: Skill at games in which there are a large number of common cards is mainly a matter of comparing the value of your hand with the ranks of cards faced as common cards. Thus, if a face card is turned as a common card, and you have cards which match it, you are in a good position. Your hand has improved, and other players are unlikely to make good use of that face card. Similarly, your three-of-a-kind is strong if it ranks higher than any exposed common card, but weak if there are common cards of higher rank.

However, when there are as many as five common cards, as

in Cincinnati, three-of-a-kind is almost worthless. In fact, in-experienced players will be trapped into playing for a flush or a straight. Only a high full house which uses the ranks of the common cards (so that other players cannot use them to make four-of-a-kind), or an actual four-of-a-kind, can be considered an adequate hand.

Lamebrain Pete, or **Cincinnati Liz.** This is the same game as Cincinnati except that the *lowest* exposed card and all other cards of the same rank are wild.

How to play: Games in which *the rank of the wild card can suddenly change* are almost beyond calculation! The only way to judge the chances accurately in Lamebrain Pete is to compute the probability that each rank will eventually become the rank of the wild cards. Such a calculation must be based on the cards held by the player, the cards exposed, and the number of cards yet to be exposed.

Since no one wishes to make a calculation of this sort, the most practical technique is to judge roughly the chance that the current lowest common card will eventually become the rank of the wild cards. Unless there is a good chance that this card will remain wild, and you have a strong hand under this assumption (such as five-of-a-kind!), do not bet strongly.

The only exception to this is a hand whose value can be *transferred to any wild card.* A hand such as three aces qualifies, as any wild card will make it four aces, and the holder need have only one other favorable card for an unbeatable high. Needless to say, nothing less than five aces can be backed strongly in games with both a large number of common cards and a large number of wild cards.

Round the World. This is the same game as Cincinnati except that only four cards are dealt face down to each player and only four cards are dealt as a widow to the center of the table. In the showdown each player selects his hand from the eight available cards.

How to play: This game should be played along the same lines as Cincinnati, but with more emphasis on straights and flushes.

A high flush is now a reasonable hand, and may win a pot in which no pairs appear in the common cards.

When playing to win on a flush, be especially wary of any pair formed in the common cards, no matter how low. Not only is this pair likely to make three-of-a-kind for some other player (since players tend to stay in the pot if they match the common cards), but if another common card matches a pair in some player's hand, he has a full house. Thus, when holding or playing for a flush, tend to drop out if a pair appears in the common upcards.

Procter and Gamble. (From George Coffin's book, "Fortune Poker.") This is a seven-card variant of Spit-in-the-Ocean. Each player has four face-down cards and three cards are dealt face down to the center. These are exposed one at a time, with a betting interval after each, and with the last exposed card and all other cards of the same rank being wild. In the showdown each player selects any five cards from among his four and the three on the table.

How to play: It is extremely difficult to establish superior tactics for this game because the value of a hand changes so drastically when the final card (which determines the rank of wild cards) is exposed. Nonetheless, since there are only four wild cards, hands should not be valued as highly as at deuces-wild (there are seven cards and everyone has at least one joker). Four-of-a-kind is a solid value, but anything less cannot be trusted too far. Bear in mind that a good final card can turn your opponents' potential three-of-a-kind or full house into a straight flush! (You, of course, would not stay in the pot on such a slim chance.)

Bedsprings. Five cards are dealt face down to each player, and two rows of five cards each to the center of the table. A card is turned up in the center and there is a betting interval; then another card in the same row, followed by a betting interval; and so on through that row, after which the cards of the other row are turned up one by one with a betting interval following the turn-up of each. After the tenth card has been turned up in the center, there is a final betting interval and a showdown in which each active player must select his hand from his own five cards plus any two cards in line, one card of each row. Thus, each player has seven cards from which to choose the best five.

How to play: The crucial feature of this game is the large number of betting intervals. Most of the money losses in this game are caused by playing through the early rounds on "possibilities." Bear in mind that it is not until after the fifth betting interval that the cards of any line (two cards across the layout) are revealed.

Therefore, with uncertain values drop as soon as possible! The average winning hand is only slightly higher than in seven-card stud for high, for each player must choose a complete set of two cards to make his seven cards (from which five are to be selected).

An original hand of a high two pairs or three-of-a-kind is worth staying on through at least the first phase of potential common cards turned. A four-flush is a doubtful possibility, although an ace-high flush may be a strong hand if inferior combinations of cards are turned as the upcards.

As always in common-card games, compare the ranks of your cards to those appearing as common cards.

Twin Beds. This is the same game as Bedsprings except that the cards are turned up one by one from each row alternately, and in the showdown a player may select his five-card hand from his own hand plus the five cards of either row, giving him ten cards from which to choose. It is often played that the last card turned up and all other cards of the same rank are wild.

How to play: Strategy must combine the best features of play of both Cincinnati and Bedsprings. The average winning hand being slightly higher than in Cincinnati, hand values are slightly lower than in that game. However, the large number of betting intervals makes it even more important that you have sound values going in.

In theory, games with a large number of betting intervals should be considered from the same point of view as seven-card stud (especially high-low) in that one should not call "near the end" unless one is prepared to see the hand through to the final stage. In Twin Beds and similar games involving a large number of betting intervals, "near the end" means the last few betting rounds. (In seven-card stud, this "rule" is usually phrased, "Don't call on the sixth card unless you are prepared to call on the seventh card.")

Other Variations

Southern Cross. Each player receives five cards face down, after which the dealer lays out nine cards in the center of the table, face down, in a pattern of five cards crossed by four cards. These cards are turned up one at a time (center card last), with a betting interval following each turn-up. After the final betting interval, each active player may select a five-card poker hand from his own five cards plus either of the five card crossbars of the cards in the center. Sometimes it is played that the center card of the cross and all other cards of the same rank are wild.

X Marks the Spot. This is the same as Southern Cross, five cards being dealt face down to each player, except that only five cards are dealt to the center, in a three-by-two cross; these are turned up one by one (center card last), with a betting interval following each. The center card of the cross and all other cards of the same rank are wild. In the showdown each active player may select his five-card hand from his own hand plus all five of the cards in the center.

Criss-Cross. Five cards are dealt to each player, then five cards are laid out in the center in a three-by-two cross, face down. These cards are turned up one by one, with a betting interval following each turn-up. The center card is turned up last. It and all other cards of the same rank are wild. Each active player in the showdown may select his five-card poker hand from his own five cards plus *either arm of the cross* — eight cards in all.

How to play: These games (as well as numerous unlisted minor variations) are best considered by comparing them with other games in the Spit-in-the-Ocean family. In judging the value of hands, the number of potential wild cards is paramount; in gauging your betting, make note of the number of intervals remaining (assuming a limit game, which is usual when dealer's choice is played and peculiar variations are allowed); in deciding late-round tactics, be governed by the rank of your hand in relation to the exposed common cards.

Each of these games is nothing more than a minor variation of one of the others, and is possibly slightly different from the particular form called in your own game. In each case you must judge the value of a hand by experience. This value will depend not only on the mathematical expectations (which are all I could give here), but on the style of players. These games are usually played loosely—but not so loosely that you should violate the fundamental principle of undervaluing your hand and playing conservatively when a close situation arises.

B. THE KNOCK-POKER FAMILY

Knock Poker. Three to five players make the best game. Each antes one chip before the deal. Five cards are dealt to each player, face down, as in draw poker; the undealt cards are placed in the center to form the stock, and the play is as in rummy. Eldest hand (player at the dealer's left) draws the top card of the stock and discards, and thereafter each player in turn has his choice between the top card of the stock and the top discard. The discard pile should be kept squared up and is not open to inspection.

Any player, in turn, after drawing and before discarding, may knock. This means there will be a showdown when his turn comes again. The knocker then discards, and each player has one more turn, in which he may draw as usual, and then he must either drop and pay the knocker a chip, or discard and stay in.

When the knocker's turn comes again, he does not draw—there is a showdown among all players who stayed in. If the knocker has the high hand, every player who stayed in pays him two chips. If any other player ties the knocker, they divide the winnings, except that the knocker keeps chips paid to him by players who dropped out. If anyone beats the knocker, he gets the antes, and the knocker pays two chips to every player who stayed in.

It is customary for bonuses to be paid (by every player, including those who may have dropped) as follows: two chips each for knocking on the first round and winning without drawing a card (in this case, the player who knocks passes his turn to draw to the player at his left); one chip each for knocking before drawing on the first round, then drawing the top card of the stock and winning; four chips each for winning with a royal flush, two chips each for winning with any other straight flush, and one chip each for winning with four-of-a-kind.

Irregularities. On the first round, a hand with six cards may discard without drawing, and a hand with four cards may draw without discarding; thereafter, an irregular hand discovered at any time is fouled. If such a hand is discovered before anyone has knocked, the holder pays two chips to the pot; if discovered after a knock but before the showdown, he pays two chips to the knocker; if discovered after the showdown, he pays two chips to the winner of the hand; and in no case can he collect.

If the knocker's hand is fouled, he pays as for any losing hand.

If a player draws more than one card from the stock, his hand is fouled; the cards he drew go on the top of the discard pile and the next player has his choice of them, as well as the right to draw from the stock if he wishes.

How to play: The knocker accepts one disadvantage in that every other player will have one more draw than he has, but a compensating advantage is that he irrevocably wins the chips of players who drop out—the same advantage that makes Blackjack so profitable a game for the dealer—and he has a chance to win the antes, in addition to which he pays no more when he loses than he collects when he wins. For this reason it pays to knock when it is probable that your hand is better than other hands are likely to be even with one more draw than you have had.

In general, two pairs are good enough for a knock on the first round, though in a game of five or more players the fourth and later players should have at least queens-up. On the second round you need three-of-a-kind; and on the third round a high straight or a flush.

A player who stays in, instead of dropping when someone has knocked, receives, in effect, three-to-one odds on the extra chip it may cost him to stay. He has a further advantage if there is any possibility that he may win the pot; and he will win, regardless of how weak his own hand is, if some other player can beat the knocker. This does not mean that it pays to stay in blindly, but too much conservatism is losing play.

Whiskey Poker. Each player receives five cards face down, and an extra hand of five cards is dealt face down in the center of the table to serve as the widow.

A pool may be formed by equal antes from all players before the deal, the pool going to the highest hand in the showdown; or the lowest hand in the showdown pays for the drinks (which was apparently the original purpose of this game and the origin of its name).

Eldest hand (to the dealer's left) plays first. He may pass, or knock, or exchange his hand for the widow. If he knocks, it means there will be a showdown when his turn comes next. If he exchanges, he lays his own hand face up on the table. If he passes, the next player in turn has the same privileges.

When any player exchanges his hand for the widow, the player in turn after him may discard one or more of his cards (up to all five) and select cards from the widow to replace them. The discarded cards are added to the widow. Once the widow has been taken, each player must either exchange or knock—he may no longer pass without knocking.

If no one exchanges on the first round, the dealer turns the original widow face up, and play continues until someone knocks. Whenever the play comes around to a player who has knocked, there is a showdown.

How to play: Although similar to knock poker, Whiskey Poker involves more disadvantage for the first knocker because of the increased likelihood that the other players will improve their hands on that round. Against this is the fact that a player cannot improve his hand without committing himself to some definite course of action. Thus, the standards for knock poker should be applied, except that moderate hands capable of improvement *if another player knocks* (such as a low two pairs) should be passed.

C. OTHER FORMS OF CLOSED POKER

Mike. All cards are dealt face down. After each player has been dealt two cards there is a betting interval; and another after each subsequent round of one card to each active player. After the last card has been dealt there is a final betting interval and a showdown. There is no draw, but it is customary to deal six, seven or eight cards to each player, depending on the rules stated by the dealer, and from these cards each player selects any five for his poker hand in the showdown.

How to play: Hand valuation in this game is the same as that in the corresponding stud game with the same number of cards. With the large number of betting intervals it is usually poor strategy to try for an unlikely powerful hand. Tend to stay in the early rounds with a high pair. Your best opportunity to try for all your possibilities while maintaining strong winning chances is with high triplets (a potential full house).

Two-card Poker. Two cards are dealt face down to each player; there is a betting interval, after which each active player may discard one or both of his cards and draw to replace them, or may stand pat. After the draw there is a final betting interval, and then a showdown in which the highest two-card poker combination wins (two-card flushes and straights not counting). This game is most often played high-low — see Hurricane, below.

How to play: A pair of aces being the highest hand, and an ace-high winning in the absence of a pair, play only when you have an ace or are dealt a pair. If you have an ace, stand pat if you also have a king or a queen and all your opponents have drawn one card.

Hurricane. Hurricane is two-card poker played at high-low. It is sometimes played with deuces-wild.

How to play: In the basic game, the ace (being high and low) maintains its significance. It is possible to win both high and low if your hand contains an ace (or even a pair of aces!). When deuces are wild, you should not consider playing unless you have a deuce or an ace (preferably both, since *this* "pair of aces" is an immortal for both high and low).

Three-card Poker, or Monte. Three cards are dealt face down to each player, and after a betting interval each player may discard one, two or three cards and draw to replace them, or may stand pat. After the draw there is a final betting interval, then a showdown in which the highest three-card poker combination wins the pot—straights and flushes not counting. (In one variation the hands rank as follows: three-of-a-kind, pair, three cards of the same suit in sequence, three-card flush, three cards in sequence of any suit, then high card.) This game is most often played high-low.

How to play: When playing for high it is enough to know that a pair is a good hand. The game is somewhat deceptive at high-low because of the relative ease with which a low hand can be made. Beware of valuing "good" lows too highly.

II. Dealer's-Choice Games of Stud Poker

A. THE BASEBALL FAMILY

Baseball with five cards. (Baseball is most often played in seven-card stud—see below.) Five-card stud is played with all nines wild; any three in the hole is wild; any player who is dealt a three face up must either drop or pay to the pot as many chips as are already in the pot, and in the latter case his facing three is wild; and any player who is dealt a four face up is *immediately* given an additional *face-up card* by the dealer. In the showdown a player with more than five cards selects any five to be his hand.

How to play: Even though there are only five cards in each hand (plus possible "extra" cards), the rank of hands runs very high because there are eight potential wild cards. All computations should be based on the assumption that a player who has stayed in during the early stages has a joker in the hole.

In deciding whether or not to match the pot, one must judge the odds carefully. Do not match the pot unless you are an odds-on favorite to win the hand.

Always credit an opponent who has stayed late in the hand with a joker in the hole.

Baseball. Seven-card stud is played with all nines and threes wild, except that when a three is dealt face up the player must either put up the size of the pot or drop. When a four is dealt face up, the dealer gives that player an additional *hole* card immediately.

Football. This is the same as Baseball, except that all sixes and fours are wild, a four dealt face up requires the player to match the pot or drop, and a deuce dealt face up entitles the player to a free hole card, dealt immediately.

Heinz. Seven-card stud is played with fives and sevens wild, but a player dealt one of these cards face up must match the pot or drop.

Woolworth. This is seven-card stud with fives and tens wild, but a player dealt a five face up must pay five chips (where the betting limit is one chip) to the pot, or drop, and a player dealt a ten face up must pay ten chips to the pot, or drop.

Innumerable other wild-card variations are played, including (listed by George Coffin in "Fortune Poker"): *Dr. Pepper:* seven-card stud with all tens, fours and deuces wild; *Four Forty-Four:* eight-card stud with four cards face down and one up, with a betting interval after each, and all fours wild. In *Four Forty-Two,* deuces are wild. In *Three Forty-Five,* three face-down cards are dealt and one up, then a betting interval, then three more face up with a betting interval after each, then an eighth card face down and a final betting interval. All fives are wild.

How to play: All these games are roughly or exactly equivalent to Baseball, and can be treated together.

When Baseball is played with seven cards, the hands run very high. Five-of-a-kind is quite common, and in a pot with any serious betting, nothing less than four aces should be given consideration.

You should be even more wary of matching the pot in the seven-card game. An opponent may always be lurking with *two* jokers in the hole, and the pot should not be matched unless you are a *very strong odds-on favorite to win.* When your opponents may have two concealed jokers it is usually impossible to assure yourself of the necessary odds.

B. BASIC VARIATIONS OF STUD GAMES

Pistol Stud. Regular five-card stud is played, except that there is a betting interval after the hole cards are dealt, and another after each round of face-up cards is dealt, making five betting intervals in all.

How to play: The only change from ordinary stud is the round of betting after the hole cards are dealt. This furnishes a good opportunity for the conservative player to save money, i.e., to get out while the getting is good, right after his first bad card!

A new set of inferences is available based on the "stays" on the first round. If most of the players stay automatically on the first round, play as in ordinary stud. If not, you can usually count on all but the most aggressive players to have at least a fairly high card in the hole. However, good players will mix up their strategies on the first round. They may hold *any* hole card for a first-round raise. So, on occasion, may you!

Joker Stud. This is regular stud poker played with a 53-card pack, with the joker as a wild card or as the bug (see page 104). The game with the joker wild has the drawback that if the joker is dealt face up, the betting usually stops abruptly and the player who got the joker gets the pot. This is not true when the joker is used as the bug, and the latter game is not a bad one.

How to play: When the joker is in the game, allowance must be made for an opponent's holding it as his hole card. Hands should be valued somewhat conservatively as compared with ordinary stud.

When the bug is used, play can be relaxed a little. Beware, however, of aces, which assume great significance when the bug is in play. There are now *five* aces in the deck and only four of each other rank. When holding the bug, consider your potential carefully. (See Chapter 4 for a discussion of how the bug fits into poker combinations.)

Four-Flush beats a pair. This is occasionally referred to as Canadian Stud or New York Stud. In the showdown, a four-flush beats a single pair but loses to two pairs or any higher hand. In the final betting interval a player with a four-flush showing bets first as compared to a player with any single pair showing. An open-end four-straight is often given similar rank, but below a four-flush.

How to play: In five-card stud the four-flush possibility is often rather important. A hand with two high cards of the same suit is usually worth a play if few cards in this suit appear on the table. If four-card straights also beat a pair, two near cards *in suit* (such as ♡ 7 ♡ 8) are also worth a play, even if many higher cards appear on the board.

Mexican Stud. Flip, Pedro, and Peep-and-Turn are other names for this game.

The betting is as in regular five-card stud except that all cards are dealt face down. After receiving his first two cards, and then after each other card is dealt to him, every player turns up a card—either of his two hole cards. The game is often played with four-card straights and flushes (see above).

Rickey de Laet is the same game except that every player's hole card, and every other card of the same rank in his hand, is wild.

Shifting Sands is the same as Mexican Stud except that the first card a player turns up, and every other card of the same rank in his hand at the showdown, is wild.

How to play: Mexican Stud has many variations which hinge on when a player must decide which hole card he will keep. Because of the difficulty of achieving simultaneous announcements, these options are usually elected consecutively, with the highest hand, or hand to the left of the dealer, forced to make the first decision. Also, since the advantage of deciding last would be so great if the new cards were known to the players, some Mexican Stud players have adopted the rule that all options must be elected before any cards are dealt.

In any case, these options greatly determine the strategy of the game. As a general rule you should attempt to expose cards which give you the highest potential hand with a perfect hole card, unless this hand is too strong. In other words, your board must be strong enough to prevent an opponent from risking a bluff, while you must not display so much power (on your winning hands) that you will have no one calling your bets. Thus, if picture cards are showing against you, expose your low pair, but if no opponent shows a pair or an ace, keep your pair of kings concealed.

Rickey de Laet is such a wild game that proper (conservative) strategy probably dictates playing only with a pair back-to-back on the first two cards. The potential danger that an opponent may have an extra joker is too much to try to overcome later in the hand. Shifting Sands is a more stable game, allowing closer calculation, but the basic strategy should be much the same as in Rickey de Laet, especially in large games.

Six-card Stud. This is the same as five-card stud except that after the fourth face-up card is dealt, and after the betting interval that follows, a sixth card is dealt face down to each player and there is a final betting interval. In the showdown, each player may select five of his six cards to be his hand. (Some prefer to deal the fifth card down and the sixth card up.)

How to play: Since everyone is playing for high (compare with six-card stud high-low), the average winning hand in a seven-handed game will be a low two pairs. The values at the early stages are about the same as in five-card stud.

In the variation in which the fifth card is dealt down, the betting round before and after the second hole card is of great significance. If you have the lead going into the second hole card, it is impossible for your opponents to judge whether you have improved or not. Therefore, especially in pot limit or table stakes play, be wary of committing yourself just before the second hole card unless you have strong values. (In a limit game, this factor is less important, although it should still be reckoned with.)

Seven-card Flip. The first deal is four face-down cards to each player (one at a time), after which each player may turn up any two of his cards after examining them all. After this the game is the same as seven-card stud from the second betting interval on.

How to play: The only change from seven-card stud is the choice of hole cards. In general, it will pay to keep surprises in the hole (such as pairs, near cards in suit, etc.) but this strategy must be varied if the game is called often lest you become a "typed" player.

Kankakee. A joker is used, but is not shuffled in with the pack. It is placed in the center of the table, is fully wild, and is common to all hands. Seven-card stud is played, except that after each player has been dealt his two original hole cards there is the first betting interval, the wild joker representing the first face-up card for each player and the player at dealer's left being the first bettor. Three more face-up cards and one final face-down card are dealt to each active player, with a betting interval after each.

How to play: Kankakee calls for little more than an adjustment of values. Every player has a joker; thus, hands which can be helped more easily by a joker (e.g., straight flush) become more common. A full house is not too strong a hand in this game, a low four-of-a-kind being the average winning hand.

Seven-card Stud, English Style. As stud poker is played in England, each player receives two cards face down and one card face up, as in seven-card stud. There is a betting interval, then two more face-up cards are dealt, with a betting interval after each. Each active player may then discard one card and draw a replacement as in draw poker, the replacement being dealt face up or face down according to the card discarded, and there is then a fourth betting interval. Each player may then discard and draw one more card, as before, after which there is a final betting interval and a showdown. Each player has only five cards for the showdown.

A player may stand pat instead of drawing, but if he stands pat for the first draw he must remain pat for the second draw.

How to play: In the early stages, hands can be judged as in seven-card stud. It must be remembered that the hands will run a little lower than in seven-card stud because a player cannot keep all his possibilities when obtaining his sixth and seventh cards. Thus, for example, a player with a full house possibility must sometimes throw away one possibility to obtain a sixth or seventh card. Three-of-a-kind is therefore a fairly good hand, and three aces will win very often.

Eight-card Stud. There are many variations of this game, the feature common to all being that each player ends with four cards face down and four cards face up. Two cards may be dealt face down and four face up, then two more face down, with a betting interval after each of the face-up cards and after each of the last two face-down cards; or three cards may be dealt face down and one face up, followed by the first betting interval with three more face-up cards and one more face-down card and a betting interval after each; or the first four face down, a betting interval, and then four face up with a betting interval after each. In any case, each player in the showdown selects five of his eight cards.

How to play: When each player has eight cards, straights and flushes really come into their own; but so, of course, do full houses. Thus, it is still doubtful strategy to back a possible straight or flush. The average winning hand (in a seven-handed game) is three kings.

Low Hole Card Wild. In this form of seven-card stud (usually restricted to social games), the lowest-ranking of a player's three hole cards, and every other card of like rank in that player's hand, is wild. This, with the exception of seven-card high-low stud (page 149), is probably the most popular form of seven-card stud. The appeal of the game lies partly in its uncertainty: having paired the lower of his first two hole cards, a player has a winning hand subject only to the danger that he will be dealt a still lower card for his seventh card (and third hole card), nullifying the value of the low cards previously dealt him.

How to play: It is the opinion of most poker analysts that except for the most obvious situations, this game defies analysis. I am constrained to agree. However, one hint: Be ultraconservative!

III. *Miscellaneous Games*

A. GAMES <u>COMBINING</u> CLOSED POKER AND STUD POKER

Shotgun. Shotgun is a combination of draw poker dealing and stud poker betting. Each player receives three cards face down; then the deal is interrupted for a betting interval. Each player next receives another face-down card, followed by another betting interval; then a fifth face-down card, and still another betting interval. There is then a draw, and a final betting interval as in draw poker.

How to play: The values of hands are the same as in five-card poker. One must learn to judge how good the possibilities are when only three or four cards are held. As a general rule, straight and flush possibilities should be disregarded *unless the cards held are of high rank* and can therefore be turned into high pairs. A high pair is a reasonable start in three cards, but a low pair should be dropped.

Remember that *at each stage* the best hand going in figures to be the best hand coming out.

Anaconda. This game combines the feature of betting on partially exposed hands with the basic principle of the knock-poker family (ability to obtain cards from other players). The combination appears to be a happy one, and Anaconda has gained considerable popularity, especially among high-school and college students.

Each player is dealt seven cards, face down. There is a round of betting (this betting round is omitted in some games), after which each player still in the pot passes three cards to his left (or right, as agreed). Each player then discards two cards, leaving himself five cards for his final hand. After a round of betting, each remaining player stacks his five cards in the order in which he intends to expose them. (*This order may not be changed during the course of the hand.*) After each player has determined his order, each turns a card. There is then another round of betting. Each player then flips (turns over) a second card and there is another round of betting, and so on, until a showdown is reached.

How to play: Anaconda can be made even more interesting by playing it high-low, or with wild cards. I will consider the play of the basic game described above, leaving it to the reader to make minor modifications to fit his own group's variation.

It is first essential to realize that at least one card of the "pass" becomes part of a player's final hand. If, therefore, it seems that you may be competing against the player who passed cards to you, you will expose one card he passed you early in the play. On the other hand, if the player who passed cards to you has dropped out, you may conceal the card(s) of his pass as long as seems best for strategic reasons.

Most considerations revolve around the full house (or four-of-a-kind). Since it is very likely (in any but the smallest game) that at least one player will make a full house, straight and flush possibilities should be disregarded. Not only do these latter figure to be inferior hands, but the early upcards of the opponents of a man with (say) a flush will certainly not eliminate the full house possibility. It will require continual calls to see the hand through. (With its large number of betting rounds, Anaconda is usually played only in a limit game — and with a limit of three raises per round.) These calls cannot be justified by the strength of the hand. Therefore, trying for a straight or a flush is a losing play. The best hands are the ones which offer full house or four-of-a-kind possibilities.

Two high pairs (the rank of the second pair is important because the relative ranks of full houses is often crucial) or three-of-a-kind is a good hand to play at the outset. With less, tend to drop out at once. After the pass, do not play with less than a full house, except as a bluff. Remember that a bluff will be possible only if you can represent a hand higher than your opponent's maximum. Therefore, do not play a bluff with (for example) queens and tens. Any of your opponents with aces or kings need not be scared away since he can represent a stronger hand. Furthermore, you may not see a king or an ace on board until the third round of flipping. This makes it very expensive to stay in just to try the bluff. A hand with a pair of aces or three aces is more suitable for a bluff—your opponents will have something to fear!

Complicated games such as Anaconda frequently offer very good odds near the end of the pot, and these favorable situations are often overlooked. Always be on the lookout for very good odds in your favor at the end of a hand. It may pay to throw in an extra chip or two, just in case your opponent is bluffing. However, try to avoid getting into situations of this type! Don't start playing during the flipping rounds of betting unless you feel there is a very good chance that you will want to see the hand all the way through.

Double-Barreled Shotgun. This game is also called Texas Tech. It begins like Shotgun (page 209), but after each player has been dealt three cards face down, the deal is interrupted for a betting interval. One more face-down card is dealt to each active player, with another betting interval; and one more face-down card is dealt to each active player, after which each player may discard and draw, as in draw poker. After the draw, each player turns up one card—any card he chooses—and there is a betting interval; then each successively turns up a second, a third, and a fourth card, with a betting interval after each, so that the hands at the end are as in five-card stud, with four cards up and one hole card.

How to play: The first phase of the game should be played as Shotgun (with an eye to potential bluffs or concealments in the second half of the game). The second part is a simplified form of the flipping stage of Anaconda—simplified, because there is no player who knows one or more of your cards.

B. OTHER GAMES

Take It or Leave It, or **Shove 'em Along.** After the hole cards have been dealt, the dealer deals the first face-up card and pauses; the player may either accept or reject this card. If he rejects it, he shoves it along to the second player and the dealer replaces it. (The player must keep the replacement.) The player to whom the card is "shoved" may either accept or reject it, as did the first player. If no one accepts a card before it comes back to the dealer, it is discarded. When a player accepts a card, the dealer gives a face-up card to the next player in turn and the same process is repeated. Each time that all players have the same number of face-up cards, there is a betting interval. (In some games, every time a player rejects a card he must pay a chip to the pot.)

How to play: When there is no penalty for refusing a card, you should reject any card which does not directly help your hand, unless you are certain it will help some other player (particularly the one to your left). On occasion, you may be able to let a card go by that is needed on your right; the theory is that some intermediate player will not be able to allow the player who needs it to have that card. This "forcing" a player to accept a card can lead to strained situations. It might be good policy (if this game is called often) deliberately to allow a good card to be passed to a late player so that others will not dare leave it to you to "protect" the interests of the players who do not need the card, yet cannot allow it to be given to a certain player.

If there is a penalty for rejecting a card, the expense must be taken into consideration when deciding whether or not to accept the card. If the penalty is roughly the same as the minimum bet per round, it will generally be advantageous to accept the penalty in order to see another card (especially in a loose game). There is no substitute for having the winning hand.

Beat Your Neighbor. Each player is dealt five cards face down, but no one looks at any of his cards. The first player in turn exposes a card, and there is a betting interval. After this, the next player turns up his cards, one by one, until he has a higher-ranking poker combination than the first player, at which point there is another betting interval. Play continues in this way until the last active player has gone through the process of turning up his cards. If anyone turns up all five of his cards without beating his right-hand neighbor, he is out of the pot and the player at his left begins to turn up cards. When the turn comes back to any player still in the pot, he may turn up additional cards in an effort to beat his right-hand neighbor. The highest hand or poker combination showing at the end wins the pot.

How to play: While the showing of certain cards changes the probabilities to some extent, it suffices to know that an "average" poker hand is ace-king high. Therefore, if none of your cards has yet been exposed, your expectation is that you cannot beat a pair.

Butcher Boy. All cards are dealt face up, one at a time. When a card of the same rank as a previously dealt card shows up, it is transferred to the player who was previously dealt that rank, giving him a pair. There is then a betting interval, and the deal is resumed with a face-up card to the player from whom the card was transferred (or, if he has dropped, to the next active player in turn). The deal continues in this way, with a betting interval after the transfer of each card, and the pot goes to the first player to get four-of-a-kind.

How to play: Don't—unless you are closer to making four-of-a-kind than anyone else. Since this strategy will have a stultifying effect on the game, Butcher Boy is a poor choice unless the game is a casual one.

Four-of-a-Kind. This is less a poker game than a drinking bout. After the pack is shuffled and cut, the dealer turns up the top card. He then deals one card face up to each player in rotation, dealing continuously; when the first card of the same rank as the first exposed card is dealt, the player who gets it orders a drink (any drink). When the second card of that rank shows up, the person to whom it is dealt pays for the drink; and when the third and last card of that rank shows up, the person to whom it is dealt drinks the drink! The cards are then shuffled and cut for a new deal by the next player in rotation. Every player antes before each deal, and the entire pot goes to the last player on his feet.

POKER
PROBABILITIES

I SAID BEFORE that the higher mathematics of poker is not very important. It doesn't help a player much to know the chances of being dealt a straight flush or a full house or even a pair. Yet, most of the published tables of poker probabilities are confined to that kind of information.

It *does* help to know the odds against *improving* any particular hand. *Memorize these odds*. At the very least, they will tell you when the pot is offering you good odds on a speculative play.

In the following pages I give some phases of poker mathematics.

THE POSSIBLE POKER HANDS

The following tables give the frequencies of the different poker hands, using various packs and wild cards.

Possible Poker Hands in a 52-Card Pack

HAND		NUMBER	FREQUENCY
Straight flush		40	1 in 64,974
Four-of-a-kind		624	1 in 4,165
Full house		3,744	1 in 694
Flush		5,108	1 in 509
Straight		10,200	1 in 255
Three-of-a-kind		54,912	1 in 47
Two pairs		123,552	1 in 21
One pair		1,098,240	1 in 2½
No pair			
Ace-high	502,860		
King-high	335,580		
Queen-high	213,180		
Jack-high	127,500		
Ten-high	70,380		
Nine-high	34,680		
Eight-high	14,280		
Seven-high	4,080		
		1,302,540	1 in 2
		2,598,960	

Chances of Holding Any Particular Hand or Better in First Five Cards

		APPROXIMATE NUMBER OF TIMES	
Any pair	or better	Once in	2 deals
Pair of jacks	" "	" "	5 "
Pair of queens	" "	" "	6 "
Pair of kings	" "	" "	7 "
Pair of aces	" "	" "	9 "
Two pairs	" "	" "	13 "
Three-of-a-kind	" "	" "	35 "
Straight	" "	" "	132 "
Flush	" "	" "	270 "
Full house	" "	" "	588 "

Possible Poker Hands in a 52-Card Pack Including the Joker Used as the "Bug"

HAND	NUMBER	FREQUENCY
Five-of-a-kind	1	1 in 2,869,685
Straight flush	204	1 in 14,067
Four-of-a-kind	828	1 in 3,466
Full house	4,368	1 in 657
Flush	7,804	1 in 368
Straight	20,532	1 in 140
Three-of-a-kind	63,480	1 in 45
Two pairs	138,600	1 in 21
One pair	1,154,560	1 in 2½
No pair	1,479,308	1 in 2
Total hands possible	2,869,685	

Possible Poker Hands with Deuces-Wild

	NONE	ONE	TWO	THREE	FOUR	TOTAL
			NUMBER OF DEUCES			
Five-of-a-Kind		48	288	288	48	672
Royal Flush	4	80	240	160	—	484
Straight Flush	32	576	2,232	1,232	—	4,072
Four-of-a-Kind	528	8,448	19,008	2,832	—	30,816
Full House	3,168	9,504	—	—	—	12,672
Flush	3,132	7,264	2,808	—	—	13,204
Straight	9,180	37,232	19,824	—	—	66,236
Three-of-a-Kind	42,240	253,440	59,376	—	—	355,056
Two Pairs	95,040	—	—	—	—	95,040
One Pair	760,320	461,728	—	—	—	1,222,048
No Pair	798,660	—	—	—	—	798,660
Total	1,712,304	778,320	103,776	4,512	48	2,598,960

Possible Poker Hands in a 40-Card Pack
(Stripped of 2s, 3s, and 4s)

Straight Flush	28
Four-of-a-Kind	360
Flush	980
Full House	2,160
Straight	7,140
Three-of-a-Kind	23,040
Two Pairs	51,840
One Pair	322,560
Less than one Pair	249,900
Total	658,008

Possible Poker Hands in a 32-Card Pack
(Stripped to the sevens)

Straight Flush	20
Flush	204
Four-of-a-Kind	224
Full House	1,344
Straight	5,100
Three-of-a-Kind	10,752
Two Pairs	24,192
No Pair	52,020
One Pair	107,520
Total	201,376

ODDS AT DRAW POKER

The following tables give the odds against various draws at draw poker (high hand wins). The ace is assumed to make a straight in two combinations: A-K-Q-J-10 and 5-4-3-2-A. In each case the odds have been approximated to a convenient fraction.

Drawing Three Cards to a Pair
(Total Number of Cases: 16,215)

RESULT	FAVORABLE CASES	APPROXIMATE ODDS AGAINST
Two pairs	2,592	5¼ to 1
Triplets	1,854	7¾ to 1
Full House	165	97 to 1
Four-of-a-Kind	45	360 to 1
Any improvement	4,656	2½ to 1

Drawing Two Cards to a Pair and an Ace Kicker
(Total Number of Cases: 1,081)

RESULT	FAVORABLE CASES	APPROXIMATE ODDS AGAINST
Aces-up	126	7½ to 1
Another pair	60	17 to 1
Total two pairs	186	4¾ to 1
Triplets	84	12 to 1
Full House	9	120 to 1
Four-of-a-Kind	1	1,080 to 1
Aces-up or better	220	4 to 1
Any improvement	280	2¾ to 1

Drawing Two Cards to Triplets
(Total Number of Cases: 1,081)

RESULT	FAVORABLE CASES	ODDS AGAINST
Full House	66	15⅓ to 1
Four-of-a-Kind	46	22½ to 1
Any improvement	112	8⅔ to 1

Drawing One Card to Triplets
(Total Number of Cases: 47)

RESULT	FAVORABLE CASES	ODDS AGAINST
Full House	3	14⅔ to 1
Four-of-a-Kind	1	46 to 1
Any improvement	4	10¾ to 1

Other Draws

DRAW	RESULT	APPROXIMATE ODDS AGAINST
Four to an ace	Aces or better	3 to 1
	Two pairs or better	11 to 1
	Aces-up or better	14 to 1
Three to A-K of the same suit	Two pairs or better	12 to 1
Two to a three-straight-flush	Two pairs or better	7½ to 1
(such as ♠ J 10 9)	Straight or better	11 to 1
(such as ♠ Q J 10		
or ♠ 4 3 2)	Straight or better	13½ to 1
(such as ♠ A K Q		
or ♠ 3 2 A)	Straight or better	20 to 1
Two to a straight (open end)	Straight	22 to 1
Two to a flush	Flush	23 to 1
One to two pairs	Full House	10¾ to 1
One to a four-flush	Flush	4¼ to 1
One to a straight		
(open end)	Straight	5 to 1
(inside)	Straight	10¾ to 1
One to a straight-flush		
(open end)	Straight flush	22½ to 1
	Straight or better	2 to 1
(inside)	Straight flush	46 to 1
	Straight or better	3 to 1

The following tables present the chance of a given hand being high at draw poker, and the chance that one (or more) opponents improved a pair by drawing three cards. These tables are expressed in decimals; thus, .97 means that this event will occur 97 times out of 100.

Chance of Being High in the First Five Cards with the 52-Card Pack, Nothing Wild

YOUR HAND	NUMBER OF OPPONENTS						
	1	2	3	4	5	6	7
Three-of-a-kind	.97	.94	.92	.89	.87	.84	.82
Two pairs	.93	.86	.80	.74	.68	.63	.59
Pair of aces	.89	.79	.70	.62	.55	.49	.43
kings	.88	.78	.69	.61	.54	.48	.42
queens	.83	.68	.56	.46	.38	.32	.26
jacks	.79	.63	.50	.40	.32	.25	.20
tens	.76	.58	.44				
nines	.73	.53	.39				
eights	.70	.49					
sevens	.66	.43					
sixes	.63	.40					
fives	.60	.36					
fours	.57	.32					
threes	.53	.28					
twos	.50	.25					

Draw Poker—Chance That an Opponent Improved (Each Player Drew Three Cards)

HAND	CHANCE THAT IT WAS DRAWN BY ANY ONE OF					
	1 OPP.	2 OPP'S.	3 OPP'S.	4 OPP'S.	5 OPP'S.	6 OPP'S.
Two pairs	.16	.30	.41	.50	.58	.64
Three-of-a-kind	.12	.24	.34	.43	.52	.59
Full house	.01	.03	.04	.05	.07	.08
Four-of-a-kind	.003	.01	.01	.015	.02	.025
Chances of any improvement by any opponent	.29	.50	.65	.76	.83	.88

MATHEMATICS OF BLIND-OPENING DRAW POKER

As discussed in Chapter 4, special considerations apply to the blind opener who must decide whether or not to call the blind raiser. This situation can be reduced to mathematical consideration to a greater degree than most other forms of poker. The following table gives the odds against the blind opener being able to defeat the blind raiser with various draws.

Blind-Opening Draw Poker

Chance of beating one opponent who has not bet voluntarily (that is, chance of beating the blind raiser when you are the blind opener):

If you draw 5 cards	9 to 1 against you
If you draw 4 cards to an ace	1½ to 1 against you
If you draw 3 cards to an A-K	2 to 1 against you
If you draw 2 cards to a flush	8 to 1 against you
If you draw 2 cards to a straight	8 to 1 against you
If you draw 2 cards to a straight flush	6 to 1 against you
If you draw 3 cards to a low pair (4, 3, 2)	Even
If you draw 3 cards to a medium pair (5 to 9)	1½ to 1 *for you*

On any hand better than a medium pair you should raise.

Comment: The pot usually offers 4 to 1. It will be seen that the usual plays stand to lose. However, the figures are complicated by the high cards in the hand that may pair.

The same principles apply to straight draw poker when you are next-to-last man and everyone but the dealer is out.

Every additional opponent reduces the odds in your favor on a particular hand. *But every additional opponent has to put his money into the pot, thus increasing the odds you are getting for your own money.* All poker calculations come to the same thing, though in varying degree: If you had the high hand to begin with, you figure to win. The more players there are against you, the fewer pots you will win but the more you will win each time you win the pot, and in the long run you still show a profit.

ODDS AT LOWBALL (DRAW POKER FOR LOW)

The following table gives the odds against making a low hand at lowball when drawing one or two cards. This table assumes that the "bug" is in play but is not in the hand. (If the bug is not in play, the odds are higher by a factor of *approximately* one-quarter—for the very good hands—to one-tenth—for the moderate hands. If the bug is in the hand, the odds against making each hand are much lower, and are comparable to the odds against making the next-worst hand when the bug is not held.)

The table of odds is more deceptive in lowball than in any other form of poker, and the lowball player should take this table with a grain of salt for reasons set forth in the comment. (For a more complete discussion, see Chapter 5.)

Lowball (with the Bug)

The following odds apply to lowball played with the bug. In each case it is assumed that the bug is not in the hand.

One card to 7-high	$3\frac{1}{2}$ to 1 against
One card to 6-high	$5\frac{1}{2}$ to 1 against
One card to 5-high	9 to 1 against
Two cards to any three cards under 7, to make 7-high or better	$27\frac{1}{2}$ to 1 against
One card to 8-high	2 to 1 against
One card to 9-high	Even

Comment: The more players in the pot, the more low cards can be assumed to have been dealt originally, and the worse the chances are for improvement. The same fact decreases the danger of pairing, but this does not alter the fact that the chances of improvement are lessened.

ODDS AT STUD POKER

The chances of holding a given hand in five-card stud are the same as in five-card draw. However, it must be remembered that players will drop out of the pot at an early stage if they do not have potentially good hands. Thus, the players who remain in a stud pot have a higher average potential than those who remain in a pot of draw poker.

The following table gives the chance that a particular hole card is the high hole card, depending on the number of opponents. This table is expressed in decimals; thus, .94 means that this event will occur 94 times out of 100.

Stud Poker — Chance of Having the High Hole Card

| YOUR HOLE CARD | NUMBER OF OPPONENTS | | | | | | | |
	1	2	3	4	5	6	7	8
Ace	.94	.89	.83	.79	.74	.70	.66	.62
King	.86	.74	.63	.55	.47	.40	.35	.30
Queen	.78	.61	.48	.37	.29	.23	.18	.14
Jack	.70	.49	.34	.24	.17	.12	.08	.05

FIVE-CARD STUD

The following table gives the odds against eventually pairing your hole card at five-card stud. (Needless to say, you will be using this table in practice only when you have a high hole card!)

Number of players	Odds against pairing if your hole card is unmatched on the table	Odds against pairing if your hole card is matched once on the table
Seven or eight	4 to 1	6 to 1
Five or six	5 to 1	7 to 1

The next table gives the chance of pairing your hole card after you have received an unmatched card for your third card. This table is listed as a function of the number of cards that other players have shown (whether or not they are still in the game).

Number of other players' cards you have seen	Odds against pairing if your hole card has not been matched	Odds against pairing if your hole card has been matched once
Nine to twelve	$5\frac{1}{2}$ to 1	9 to 1
Five to eight	$6\frac{1}{2}$ to 1	10 to 1

These two tables are approximations. Clearly, the odds will vary slightly with the *exact* number of opponents and the *exact* number of cards you have seen. Such precise figures, however, are unlikely to be of value under actual playing conditions.

Another common situation in five-card stud is when you find yourself with a low pair. If several other players have high cards showing, there is a good chance that one or more of them has, or will eventually have, a higher pair. Therefore, it is valuable to know the approximate odds against improving your hand to *better than a high pair*.

Under normal conditions, if you have a pair and an odd card, the odds against such improvement are $2\frac{1}{2}$ to 1 if you have seen no card matching either of the ranks you hold, but $3\frac{1}{4}$ to 1 if a card matching your pair or odd card has appeared. (If two matching cards have appeared, you should almost always drop out, the odds against eventual improvement being prohibitive.)

SEVEN-CARD STUD (HIGH)

The following tables give the odds against improving various combinations in seven-card stud high poker. For purposes of strategy, these figures are somewhat deceptive, for a player with only a potential hand may be forced to drop out of the pot before he has seen his final card(s).

Odds Against Making a Full House or Better

HOLDING	APPROXIMATE ODDS AGAINST MAKING A FULL HOUSE OR BETTER
Three-of-a-kind or three-of-a-kind and one odd card	$1\frac{1}{2}$ to 1
Three-of-a-kind and two odd cards	2 to 1
Three-of-a-kind and three odd cards	4 to 1
One pair and an odd card	13 to 1
One pair and two odd cards	19 to 1
One pair and three odd cards	39 to 1
Two pairs	4 to 1
Two pairs and an odd card	7 to 1
Two pairs and two odd cards	10 to 1

Odds Against Making a Flush

HOLDING	APPROXIMATE ODDS AGAINST MAKING A FLUSH
Three of a suit	4½ to 1
Three of a suit and one odd card	9 to 1
Three of a suit and two odd cards	23 to 1
Four of a suit	1¼ to 1
Four of a suit and one odd card	1¾ to 1
Four of a suit and two odd cards	4¼ to 1

Odds Against Making a Straight

HOLDING	APPROXIMATE ODDS AGAINST MAKING A STRAIGHT
J 10 9	4¼ to 1
J 10 9 2	8 to 1
J 10 9 3 2	20 to 1
J 10 9 8	1⅓ to 1
J 10 9 8 2 (or A Q J 10 8)	2¼ to 1
J 10 9 8 3 2 (or A Q J 10 8 2)	4¾ to 1
J 10 9 7	2¾ to 1
J 10 9 7 2	4½ to 1
J 10 9 7 3 2	10 to 1
K Q J (or 4 3 2)	6¾ to 1
K Q J 2 (or K 4 3 2)	12 to 1
A K Q (or 3 2 A)	13 to 1
A K Q 2 (or J 3 2 A)	24 to 1

SEVEN-CARD HIGH-LOW STUD

In many hands of seven-card high-low stud, you will find your-self trying to make a low hand. The following table gives the approximate odds against completing various low hands under the assumption that a straight does *not* count as a low hand. (If aces are low cards, the chances are given by those for the next-worst hand.)

Your hand	Odds against making a seven-low	Odds against making no worse than an eight-low	Odds against making no worse than a nine-low
7 3 2	4 to 1	2 to 1	Even
7 3 2 K	8 to 1	4 to 1	2 to 1
7 3 2 K Q	24 to 1	10 to 1	6 to 1
7 4 3 2	1½ to 1	2 to 3	1 to 3
7 4 3 2 K	2 to 1	1¼ to 1	2 to 3
7 4 3 2 K Q	5 to 1	3 to 1	2 to 1
*4 3 2	6½ to 1	2¾ to 1	Even
*4 3 2 K	13 to 1	5 to 1	2¼ to 1

* These holdings are somewhat inferior to the same with the seven replacing the four because of the chance that certain "good" cards will turn the holding into a straight. If straights *do* count as low hands, use the figures given for 7 3 2, 7 3 2 K, etc., which are very slightly lower than the true odds.

THE MATHEMATICAL THEORY OF GAMES AND ITS APPLICATION TO POKER

Iₙ ᴘᴏᴋᴇʀ, each of the players makes a series of strategy decisions upon which the outcome of the game depends. Poker thus comes within the scope of the "theory of games" originally developed by John von Neumann.

Unquestionably, one can be a good poker player without understanding this theory. In fact, the "game-theoretic" considerations are usually outweighed by simple psychological considerations when a hand of poker is played *at the table* instead of on a mathematician's note pad.

However, as the theory of games *may have* significant effects on the play of a hand of poker, and since an understanding of the basic results of this theory may provide an insight into the nature of the game, I will describe some of the basic game-theoretic considerations of poker.

Matching coins. Imagine that A and B want to "match pennies." Each player has a stack of pennies (say) which he prepares in advance, the coins being placed in the stack so that either a head or a tail will appear when it is exposed. They play a game in which each exposes the coins of his stack one at a time; if, on comparison, the faces match, A wins those two coins; if the faces do not match, B wins the two coins.

Clearly this is a fair game, with equal chances for A and B. On any one comparison, each has an equal chance to win, and each bet is made at even money.

One question we might ask with relation to this game is the following: Is there any strategy that A or B might adopt (in the stacking of his coins) so as to place a limit on his losses, or to guarantee a certain minimum gain in the long run? The answer to this is yes. Furthermore, the most important significance of von Neumann's theory is that in any two-person, choice-of-strategy game in which, at each phase, one player wins what the other loses (and vice versa), *such a strategy* (called an optimum strategy) *exists for each player.*

In the coin-matching game described above, the optimum strategy (for either player, as this is a symmetrical game) is to stack the coins at random, half of them heads and half tails. It is clear that if A, for example, stacked his coins with more heads than tails, B could do better than break even (in the long run) by stacking his coins with more tails than heads; in fact, if B put *all* of his coins so as to come up tails, he would be assured of a profit. Similarly, if A weights his stack toward heads, B can profitably weight his toward tails. (Of course if B guesses A's strategy wrong, A will win.)

However, if A aligns his stack on a 50-50 basis, the game will result in a draw (in the long run), no matter how B places his coins. (The reader should verify this for himself.)

If A (say) does *not* adopt his optimal strategy (half and half) and instead weights his stack in one direction or the other, he is, in essence, gambling that he can outguess B. Use of the optimal strategy can guarantee A no worse than an even split (the "fair" result) in the long run.

Application to poker. When a "game theory situation" arises in poker, there is similarly an optimum strategy for each player. Just as in coin-matching a strategy consists of taking different actions (placing a coin as heads or tails) *on a percentage basis,* so in poker does a strategy consist of making a betting decision on a percentage basis. Some strategical questions at poker which can be analyzed on a game-theory basis are: How often to bluff; how often to call a possible bluff; how often to bet into a potential high-low call; how often to call high low without an "immortal" in each direction.

According to the so-called "fundamental theorem of the theory of games," there is always an optimum percentage strategy which will guarantee the player no worse than his true equity in the situation. This corresponds to the half-and-half strategy in coin-matching. However, just as in the coin-matching game, *when one player deviates from his optimum strategy, his opponent can take advantage of him by making a corresponding change from his own optimum strategy.* Thus, if A has a tendency to stack heads, B should tend to stack more tails.

The precise percentage of the time each choice of action should be adopted in the poker-strategy situations listed above depends on the amount of a potential bet, the amount in the pot, the importance of the particular amounts of money to each player involved, and so forth. For the practical player, it is important to appreciate two facts:

(1) A theoretical optimum strategy always exists. (This strategy, remember, consists of taking each of the possible actions a certain percentage of the time.)

(2) A player can take advantage of his opponents' deviation from his own optimum strategy; but by doing so, he runs the risk that he has misjudged the direction in which his opponent deviated from the theoretical ideal. (Examine the coin-matching game if you are having trouble visualizing this.)

As stated before, it is unclear whether or not this theory has any practical application in a poker game. We *can* use this theory to make a simplification of one particular poker *analysis*. Poker situations do *not* necessarily consist of endless bluff and double-bluff. In each strategy situation, there is theoretically optimum (percentage) strategy, and it is only through deviations from this strategy that a player can win or lose against his fair share of the pot (in long-range considerations).

The percentage calculation of optimum strategies is quite complicated, even if the proper values (of the bets, the pot, and so forth) are known. It is virtually impossible to compute them during the play of an actual deal. What should be taken into account, instead, are the peculiarities and tendencies of the particular opponent(s) on the deal in question.

APPENDIXES
GLOSSARY
INDEX

Appendix

THE EVOLUTION
OF POKER

POKER IN ITS PRESENT form is relatively new as games go. Its ultimate ancestor was perhaps the Persian game As Nas, or perhaps an earlier oriental game. A similar game of structures appeared in England in the 18th century as Brag; in France as Commerce, an ancestor of the Whiskey Poker of today. The German equivalent was Pochen (to bluff), which the French called Poque and the Americans corrupted to Poker. This name became so thoroughly identified with the game that at first any game of structures was called a poker game: The Spanish Conquian became not merely Rum, but "Poker Rum" ("rum," that is, "queer," poker).

At first poker was a rough, tough, ask-no-quarter-give-no-quarter gamblers' game played by men in shirtsleeves. In the 20th century, however, it has become a social game for both sexes, played in the parlor for nominal stakes and sometimes for none at all. Originally it was a slow, serious game; more lately it has been "pepped up" by the introduction of new variants and by promiscuous use of "wild cards." Nearly all poker games today are of this "pepped-up" variety.

The laws and customs of poker have not kept up with the changing times. When R. F. Foster drafted a code of poker laws in the 1890s, his object was to prevent cheating, which was then prevalent. The code of ethics was amoral; there was no ban on lying or trickery in almost any form. In almost no case did a violation call for a penalty.

Such laws and ethics are not compatible with the drawing-room atmosphere of present-day poker, but it has proved difficult for would-be lawmakers to break through the old traditions or to standardize laws which are traditionally subject to an unlimited number of "house rules" established by any club or host who has his own ideas of propriety. Yet it was just such a task that was eventually accomplished in the standardization of the Bridge laws. In many cases the old poker customs are inequitable or unjust, and sensible players will continue to improvise improvements on the laws until they are given a code they can adopt without outrage to their sense of equity and justice.

A start in that direction was made in a code of laws written by Oswald Jacoby in 1940. A code of poker laws was published by the United States Playing Card Company in 1941; and during World War II, when much poker was played in the armed services, Lieut. George S. Coffin made a complete revision of that code. A description of poker procedure in both casual and professional games was published in my book, "The Modern Hoyle" (1944). Jacoby and I later participated in a re-editing of Coffin's code.

OBSOLETE POKER GAMES

Poker with the Buck. This, one of the earlier forms of Poker, is listed in many books as Straight Poker, of Bluff. There is a deal of five cards face down to each player, a betting interval and a showdown – no draw. Some token, such as a penknife (originally a buckhorn-handled knife, whence the name) is called the buck. The first dealer antes one chip for each player and passes the buck along to the player at his left. That player will ante for the next deal and pass the buck, so that the obligation to ante is always marked by the buck. The winner of each pot deals the next. Betting begins with the player at the dealer's left; a player may pass and come back in if anyone bets. If no one bets, there is another ante by the player who has the buck, and the deal passes to the player at the previous dealer's left.

As, or **As Nas.** An ancient Persian game, this may be the ultimate ancestor of poker. The pack consists of five cards (ace to ten, or the equivalent) in each suit, and as many suits as there are players. For example, four players use a 20-card pack. All the cards are dealt out, face down, five to each player. Each player, after looking at his hand, may make a bet or may drop; once a bet has been made, the betting process of calling, raising, or dropping is the same as in poker, and in the showdown four-of-a-kind is the highest hand, next, three-of-a-kind, then two pairs, then a single pair. There are no straights or flushes; if no one has a pair, then all hands must tie. (Poker, as originally played in the United States, was almost identical to this game.)

Glle, Gllet, Gillet or **Trionfetti.** This may be the most ancient European ancestor of poker. Four play, and the 32-card Piquet pack is used, ace to seven in each suit. Each player antes equally to each of two pots. Three cards are dealt, face down, to each player. First there is betting and a showdown for the first pot, for which the highest hand is three-of-a-kind (a *tricon*) and the next-highest a pair (a *ge*). If no pair or better is held, this pot is combined with the second; there is a betting interval and then a showdown for *point*; in this showdown the highest hand is a *flux* or flush, three cards of the same suit; if there is no flush, or as between two flushes, the highest point wins, two aces counting 21, an ace and a face card counting 20½, an ace 11, a face card or ten 10, and other cards their index values; but if any player has two or more cards of the same suit, no player may count the cards of more than one suit in his hand.

Brelan, or **Bouillotte.** Four usually play, each for himself, with a 20-card pack including ace, king, queen, nine and eight of each suit. Each player is dealt three cards, and the next card is turned up and is counted by each player as part of his hand. Rotation and order of preference are to the right, beginning with the dealer. The dealer makes a blind bet, which may be straddled by the players in order to his right. After the betting there is a showdown in which four-of-a-kind (*brelan carré*) is the highest hand and *brelan* (three-of-a-kind) is next-highest. The holder of the former receives a bonus of four chips from each player, and the holder of the latter a bonus of one chip from each player (if it is the winning hand). If no one has a *brelan,* the winner is determined by the *point*: All hands are shown, and the suit having the highest point-count in all four hands and the exposed card (counting ace as 11, face cards 10 each, and nine and eight their index values) is the winning suit; the active player having the highest point count in this suit wins the pot. In case of ties the dealer, and after him each player in order of preference to the right, wins. If two suits tie for point, the active player in order of preference may select one of them as the suit that wins. If no active player has a card of the suit that wins, the suit having the next-highest point in all 13 cards becomes the suit that wins.

Ambigu. This old French game was played by two to seven players with a 40-card pack—ace to ten in each suit, with no face cards, ace ranking low. At the start each player antes equally to the pool. Two cards are dealt to each player, and each in turn may stand pat or may discard one or two cards and draw replacements, and may bet, as in poker. If no one calls a bet in this interval, the lone bettor withdraws his wager and is paid a penalty equal to a player's ante by the last player who refused to call. If anyone calls, the betting proceeds as in poker, and all players who have passed after the bet, or who pass after the call, are out.

When this betting interval ends, each active player receives two more cards, and each in turn may now discard from his four cards and draw. There is now a betting interval, as in poker, followed by a showdown, but if no one bets, everyone antes again and there is a new deal. In the showdown the hands rank as follows: Four-of-a-kind (*frezon*), high; three-of-a-kind with a fourth card of a different suit; flush; three-of-a-kind with a fourth card of the same suit as one of the three; sequence, or four-card straight; prime, or Dutch flush—four cards of different suits; point, or the highest point count of cards of the same suit in the same hand, each card counting its index value (ace counting 1). The highest-ranking hand wins the pot, plus bonuses from all players, active and inactive, of one chip if he won on point; or, if he won with a higher-ranking hand, one extra chip for each combination he holds or can beat. For example, with three-of-a-kind and the fourth card of another suit, he would collect six chips, because he has two combinations—three-of-a-kind and a prime—and can beat four others: point, prime, sequence, and three-of-a-kind without the prime.

Brag. This is the English representative of the poker family. The full 52-card pack is used. There are three wild cards: ace of diamonds, jack of clubs and nine of diamonds, ranking in that order and called *braggers*. (In other forms of the game, all jacks and nines were braggers.) The dealer alone antes, his ante being a blind opening bet. Three cards are dealt face down to each player, and there is a betting interval as in poker, each player in turn having the privilege of dropping, calling or raising until the bets are equalized. If no one calls, each other player pays the dealer one chip. After the betting interval, if anyone has called, there is a showdown in which three-of-a-kind and pairs are the only combinations of value, and in which natural cards beat combinations including wild cards. As between two combinations including wild cards and otherwise of equal rank, the one including the highest-ranking wild card wins. [There were several variants of Brag, most of them representing combinations of the basic game with other similar games.]

Commerce. The 52-card pack is used, and the dealer gives each player three cards, one at a time, in each round of dealing turning up one card in the center of the table to make a three-card widow. The dealer may exchange his hand for the widow; whether or not he does so, each player in turn may then exchange one card for a widow card until someone knocks. When any player knocks, play ends and there is a showdown in which the hands rank: three-of-a-kind, pair, and point (as in

Ambigu). [In later developments of the game, the highest hands were: three-of-a-kind, then a three-card straight flush, then a three-card flush, then a pair, and finally point.]

Poch or **Pochen** was a gambling game for three to six players. Equal antes are first distributed to compartments of a layout labelled: ace, king, queen, jack, ten, marriage, sequence, poch. Five cards are dealt to each player, the next card is turned for trump, and the holders of the trump ace, king, etc., collect at once from the layout. The only real competition comes with *poch* — the best pair, three-of-a-kind, or four-of-a-kind. There is a betting interval, as in poker. To open or stay, a player has to have at least a pair. After due betting, raising, etc., there is a showdown of all hands still in, and the best takes the pot together with the chips on poch in the layout. (When a high trump is missing from the cards dealt, chips on that compartment of the layout stay and are increased by subsequent antes.) The hands are then played out as at whist (except that a player who cannot follow suit does not play at all to that trick) and the first to get rid of all his cards collects from each other player — one chip for every card they still have.

Appendix

THE LAWS
OF POKER

THERE ARE several worthy sets of poker laws. It is not so important that players adopt any particular set of laws as that they adopt some set of *written* laws and follow it strictly. If players wish to add house rules or special customs, it is their privilege to do so, but these too should be written. The following laws are recommended because experience has shown that they answer virtually every question that is likely to arise in a poker game.

The laws have three main sections: General laws, applying to all forms of poker; laws applying to draw or closed poker; and laws applying to stud or open poker.

Penalties for breaches of law represent a problem that has never been satisfactorily solved in any poker laws. A penalty can punish an offender but it cannot restore the rights of players who were damaged by the irregularity. Therefore, no penalties are provided by the following laws. In extreme cases the players can constitute themselves a kangaroo court and make some equitable adjustment, but generally the following laws are confined to rectification rather than penalization of irregularities.

GENERAL LAWS

(This section covers the pack of cards; the rank of hands; the shuffle, cut, and deal; the betting; and the showdown.)

1. *Players.* Poker may be played by two to ten players. In every form of poker each person plays for himself.

240

2. *Object of the game*. The object of poker is to win the pot, either by having the best hand (as explained below) or by making a bet that no other player meets.

3. (a) *The pack*. The poker pack consists of 52 cards, divided in four suits: spades (♠), hearts (♡), diamonds (◊), clubs (♣). In each suit there are 13 cards: A, K, Q, J, 10, 9, 8, 7, 6, 5, 4, 3, 2.

(b) *Joker*. The joker may be added to the pack as a wild card.

(c) *Wild cards*. The joker or any other card or class of cards may be designated as wild by any of the following methods. The method must be selected in advance by the players in the game.

(1) The wild card may be designated by its holder to represent any other card that its holder does not have.

(2) The joker (in this case called the bug) may be designated by its holder to represent a fifth ace or any card needed to complete a straight, a flush, or any special hand such as a dog, cat, etc.

(3) Any wild card may represent any other card, whether or not the holder of the wild card also has the card designated. [This permits double- or even triple-ace-high flushes, etc.] A wild card, properly designated, ranks exactly the same as a natural card.

4. *Rank of cards*. (a) A (high), K, Q, J, 10, 9, 8, 7, 6, 5, 4, 3, 2; A (low) only in the sequence 5-4-3-2-A.

(b) *Optional*. The ace may rank low in low poker (lowball) or in high-low poker. When the ace is by agreement designated as low:

(1) In low poker, the ace is always low, so that A-A is a lower pair than 2-2.

(2) In high-low poker, the holder must designate the relative rank of the ace at the time he shows his hand in the showdown, e.g., by saying "aces high" (in which case A-A beats K-K for high) or "aces low" (in which case A-A beats 2-2 for low but loses to 2-2 for high).

(c) In any pot to be won by the high hand, the ranking follows subsection (a) of this law, so that, for example, between two little dogs, 7-6-4-3-2 beats 7-5-4-3-2.

5. *Seating*. (a) Players take seats at random unless any player demands, before the game begins, that the seats of the respective players be determined as provided in the next paragraph.

(b) When any player demands a reseating, the banker has first choice of seats. The first dealer (see paragraph 7) either may take the seat to the left of the banker or may participate with the other players in having his position determined by chance. The dealer then shuffles the pack, has the cards cut by the player to his right, and deals one card face up to each player in rotation, beginning with the player at his left. The player thus dealt the highest-ranking card sits at the right of the banker, the player with the next-highest card at the right of that player, and so on. If two players are dealt cards of the same rank, the card dealt first ranks higher than the other.

(c) After the start of the game no player may demand a reseating unless at least one hour has elapsed since the last reseating. A player entering the game after it begins must take any vacant seat. A player replacing another player must take the seat vacated by that player. Two players may exchange seats, after any showdown and before the next deal begins, provided no other player objects.

(d) When there is no banker, the dealer has first choice of seats.

6. *The shuffle and cut.* Any player, on demand, may shuffle the pack before the deal. The pack should be shuffled three times in all, by one or more players. The dealer has the right to shuffle last and should shuffle the pack at least once.

(a) The dealer offers the suffled pack to his right-hand opponent, who may cut it or not as he pleases. If this player does not cut, any other player may cut. If more than one player demands the right to cut, the one nearest the dealer's right hand shall cut. Except in case of an irregularity necessitating a new cut, the pack is cut only once.

(b) The player who cuts divides the pack into two or three portions, none of which shall contain fewer than five cards, and completes the cut by placing the packet that was originally bottom-most on top. [If a card is exposed in cutting, the pack must be shuffled by the dealer and cut again. Irregularities requiring a new shuffle and cut are covered under point 11.]

7. *The deal.* (a) At the start of the game any player shuffles a pack and deals the cards face up, one at a time to each player in rotation beginning with the player at his left, until a jack is turned up. The player to whom the jack falls is the first dealer. Thereafter, the turn to deal passes from each player to the player at his left. A player may not voluntarily pass his turn to deal.

(b) The dealer distributes the cards from the top of the pack, one card at a time to each player in clockwise rotation, beginning with the player at his left and ending with himself.

8. *Rank of hands.* Poker hands rank, from highest to lowest:

(a) Straight flush—five cards of the same suit in sequence. The highest straight flush is A, K, Q, J, 10 of the same suit, called a royal flush. The lowest straight flush is 5, 4, 3, 2, A of the same suit. As between two straight flushes, the one headed by the highest card wins. [When any card of the pack is designated as wild—see 3(c)—a straight flush loses to five-of-a-kind, which is the highest possible hand.]

(b) Four-of-a-kind—four cards of the same rank. This hand loses to a straight flush but beats any other hand. As between two hands, each containing four-of-a-kind, the four higher-ranking cards win. [When there are several wild cards it is possible for two players to hold four-of-a-kind of the same rank. In this case the winning hand is the one with the higher-ranking fifth card.]

(c) Full house—three cards of one rank and two cards of another rank. As between two full houses, the one with the higher-ranking three-of-a-kind is the winner. [When there are several wild cards, two players may have full houses in which the three-of-a-kind holdings are of the same rank; the higher of the pairs then determines the winning hand.]

(d) Flush—five cards of the same suit. As between two flushes, the one containing the highest card wins. If the highest cards are of the same rank, the higher of the next-highest cards determines the winning hand, and so on; so that ♠ A K 4 3 2 beats ♡ A Q J 10 8, and ♠ J 9 8 6 4 beats ♡ J 9 8 6 3.

(e) Straight—five cards, in two or more suits, ranking consecutively; as 8, 7, 6, 5, 4. The ace is high in the straight A, K, Q, J, 10, and low in the straight 5, 4, 3, 2, A. As between two straights, the one containing the highest card wins, so that 6, 5, 4, 3, 2 beats 5, 4, 3, 2, A.

(f) Three-of-a-kind—three cards of the same rank. As between two hands, each containing three-of-a-kind, the one with the higher-ranking three-of-a-kind wins. [When there are several wild cards, there may be two hands containing identical threes-of-a-kind. In such cases the highest-ranking unmatched card determines the winner. If these cards are of the same rank, the higher-ranking fifth card in each hand determines the winner.]

(g) Two pairs—two cards of one rank and two cards of another rank, with an unmatched fifth card. As between two hands, each containing two pairs, the one with the highest pair wins. If the higher pairs are of the same rank, the one with the second-ranking pair wins. If these pairs too are of the same rank, the hand containing the higher of the unmatched cards is the winner.

(h) One pair—two cards of the same rank, with three unmatched cards. Of two one-pair hands, the one containing the higher pair wins. As between two hands containing pairs of the same rank, the highest unmatched card determines the winner; if these are the same, the higher of the second-highest unmatched cards, and if these are the same, the higher of the lowest unmatched cards. For example, 8, 8, 9, 5, 3 beats 8, 8, 9, 5, 2.

(i) No pair. This loses to any hand having a pair or any higher-ranking combination. As between two no-pair hands, the one containing the highest card wins; if these two cards are tied, the next-highest card decides, and so on, so that A, 8, 7, 4, 3 loses to A, 9, 7, 4, 3 but wins from A, 8, 7, 4, 2.

Two hands that are identical, card for card, are tied, since the suits have no relative rank in poker.

9. *Betting*. (a) All the chips bet go into the center of the table, forming the pot. Before putting any chips in the pot, a player in turn announces whether he is betting, calling, or raising; and, if he is betting or raising, how much. A player may not raise by any amount less than the bet he calls, unless there is only one player besides himself in the pot.

(b) If every player in turn, including the dealer, passes, there is a new deal by the next player in rotation and the ante (if any) is repeated. If any player bets, each player in turn after him must either call, or raise, or drop.

(c) In each betting interval, the turn to bet begins with the player designated by the rules of the variant being played, and moves to each active player to the left. A player may neither pass nor bet until the active player nearest his right has put the correct number of chips into the pot or has discarded his hand.

(1) In draw poker, the first in turn before the draw is the player nearest the dealer's left. The first in turn after the draw is the player who made the first bet before the draw, or, if he has dropped, the active player nearest his left.

(2) In stud poker, the first in turn in each betting interval is the player whose exposed cards are higher than those of any other player. If two or more players have identical high holdings, the one nearest dealer's left is first in turn. In the first betting interval, the high player must make a minimum bet. In any later betting interval, he may check without betting.

(d) Unless a bet has been made in that betting interval, an active player in turn may check, which means that he elects to remain an active player without betting. [In some variants of poker, checking is specifically prohibited.]

(e) If any player bets, each active player in turn after him (including players who checked originally) must either drop, or call, or raise.

(f) No player may check, bet, call, raise, or drop, except in his proper turn. A player in turn may drop even when he has the privilege of checking. At any time that a player discards his hand, or permits it to be mixed with any discard, he is deemed to drop and his hand may not be reclaimed.

(g) Whenever only one active player remains, because every other player dropped, the active player wins the pot without showing his hand and there is a new deal by the next dealer in turn.

(h) No two players may play in partnership, and there may be no agreement between two or more players to divide a pot.

10. *The showdown*. When each player has either called the highest previous bet, without raising, or has dropped; or when every active player has checked; the full hand of every active player is placed face up on the table and the highest-ranking hand wins the pot. If two or more hands tie for the highest rank, they divide the pot evenly, an odd chip going to the player who last bet or raised.

IRREGULARITIES

11. *Redeal*. Any player, unless he has intentionally seen the face of any card required to be dealt to him face down, may call for a new shuffle, cut, and deal by the same dealer if it is ascertained, before the dealer begins dealing the second round of cards, that:

(1) a card was exposed in cutting;

(2) the cut left fewer than five cards in either packet;

(3) two or more cards are faced in the pack;

(4) the pack is incorrect or imperfect in any way [see paragraphs 3(a), 14, and 15];

(5) a player is dealing out of turn [see next paragraph].

If a player is dealing out of turn, and a redeal is called, the deal reverts to the proper player in turn. In a game in which every player antes, no one need ante again. Any other bet that has been put in the pot is forfeited to the pot. If no redeal or misdeal is called within the time limit provided, the deal stands as regular and the player at the left of the out-of-turn dealer will be the next dealer in turn.

12. *Misdeal*. If a misdeal is due to the dealer's error, and attention is drawn to it by a player who has not intentionally seen any face-down card dealt to him, the deal passes to the next player in turn. Any ante made solely by the dealer is forfeited to the pot. If all players have anteed equally, their antes remain in the pot and no one need ante again. A blind bet or raise may be withdrawn.

A misdeal may be called:

(a) by any player who has not intentionally seen any face-down card dealt to him, if before the dealer begins the second round of cards it is ascertained that the pack was not shuffled or was not offered for a cut;

(b) by any player to whom the dealer gives two face-up cards in draw poker or any other form of closed poker, provided that player has not intentionally seen any face-down card dealt to him and has not con-

tributed to the error; and provided he calls for the misdeal immediately;
(c) if the dealer gives too many cards to more than one player.

If the dealer stops dealing before giving every player enough cards,
due solely to his omission to deal one or more rounds, it is not a misdeal
and the dealer is required to complete the deal whenever the irregularity is discovered. [For example, if the dealer stops dealing after giving
each player only four cards; or if the dealer gives the first five of seven
players five cards each and the sixth and seventh players only four cards
each, having stopped dealing after the fifth player on the last round.]

If the dealer deals too many hands, he shall determine which hand
is dead, and that hand is discarded; but if any player has looked at any
face-down card in any hand, he must keep that hand.

If the dealer deals too few hands, he must give his own hand to the
first omitted player to his left. Any other player who has been omitted
and who has anteed may withdraw his ante.

13. *Exposed card.* (a) If the dealer exposes one or more cards from
the undealt portion of the pack, after the deal is completed, those cards
are dead and are placed among the discards. (See also stud poker,
paragraph 35.)

(b) There is no penalty against any player for exposing any part of
his hand, and he has no redress. A player who interferes with the deal
and causes the dealer to expose a card may not call a misdeal.

(c) Each player is responsible for his own hand and has no redress if
another player causes a card in it to be exposed.

14. *Incorrect pack.* If it is ascertained at any time before the pot has
been taken in that the pack has too many cards, too few cards, or a
duplication of cards, the deal is void, and each player withdraws from
the pot any chips he contributed to it, any other laws of the game to the
contrary notwithstanding; but the results of pots previously taken in
are not affected.

15. *Imperfect pack.* If the pack contains any card that is torn, dis-
colored or otherwise marked so as to be identifiable from its back, the
pack must be replaced before the deal in progress or any other deal can
be completed; but the play of the pot in progress is not affected if the
deal has been completed.

16. *Incorrect hand.* A hand having more or fewer than five cards (or
any other number of cards designated as a player's hand in the poker
variant being played) is foul and cannot win the pot. If every other
player has dropped, the pot remains and goes to the winner of the next
pot. [Players may agree that a hand with fewer than five cards is not
foul, in which case its holder may compete for the pot with the best
poker combination he can make with the cards he has.]

17 *Irregularities in betting.* Chips once put in the pot may not be withdrawn except:

(a) By a player who, after he has anteed, is dealt out — see paragraph 12;

(b) In jackpots, when another player has opened without proper openers — see paragraph 30(c);

(c) In draw poker, by the players who opened or raised blind, in case of a misdeal — see paragraph 12;

(d) In stud poker, when the dealer has failed to deal a player any card face down — see paragraph 34.

18. *Installment or string bets.* A player's entire bet must be put in the pot at one time. Having put in any number of chips, he may not add to that number unless the original number was insufficient to call, in which case he may add exactly enough chips to call. If, however, he announced before putting in any chips that he was raising by a certain amount, and he puts in an amount insufficient for such a raise, he must on demand supply enough additional chips to equal the announced amount of his bet.

19. *Insufficient bet.* When a player in turn puts into the pot a number of chips insufficient to call, he must either add enough chips to call and may not raise; or he must drop and forfeit chips already put in the pot. When a player raises by less than the minimum permitted, he is deemed to have called and any additional chips he put into the pot are forfeited to it.

20. *Bet above limit.* If a player puts in the pot more chips than are permitted by the limit, it stands as a bet of the limit and additional chips are forfeited to the pot. An exception is made in table stakes, when a player's bet exceeds the number of chips an opponent has; in that event, the player may withdraw the excess and either bet it in a side pot, or, if there are no other players willing or able to meet that bet in the side pot, restore those chips to his stack.

21. *Announcement in turn of intention to pass or bet.* If a player in turn announces that he passes or drops, his announcement is binding on him whether or not he discards his hand. If a player in turn announces a bet but does not put any chips in the pot, he is bound by his announcement and must if able supply such additional chips as are necessary to bring his bet up to the announced amount. In any event, other players who rely upon an announcement of intention do so at their own risk and have no redress in case under these rules the announcement need not be made good. [In many circles it is considered unethical to announce any intention and then not make good on it.]

22. *Announcement out of turn of intention to pass or bet.* If, out of turn, a player announces his intention to pass or drop when his turn

comes, but does not actually discard his hand; or to make a certain bet, but does not actually put any chips in the pot; his announcement is void and he may take any action he chooses when his turn comes. Any other player who acts in reliance upon the announcement does so at his own risk and has no redress. [As in the case of paragraph 21, above, failure to make good on such an announcement, and especially if the announcement was intentionally misleading, is in many circles considered unethical.]

23. *Bet out of turn.* If a player puts any chips in the pot out of turn, they remain there, and the play reverts to the player whose turn it was. If any player to the offender's left puts chips in the pot, he has bet out of turn and is equally an offender. When the offender's turn comes, if the chips he put in were insufficient to call, he may add enough chips to to call; if the amount was exactly sufficient to call, he is deemed to have called; if the amount was more than enough to call, he is deemed to have raised by the amount of the excess but cannot add chips to increase the amount of his raise; if no player before him has bet, he is deemed to have bet the number of chips he put in and any amount above the agreed limit is forfeited to the pot. If the chips he put in were insufficient to call he may forfeit these chips and drop. He may never add chips to raise or to increase his raise.

24. *Pass out of turn.* The pass (act of dropping) out of turn is among the most damaging of poker improprieties, but there is no penalty therefor except by agreement of the players. In any case the offender's hand is dead and cannot win the pot.

25. *Irregularities in the showdown.* (a) *Hand misstated.* If a player in the showdown announces a hand he does not actually hold, his announcement is void if attention is called to the error at any time before the pot has been taken in by any player (including the player who miscalled his hand). ["The cards speak for themselves."]

(b) *Designation of wild cards.* If in the showdown a player orally designates the suit or rank of a wild card in his hand, or implies such designation by announcing a certain hand, he may not change that designation (e.g., an announcement of Joker-J-10-9-8 as "jack-high straight" fixes the joker as a seven). A player may always show his hand without announcement and need not designate the value of a wild card unless another active player demands that he do so.

(c) *Concession of a pot.* A player who has discarded his hand after another player's announcement of a higher hand may not later claim the pot even if the announcement is determined to have been incorrect.

DRAW POKER

26. *The draw.* (a) When each player has exactly called the highest previous bet, without raising, or has dropped, the first betting interval ends. The dealer picks up the undealt portion of the pack, and each active player in turn to his left may discard one or more cards, whereupon the dealer gives him that number of cards, face down, from the top of the pack. A player need not draw unless he so chooses.

(b) If the dealer is an active player, he must announce how many cards, if any, he is drawing. At any time following the draw and before the first player in turn bets or checks in the final betting interval, any active player may ask any other active player how many cards he drew. The latter player must answer, but the questioner has no redress if the answer is incorrect. [It is considered unethical, however, to give an incorrect answer intentionally.]

(c) The dealer may not serve the bottom card of the pack. If the pack exclusive of this card does not suffice for the draw, the dealer must assemble all cards previously discarded, plus the bottom card of the original pack; shuffle these cards; offer them for a cut; and continue dealing. The cut shall be as provided in paragraph 6 (b) except that only an active player may cut. The opener's discards and the discards of any player yet to draw are excluded from the new pack if they have been kept separate and can be identified.

27. *Irregularities in the draw.* (a) *Wrong number of cards.* If the dealer gives a player more or fewer cards than he asks for in the draw, the error must be corrected if the player calls attention to it before he has looked at any of the cards. Unless a card has been served to the next active player in turn, the dealer must correct the error by supplying another card or restoring the excess to the top of the pack, as the case may be. If the next player has been served, the player may discard from his hand additional cards to accept an excess draw without going over a five-card hand; if he has already discarded and the draw is insufficient to restore his hand to five cards, his hand is foul. If the player has looked at any card of the draw and the entire draw would give him an incorrect number of cards, his hand is foul.

(b) *Card exposed.* If any card is exposed in the draw, whether or not it was faced in the pack, the player must accept the first such card but any additional exposed card to be dealt to him is dead and is placed among the discards. After the dealer has served all other active players, he serves additional cards due the player from the top of the pack.

(c) *Draw out of turn.* If a player allows a player at his left to draw out of turn, he must play without drawing, or drop. If he has already discarded any card, his hand is foul.

(d) A player may correct a slip of the tongue in stating the number of cards he wishes to draw, but only provided the dealer has not yet given him the number of cards he first requested.

(e) If a player discards a number of cards that would make his hand incorrect after the dealer gives him as many cards as he asked for, his hand is foul.

28. *Showing openers.* The player who opens must prove that he held a legal hand of five cards including the strength (if any) required to open. If he is in the showdown he must show his entire hand face up. In any other case, before discarding his entire hand he must show his openers face up and his remaining cards, if any, face down.

29. *Splitting openers.* The player who opened may split his openers (discard one or more cards essential to them) and he need not announce that he does so. He may put his discard in the pot, face down, for reference later. [For example, having opened with ♠ Q ♡ Q J 10 9, he may discard the ♠ Q and draw one card. It is not customary for the opener to put his discard in the pot, since he can usually demonstrate to the other players' satisfaction that he held openers.]

30. *False openers.* (a) If it is ascertained at any time that a player opened without proper openers, or that his hand contains too many cards, his hand is foul and all chips he has bet are forfeited to the pot.

(b) If false openers are discovered before the draw, any other player in turn to the offender's left (excluding those who passed on their first turns) may open, and play continues; but any player except the offender may withdraw from the pot any chips he put in after the pot was falsely opened. If no one can open, the remainder of the pot remains for the next deal.

(c) If false openers are discovered after every player but the offender has dropped, each other player may withdraw from the pot any chips he put in after the pot was falsely opened.

(d) If false openers are discovered after the draw, and when any active player remains, play continues and the pot goes to the highest hand at the showdown, whether or not any player had openers. [If there is no hand at the showdown that is not foul, the pot remains and goes to the winner of the next pot. Regardless of other circumstances, a hand that has dropped can never win a pot.]

STUD POKER

31. *Betting in stud poker.* (a) In each betting interval the player with the highest exposed combination (as defined by paragraph 32) has the privilege of betting first. In the *first* betting interval, this player must bet at least the minimum established for the game. In any subsequent betting interval, this player may check.

(b) If in any betting interval every active player checks, the betting interval ends. Another round of cards is dealt, or there is a showdown, as the case may be. If in any betting interval any player bets, each active player in turn after him must at least call the highest previous bet or drop.

(c) At the start of each betting interval the dealer must announce which player bets first, naming the combination that gives such player the high exposed holding at that point (for example, "Pair of eights bets" or "First ace bets"). The dealer should also announce, after the third and fourth face-up cards are dealt, any player's combination which, when combined with his hole card, may make a one-card draw to a flush or straight (announced by saying "Possible flush" or "Possible straight").

[*Optional law.* In the final betting interval, a player may not check or call unless his full hand, including his hole card, will beat the exposed cards of the highest combination showing. Such player may, however, bet or raise. This rule, which is not recommended, is designed to protect players against making pointless calls; at the same time, it eliminates some bluffing opportunities. Like other optional rules, it should not apply unless there has been prior agreement among the players in the game.]

32. *Incomplete hands.* (a) Four or fewer exposed cards, for the purpose of establishing the first bettor in any betting interval, rank from highest to lowest as follows:

(1) Four-of-a-kind; as between two such hands, the four higher-ranking cards are high.

(2) Three-of-a-kind; as between two such hands, the higher-ranking three-of-a-kind is high.

(3) Two pairs; as between two such hands, the highest pair determines the high hand, and if the highest pairs are the same, the higher of the two lower pairs.

(4) One pair; as between two such hands, the higher pair is high; if two hands have the identical pair, the highest unmatched card determines the high hand, and if they are identical the higher of the two other cards.

(5) The highest card; if two players tie for highest card, the next-highest card in their respective hands determines the high hand, and so on.

(b) As between two holdings that are identical card for card, the one nearest the dealer's left is high for purposes of betting (but has no superiority over the other in the showdown).

[Flush and straight combinations of four or fewer cards have no higher rank, for determining the first bettor, than any other holdings including no pair, except when a four-flush is played to beat a pair, in which case a four-flush showing bets ahead of a pair.]

(c) If through the dealer's or his own error a player has all his cards exposed, all are taken into consideration for establishing the first bettor; and if at the start of the final betting interval such player has a straight, flush, full house or straight flush showing, his hand outranks any combination of exposed cards that his hand would beat in a showdown.

33. *Irregularities in dealing stud poker.* (a) At any time before the dealer begins dealing the second round of cards, a player who has not looked at a card dealt face-down to him may call for a new shuffle, cut, and deal if it is ascertained that:

(1) the pack was not shuffled or cut;

(2) a card was exposed in cutting, or the cut left fewer than five cards in either packet;

(3) two or more cards are faced in the pack;

(4) the pack is incorrect or imperfect in any way;

(5) a player is dealing out of turn.

When there is a redeal, the same dealer deals again unless he was dealing out of turn, in which case the deal reverts to the proper player in turn.

(b) If the dealer deals too many hands, he shall determine which hand is dead, and that hand is discarded; but a player who has looked at the hole card of any hand must keep that hand.

(c) If the dealer deals too few hands, he must give his own hand to the first omitted player to his left.

(d) If the dealer gives a player two face-down cards instead of one on the first round of dealing, he omits that player on the second round of dealing and (unless the rules of the game require two hole cards, as in seven-card stud) he turns up one of the cards. The player who received the two cards may not look at them and then turn up one of them.

(e) If the dealer gives a player more than two cards on the first round of dealing, that player may require a redeal if he does so before the second round of dealing has begun. If the error is not noted until later, his hand is dead.

(f) If in dealing any round of face-up cards the dealer omits a player, he moves back the cards dealt later, so as to give each player the face-up card he would have had if no irregularity had occurred; except that if attention is not called to the irregularity before the first bet is made in the ensuing betting interval, the hand of the player who was omitted is dead.

34. *Exposed card.* If the dealer gives any player a hole card face up, the player must keep that card and instead receive his next card face down. The player has no redress, except to receive his next card face down, unless the dealer repeatedly fails to correct the error until the player has four cards; at which point, if the dealer has never given him a face-down card, the player may if he wishes drop out, withdrawing from the pot all chips he has put in. If the player instead stays for his fifth card, and receives it also face up, he may withdraw his chips from the pot; but the player may elect to remain in the pot.

35. *Dead cards.* A card found faced in the pack during any round of dealing must be dealt to the player to whom it falls. A card at the top of the pack exposed during a betting interval, either because it is faced in the pack or because it is prematurely dealt, is discarded. In dealing the next round of face-up cards, the dealer skips the player to whom such card would have fallen, and deals in rotation, ending with the last player who would have received the exposed card if it had not been exposed. In each subsequent round of cards, on demand of any player the dealer must begin the rotation with the player who would otherwise have received the top card.

36. *Impossible call.* If the player last to speak in the final betting interval calls a bet when his five cards, regardless of his hole card, cannot possibly beat the four showing cards of the player whose bet he calls, his call is void and the chips may be retracted provided any player calls attention to his error before the hole card of any other active player is shown.

37. If the dealer errs in calling the value of a hand or in designating the high hand, no player has any redress; but if the first bet is made by the player incorrectly designated by the dealer, it is not a bet out of turn.

38. The dealer does not have the option of intentionally dealing a player's first card up and his second card down. A player may not turn up his hole card and receive his next card face down; if he turns up his hole card, he must play throughout with all his cards exposed.

BETTING LIMITS

39. *Table stakes.* (a) In any poker game except one with fixed limits, i.e., in any pot-limit, doubling-up or no-limit game, a player who has not enough chips to call the preceding bets and who cannot obtain more chips may stay in for the showdown by betting all the chips he has left. If there are other players in the pot and they wish to continue betting, their bets above this amount go in a "side pot" in which the short player has no interest. Play continues normally until there is a showdown, when the player who was short competes on even terms for that part of the pot to which he contributed in full.

(b) A player in a table-stakes game may obtain additional chips from the banker, and add them to his stack on the table, only in the period between a showdown and the beginning of the next deal. He may at no time reduce the number of chips he has in front of him by cashing them in or by removing them from his stack, except when he leaves the game.

(c) A player who is tapped, and calls, remains in the pot until the showdown, drawing cards on even terms with the other players, without further contributions to the pot. If he has the best hand at the showdown, he takes the main pot. He has no interest in any side pots.

(d) A player who drops rather than call a bet in a side pot must discard his hand and relinquishes his interest in all pots.

GLOSSARY

Ace: the one-spot in a pack of cards.

Ace-high: a hand with no pair or better, but with an ace.

Ace-kicker: an ace held with a pair in a two-card draw.

Acepots: draw poker in which no player may open without a pair of aces or better.

Aces-up: a hand of two pairs including aces.

Action: betting; opportunity to bet; a bet made and accepted.

Active player: one who has not withdrawn from the betting and abandoned his hand.

Advertise: make a bluff intended to be exposed.

Age: the player at dealer's left, so called because he is first to receive cards in the deal; eldest hand.

All blue, all pink, *etc:* an announcement that one has a flush; sometimes designating respectively a flush in a black or in a red suit.

All the way: a dealer's announcement in a table-stakes game that all active players have been tapped and that remaining cards will be dealt without betting intervals.

Alternate straight: same as Dutch, or skip, straight; as, Q-10-8-6-4.

Ambigu: an obsolete French game of the same family as poker.

American Brag: a variant of Brag in which a raiser and caller show each other their hands immediately, the inferior hand dropping out.

Anaconda: a game in which each player is dealt seven cards, discards two of them, and turns up the others one by one with a betting interval after each.

Angle: a situation favorable to a bet.

Announced bet: one made orally without putting up chips or money; "mouth bet."

Ante: 1, a bet made before the deal

255

or before drawing cards. 2, chips required to be put into the pot before the deal. 3, to put in such chips.

Ante up!: 1, verbal phrase = put ante in the pot. 2, announcement = all players have duly anteed.

Arkansas flush: four cards in one suit and a fifth card in another suit.

As or **As Nas:** an ancient Persian game (still played), the ultimate ancestor of poker.

Assigned first bettor: the player who has the privilege of betting first in any betting interval.

Australian Poker: blind opening.

Backer: 1, non-player who finances an active player. 2, banker.

Back in: come into the betting after having checked at one's first turn.

Back raise: (Coffin) a raise of the smallest permissible amount, to limit the cost of staying when the number of raises per interval is restricted.

Back-to-back: said of the hole card and first upcard when they are a pair.

Bait: a small bet designed to invite a raise, which may be reraised.

Bank: common gambler; gambling house; the dealer in a gambling house.

Banker: 1, dealer against whom all others bet. 2, the player who

keeps, sells and accounts for the chips.

Baseball: a stud poker variant in which threes, fours and nines have special functions.

Bay and a gray: a bet of red chip and a white chip.

Beans: = chips.

Bear: a tight player.

Beat the board: have a higher poker combination than the exposed cards of any other player.

Beat Your Neighbor: a poker variant in which each player in rotation turns up his cards, one by one, until his showing combination beats any cards previously turned; after which there is a betting interval. If he cannot beat the previous best hand, he is out of the pot.

Bedsprings: a poker variant in which each player receives five cards face down, and ten widow cards are arranged in two rows in the center; these being turned up one by one, with a betting interval after each, with each player finally entitled to choose a hand from his five cards plus any two cards in the same position in the two rows.

Behind the six: broke; short of funds.

Belly hit: a card drawn that fills an inside straight.

–Best: ranking in the ordinal position specified, from the top of the suit, as *third-best*.

Best flush: a game in which only flushes may compete for the pot: the best four-flush if there is no flush, the best three or two cards of the same suit if there is no longer flush.

Bet: 1, any wager on the outcome of a deal or game; any chips put in a pot; to put chips in a pot. 2, the first bet in a betting interval.

Bet blind: bet without looking at one's hand.

Bet the pot: bet as many chips as there are in the pot.

Bet the raise: a betting limit in which the limit for a bet or raise is the number of chips any player has previously put in the pot at one time.

Betting interval: period during which each active player in turn has the right to bet or drop out.

Betty Hutton: seven-card stud with nines and fives wild.

Bicycle: the lowest possible hand in Lowball, consisting of A-2-3-4-5, so called from a former design of Bicycle brand playing cards.

Big Bobtail: *Special Hand.* A four-card sequence in one suit; loses to four-of-a-kind, beats any lower hand.

Big Cat: *Special Hand.* King-high, eight-low, no pair. Loses to a flush, beats any lower hand; also called *Big Tiger.*

Big Dog: *Special Hand.* Ace-high, nine-low, no pair. Loses to a Little Cat, Big Cat or flush; beats a Little Dog or a straight.

Big poker: 1, a game in which only the high hand can win. 2, a game for very high stakes.

Big Tiger: a hand containing king-high and eight-low, with no pair; also called *Big Cat.*

Blaze: a hand composed entirely of face cards. Beats any two pairs, loses to three-of-a-kind.

Blind: 1, a compulsory bet or ante made before the cards are dealt. 2, widow. 3, without looking at one's cards.

Blind bargain: (Ellinger) an alternative in tactics, neither choice seeming superior.

Blind opening: compulsory opening of the pot by a blind bet, as in one form of draw poker.

Blind tiger: = blind opening.

Block system: a form of blind opening poker in which there are large compulsory bets to start the pot.

Blow back: raise an opponent's bet after having previously checked or called.

Bluff: bet on a hand the holder does not think is the best. Also, an old name for straight poker.

Board: in stud poker, the showing combinations of all active players.

Bobtail: a four-flush, or four cards in sequence that will become a straight if the card of consecutive rank at either end is drawn; in some jackpots games, one may open on a bobtail.

Bolt: drop (Brag).

Bonus: a sum of chips paid to the holder of a big hand; same as *royalty* or *premium.*

Boost: 1, bet high. 2, raise.

Bouillotte: an old French game,

one of the ancestors of modern poker.

Boys: jacks, when a pair of jacks is required to open.

Brag: an old English game, one of the ancestors of modern poker.

Braggers: jacks and nines, which are always wild, in Brag.

Brandeln: an obsolete card game similar to Commerce.

Breakers: openers.

Breathe: check the bet.

Breather: opportunity to check, rather than call or bet, in a betting interval.

Brelan: 1, an old French game, same as Bouillotte. 2, three-of-a-kind. 3, (*Brelan Carré*) four-of-a-kind.

Brother-in-law poker: buddy poker.

Buck: a token put in the pot and used to determine the next dealer, or the next player to have the option of naming the form of game to be played; originally, a buckhorn-handled knife.

Buddy poker: a practice in play of not betting against a close friend or relation.

Bug: the joker when it may be used only as an ace or a wild card to fill a flush or straight.

Bull: ace.

Bullet: ace.

Bump: raise.

Burn: discard the top card of the pack, usually by putting it on the bottom of the pack. The card may and may not be shown, de-pending on the rule or custom of the game.

Bust: 1, fail to fill a straight or flush. 2, a hand to which a player has drawn unsuccess-fully.

Butcher Boy: a poker variant in which all cards are dealt face up; when a duplicate appears, it is transferred to the player who first was dealt a card of that rank, and there is a betting interval. The transferred card is replaced and the deal continues. The pot goes to the first player to get four-of-a-kind.

Buy: draw.

Buy-in: stack or takeout; the value of the chips a player must or does buy at the beginning of a game.

Buy the pot: Put in the pot as many chips as are already there, to buy a privilege (in certain poker variants).

"By me": pass, or check.

California Lowball: Lowball.

Call: 1, put enough chips in the pot to make one's total contribution exactly equal to the total contribution of the previous active player (excluding antes that do not rank as bets). 2, an act of calling, or the amount required to call.

Cards speak: designating a seven-card high-low game in which a player may win both high and low without a declaration.

Case card: the last card of any rank to show up.

Cash in: turn in one's chips to the banker.

Cash out: quit a game, converting one's chips to money.

Cat: any Big Tiger or Little Tiger or Big Cat or Little Cat.

Catbird's seat: a position in which one can declare after all other active players have declared, when one can assure himself of half the pot.

Cat flush: *Special Hand.* A Big or Little Cat, all of the same suit, played (but very rarely) to beat a straight flush, because a Cat beats a straight.

Check: 1, a poker chip; a chip of lowest value; any token or counter. 2, a bet in effect, but one that does not require putting any chip in the pot; originally, a minimum bet or a call of a minimum bet.

Check and raise: the privilege of checking in any betting interval, and then raising if another player bets.

Chicago: a form of seven-card stud in which the pot is split between the high hand and the holder of the highest spade among hands in the showdown.

Chicago pelter: kilter.

Chip: 1, a disk or other token used in place of money; the unit of currency in betting. 2, put chips in the pot.

Chip along: stay in a pot without raising; make the smallest permissible bet.

Chip in: to ante, or to stay in for a small amount.

Chiseler: one who tries to obtain undue odds in betting.

Choice-pots: (British) dealer's choice.

Cinch hand: a hand that no other player can beat in the showdown, regardless of his hole card (stud poker); any hand sure to win.

Cincinnati: a variant in which a player may eventually select his hand from five cards dealt to him and five cards common to all hands.

Cincinnati Liz: = Lamebrain Pete.

Close: 1, call for a showdown, thus limiting each other player to one more draw (Whiskey Poker). 2, conservative; conservatively.

Closed poker: any form of poker in which all cards are dealt and remain face down until the showdown; the principal form is draw poker.

Close to the belly: 1, conservatively, in betting. 2, (of cards) held so that no one may see their faces.

Close to the chest: conservatively.

Clutch: cinch hand.

Coffee-housing: attempting to mislead opponents as to one's cards by speech and manner.

Cold deck: a pack whose cards have been prearranged, dishonestly, to create a deal advantageous to card sharpers.

Cold hands: five-card hands dealt face up, usually at the end of a

game, to determine the winner of a pot. There is seldom a draw. The pot is usually made up of odd chips too insignificant to turn in.

Come: "on the come" = needing to draw a proper card before having a hand that can win.

Come in: call, in any betting interval before the last.

Commerce: an old English game, a precursor of poker, played with three-card hands and a three-card widow.

Common card: a card considered as part of each player's hand, as in Spit-in-the-Ocean.

Complete hand: in draw poker, the five cards held by a player after the draw.

Concealed: (of cards that complete a winning combination) in the hole.

Condone: legalize or waive penalty for an irregularity.

Consecutive declaration: in high-low poker with declarations, the procedure whereby one "declares" after hearing the declarations of players before him in turn.

Conservative: describing a player who does not bet or call unless he is mathematically likely to have a winning hand.

Contract poker: high-low poker with oral declarations.

Counter: a token used in place of money; chip.

Cowboys: kings.

Crazy: wild.

Criss-cross: Same as *X Marks the*

Spot, with the center of the cross and like cards always wild.

Curse of Scotland: the nine of diamonds.

Cut: 1, divide the pack into two parts in completion of the shuffling; such division. 2, chips taken from the pot for the benefit of the house or bank.

Cut the pot: take a percentage from the pot, as to defray expenses or charges.

Cut up jackpots: boast about previous winnings.

Dame: queen.

Dark: blind; without looking at one's cards.

Dead: out of play; discarded; as applied to a hand, barred from any right to win the pot.

Dead hand: a hand that must be abandoned in penalty for an irregularity.

Dead man's hand: two pairs, aces and eights (in some definitions, black aces and black eights): the hand Wild Bill Hickok is said to have been holding when he was shot to death.

Deadwood: the pile of discarded cards.

Deal: 1, distribute cards to the players. 2, distribution of cards to players; act of dealing. 3, a player's turn to deal. 4, the period of time between service of the first and last cards by the dealer. 5, the period of time beginning with the shuffle and ending when the pot is legally taken by the winner; pot.

Dealer: 1, the player who distributes the cards or whose turn it is to distribute the cards to the players. 2, a representative of the house.

Dealer's choice, Dealer's option: a game in which each dealer may designate the form of poker to be played and what cards, if any, will be wild.

Deal off: announce, while dealing, that one will play through another round of deals, and leave the game after dealing once more.

Deal out: omit giving a card or a hand to (a player).

Deck: pack (of cards).

Declaration: in high-low poker, a statement, made before the showdown, that one is trying for high, low, or both.

Declare: 1, make a declaration. 2, state one's intention, as to call, raise, or drop.

Deuce: two-spot.

Deuces-wild: a form of draw poker in which all deuces are wild cards.

Devil's Bedpost: the four of clubs.

Dig: replenish one's stake while the play of a hand is in progress. In table-stakes play, this is not permitted.

Discard: 1, abandon (cards). 2, all the cards so abandoned by all players.

Doctor Pepper: seven-card stud with tens, fours and twos wild.

Dog: Big Dog or Little Dog.

Dog flush: a Big Dog or Little Dog, all of one suit.

Doghouse cut: a cut of the pack by pulling out cards from its center and putting them on top, without changing the position of one or more cards at the bottom of the pack.

Double: (British) raise.

Double-barreled shotgun: Shotgun with a draw after the third betting interval.

Double-ended straight: four cards in sequence, except A-K-Q-J and A-2-3-4.

Double-header: a pool not won in the same deal as formed, but left to be won subsequently.

Doubling limit: a game in which a player may raise by the amount of the previous bet or raise.

Doubling up: Betting twice as much as was previously bet and lost.

Down: (of a card) dealt or lying on the table with its face down so that its suit and rank are not expected to be known by anyone but the holder of the card.

Downcard: any hole card or card dealt face-down in stud or open poker.

Down the river: seven-card stud.

Drag: take chips out of the pot as change.

Draw: 1, pull cards from a pack spread face down, to determine seats, first deal, etc. 2, receive cards from the stock to replace discards.

Draw out (on): achieve a winning hand with the last card or cards drawn, after staying with an inferior hand.

Draw poker: closed poker in which a player may discard and receive replacement cards.

Drib: unskillful player (*slang*).

Driver's seat, in the: said of a player who holds what is sure to be the best hand.

Drop: withdraw from the current deal; discard one's hand rather than put enough chips in the pot to remain an active player.

Dry: broke; having lost heavily.

Duffer: unskillful player.

Duke: hand of cards (*slang*).

Dutch straight: = skip straight; as, J-9-7-5-3.

Edge: eldest hand; the player nearest the left of dealer; same as *age*. 2, an advantage enjoyed by one party over another. 3, an ante by dealer only.

Eight-card stud: same as seven-card stud but with five upcards.

Eldest hand: the player nearest dealer's left (because he is first to receive cards in the deal).

End bet: a bet in the last betting interval.

English poker: blind opening.

Exposed: face up, during the shuffle, dealing or betting.

Exposed pair: = open pair.

Face card: any king, queen, or jack. (The ace is not a face card.)

Faced: lying with its face up (said of a card).

Fall of the cards: the identity and order of cards as dealt.

False openers: a hand with which a pot has been opened, but which is not as good as the rules require.

Fancy buy: (Ellinger) a draw in the hope of being dealt an unlikely combination of cards.

Fast game: a game in which the players are not conservative in playing hands likely to lose, or in betting on hands that may not win.

Fatten: ante again (to a jackpot not opened on the previous deal).

Feed: contribute to (the kitty); set aside a percentage of each pot to defray expenses.

Feeler: a small bet made to find out where the power lies (Larsen); that is, to give other players an opportunity to show their strength by raising or calling.

Fever: a five-spot.

Fill: draw or be dealt a card that makes a full house, straight, flush, or straight flush.

Finger poker: a game run on credit. *On the finger* is synonymous with *on the cuff* (Larsen).

Fish-hook card: any seven or jack; also, rarely, a nine or six: a term used when such cards are designated as wild cards.

First jack deals: a popular method of selecting the first, or next, dealer: cards are dealt one by one face up in rotation, and the dealer is the player to whom a jack is first dealt.

First hand: 1, the first player in turn to call. 2, eldest hand.

Five-of-a-kind: the highest-ranking hand in poker, composed wholly of cards of the same rank plus wild cards designated to be of that rank.

Five-suit poker: poker played with a 65-card pack including a 13-card suit of "royals" or "eagles."

Fixed limit: a betting limit that is not affected by the size of the pot.

Flash: 1, expose a card, as in dealing. 2, a hand containing cards of all five suits (in poker with the five-suit pack), or a card of each suit plus the joker; beats two pairs, loses to three-of-a-kind.

Flat poker: a variant of blind opening.

Flip: 1, Mexican Stud. 2, turn over (a card).

Flush: a hand or combination comprising cards of only one suit.

Fluss, flux: = flush (obsolete).

Flying: = full, as in a full house.

Fold: drop; turn one's cards face down to signify withdrawal from the deal.

Football: a dealer's choice game similar to Baseball.

Foul hand: 1, a hand of more or less than the legal number of cards. 2, barred from winning a pot, as though discarded.

Four-flush: four cards of the same suit; often played as a special hand that beats one pair but loses to two pairs, or as openers in a jackpots game.

Four Forty-four: eight-card stud with all fours wild and four cards down, four up.

Four Forty-two: same as Four Forty-four but with deuces wild.

Four-of-a-kind: four cards of the same rank in one hand. 2, a game in which the cards are dealt face up until any card is duplicated; the recipient of this card orders a drink. The deal continues; the recipient of the next card of that rank pays for the drink, and the recipient of the last card of that rank drinks it. Players ante before each deal, and the last player to accept a drink takes the pot.

Fours: four of-a-kind.

Freak: wild card.

Freak-pots: = Deuces-wild.

Free ride: a case in which everyone checks, in any betting interval except the last. Also, the privilege of drawing one or more cards without further contribution to the pot, because of having tapped oneself.

Free shot: in a position to try for the entire pot with assurance of winning at least half the pot.

Free wheeling: the right of a losing player in Poverty Poker.

Freezeout: any game in which no player may replenish his stack and each player must drop out when he loses his entire stack; also, any game in which losers retire, leaving winners to continue play until only one survives.

Freezer: an anticipatory short call

when two or more other players are raising; further raises then go to a side pot.

Frozen out: retired from play because: 1, one has lost one's original stake; 2, one has lost a round or deal in a freezeout game.

Full hand: full house.

Full house: three cards of one rank and two cards of another rank.

Fuzzing: shuffling the pack by drawing cards simultaneously from top and bottom; milking.

Gadget: any special rule applying to a wild-card game.

Gaff: any secret device used in cheating.

Game: any standard form of poker or variant of the basic game named by the dealer to be played in that deal, as in Dealer's Choice Poker.

Garbage: 1, a dealer's choice game in which almost any five-card betting game may be elected. 2, the discards.

Gile, or **Gilet,** or **Gillet:** an old Italian and French game, perhaps the most ancient European ancestor of poker.

Gimmick: any secret mechanical device; gaff; cheating stratagem.

Girls: queens. (Larsen) a euphemism for *whores*. If the player (with queens) wins the pot, they are "ladies"; but if he loses the pot, they are "whores."

Gleek: three-of-a-kind.

Go: a directive to the (house) dealer to resume dealing.

Go in: ante, or stay in before any betting interval but the last.

Go out: drop.

Gravy: winnings; any sum held by a player in excess of his original stake.

Grec: = Greek.

Greek: any card cheat (obsolete).

Grifter: a cheat; confidence man; blackleg.

Gruged: beaten by a higher hand (obsolete).

Gruesome Twosome: (Coffin) two-card poker with the right to stand pat or draw one or two cards in each of an agreed number of rounds.

Gut shot: a card drawn that fills an inside straight.

Half-pot limit: a betting limit fixed at one-half the amount currently in the pot.

Hand: 1, the cards held by one player. 2, the period of time between the start of the deal and the winning of the pot.

Hedge: bet against a contingency formerly bet on, to reduce or limit possible losses.

Heeler: same as kicker: an unmatched card held in the hand when drawing.

Heinz: seven-card stud with fives and sevens wild, but requiring a penalty payment to the pot when they are dealt face up.

Help Me, Neighbor: variant of Commerce (Accomodez-moi).

Hidden declarations: in seven-card stud, declarations made secretly, as by holding a chip of a particular color in one's closed hand until all active players have declared.

High: 1, highest-ranking among poker combinations. 2, displaying the highest-ranking poker combination among cards showing. 3, the player who has the high hand at any juncture or in the showdown. 4, designating any poker game in which low hands have no value.

-High: headed by the card named, as *ace-high*.

High-Low: designating any form of poker in which the highest and lowest hands in the showdown divide the pot equally.

High spade: a popular side-bet among two or more players, whereby each contributes to a separate pot and the player with highest spade wins this pot.

Hilo: same as Kings Back. Also, Hi-Lo.

Hilo-Picalo: a dealer's choice game: same as Take It or Leave It.

Hit: Fill.

Hole card: a card dealt face down in stud poker, in accordance with the rules.

Holy Olie: = hole card (Larsen: jocular).

Hook: fishhook.

Hookers: queens.

House: the person or organization that provides playing space for a game and charges a fee for its use, or cuts the pot.

House cut: an amount taken out of each pot as the fee or rental charged by the house — usually no more than 5% of a small pot or 2½% of a large one.

House rules: regulations differing from or additional to the usual laws of poker, imposed by the house or adopted by agreement among the players.

Hoyle: common term for any book on intellectual games. Actually, Edmond Hoyle (1679–1769) died before poker was played, but many books of rules for card games, including poker, bear his name.

According to Hoyle: in conformance with traditional rules or strategical precepts.

Hurricane: two-card poker.

Hustler: one who seeks advantage through the ignorance of his victims.

Ice: 1, cold deck. 2, protection money paid by a house operating illegally.

Immortal hand: a hand that is sure to win; = cinch hand.

Imperfect pack: a pack containing the correct number and assortment of cards, but with a card distinguishable from its back because it is marked, mutilated, the wrong design, or the wrong size.

Improve: draw cards that better one's hand.

In: having called all preceding bets; having anteed; active in the current pot.

Incorrect pack: a pack containing an incorrect number or assortment of cards.

Index: the number or letter printed in the corner of a playing card, so that it may be read when held in a fan.

In like Flynn: (jocular) in; sometimes (Larsen) having called before one's turn.

Inside straight: four cards of incomplete sequence needing a card of interior rank to form a straight, as 8-7-6-4. The term is applied also to one-end straights such as A-K-Q-J.

Installment bet: string bet.

Interval of betting: period during which bets are made and players may drop.

In the hole: dealt face down, in stud poker.

Intricate shuffle: riffle shuffle.

Ironclad hand: a hand that is sure to win.

Iron Duke: a hand sure to win, or a hand played as though it were sure to win.

Irregularity: any departure from a rule of correct procedure (in the sense of inadvertent error, not intentional misdeed).

Jackpot: a deal in which everyone antes; usually in such a deal a pair of jacks or better is required to open.

Jackpots: draw poker in which every deal is a jackpot.

Jacks Back: a form of Jackpots in which if no one opens on the first round, every player has another chance to open for a Lowball pot, or for another type of draw poker game.

Jacks or better: a pair of jacks, or any hand that would beat a pair of jacks in a showdown; the requirement for opening in many games of draw poker.

Jack up: raise, boost.

J-bird or **J-boy:** jack.

Johns: jacks.

Joker: a card often introduced into the pack as a fifty-third card; usually it is wild, or acts as the bug.

Joker poker: any poker game, but usually draw poker, with the joker as a fully wild card.

Kankakee: seven-card stud with the joker available to every player as an extra wild card in his hand.

Kibitzer: a nonplaying spectator.

Kick: raise.

Kick a kicker: (British) draw a card that pairs one's kicker.

Kicker: an unmatched card held in the hand when drawing, either to improve the chance of making a certain hand or for purposes of deception.

Kilter: *Special Hand.* No card as high as a ten, no pair, no four-flush or bobtail straight. It beats three-of-a-kind, loses to a straight. Originally, the term was applied to a hand so bad it could not be drawn to.

Kings Back: same as Jacks Back,

except that kings or better are required to open and Lowball is played on the second round.

Kitty: a special pot, belonging equally to all players, made up of chips occasionally taken from large pots.

Knave: the jack of a suit.

Knock: rap on the table to signify: (1) check or pass, or waiver of cutting the pack; (2) in Knock Poker or Whiskey Poker, that after one round there will be a showdown.

Knock Poker: a combination of poker and Rummy. Each player is dealt five cards, and in each turn draws one card (the top of the stock or the previous discard) and discards one card, until one player knocks.

Ku Klux Klan: three kings.

Ladies: queens.

Lamebrain Pete: same as Cincinnati, except that the lowest exposed card and all other cards of the same rank are wild.

Lamebrains: Cincinnati.

Last-card Louie: a player who stays for his last card, in stud poker, when only a particular card will give him a winning hand; also, a player who has just drawn a winning hand on his last card.

Lay down: face (one's hand) in the showdown.

Lay odds: offer a bet of a larger amount against a smaller amount.

Lead. willingness to make a voluntary bet (see *Take the lead*).

Leader: the player designated by the rules to act first in a betting interval; same as *assigned first bettor*. 2, the player who is apparently willing to bet, or to raise if anyone else bets.

Light: owing chips to the pot; signified by drawing from the pot, toward oneself, as many chips as one owes.

Limit: the largest number of chips one is permitted to bet or raise.

Little Bobtail: a special hand, one containing a three-card straight flush, occasionally (very rarely) played to beat two pairs, to lose to three-of-a-kind.

Little Cat: a special hand, eight high, three low, no pair. Loses to a Big Cat, beats any Dog or lower hand.

Little Dog: a special hand, seven-high and deuce-low but no pair. Loses to a Big Dog, any Cat, or higher; beats a straight.

Little Tiger: Little Cat.

Live: (of a card) able or likely to be paired, in stud poker, because no or few cards of the same rank have shown.

Lock: a cinch.

Long Studs: (British) stud poker in which more than five cards are dealt.

Look: call, especially the final bet or raise before the showdown; see.

Lowball: a form of draw poker in which the lowest-ranking hand wins the pot.

Low hole card wild: a special rule in some stud poker variants.

Low poker: a game in which the lowest-ranking hand wins the pot.

Main pot: the first pot formed in a deal, as distinct from side pots.

Make good: add enough chips to the pot to meet a raise.

Make the pack or **Make up:** gather and shuffle the pack for the next deal.

Marker: a promissory note; IOU.

Mechanic: a crooked dealer.

Meet: call.

Mexican stud: five-card stud in which all cards are dealt face down and each player may elect the card newly dealt to him as his hole card.

Middle: 1, to be in the middle = to have potential bettors or raisers both to one's right and left. 2, the rank of the cards needed to fill an inside straight.

Middle straight: inside straight.

Mike: closed poker with betting intervals after the second, third, fourth, and last cards, and no draw.

Milk: draw top-and-bottom cards off (a new pack) to mix the cards before the first shuffle.

Minnie: the lowest possible hand in Lowball (5-4-3-2-A) or Low Poker (7-5-4-3-2).

Misdeal: any irregularity in dealing that requires a new shuffle and deal. (*Note:* this term is sometimes reserved to an irregu-larity which by rule forfeits the player's turn to deal, as distinct from *redeal,* a new deal by the same player.)

Miss: fail to draw a helpful card (antonym of *fill* or *improve*).

Mistigris: an old name for poker with the joker wild. (*Mistigris* in French means joker.)

Mites and lice: two pairs, threes and deuces.

Monkey flush: three cards of a suit, not in sequence.

Monte: three-card poker.

Mouth bet: a bet made orally, without putting up chips or money.

Natural: (of a card) used in its normal rank and suit, as distinguished from a wild card.

New York stud: stud poker in which a four-flush beats a pair.

Nits and buggers: two pairs, threes and deuces.

Nits and lice: two very small pairs.

Odds: a statement of probability in the form of a ratio.

Odds-on: odds at less than even money.

Office hours: (Coffin; jocular) a 9 to 5 or 8 to 4 straight.

One-card draw: in draw poker: 1, a draw of one card. 2, a hand that drew only one card.

One-end straight: four cards in sequence, A-K-Q-J or 4-3-2-A.

One-eyes: face cards on which the picture is in profile, showing only one eye; in the standard pack, these are the ♠ J, ♡ J, and ◇ K.

One pair: a hand containing two cards of the same rank, with three unmatched cards.

Open: 1, make the first bet in the first betting interval, in draw poker. 2, face-up on the table, as a card in stud poker.

Open-end straight: bobtail straight.

Opener: the player who opens the pot.

Openers: a hand, or that part of it, which fulfills the minimum requirement for opening a pot; usually, a pair of jacks or better.

Open game: a game that a stranger or any club member may join if a seat is available.

Open pair: in stud poker, a pair among a player's face-up cards.

Open Poker: stud poker; a poker game in which some cards are dealt face up.

Open seat: a seat in a game that does not have the maximum number of players.

Original hand: a hand as dealt, before its alteration by draw or discard.

Overcards: in stud poker, cards which if paired will give the holder a pair higher than another player's open pair.

Overhand shuffle: a shuffle executed by holding the pack in one hand and dropping packets from the top into the other hand.

Pack: deck; all the cards used in a game, collectively.

Packet: a portion of the pack, less than the whole.

Pack up: withdraw permanently from a game.

Painted: in Lowball, having drawn a face card to four low cards.

Pair: two cards of the same rank in one hand.

Palooka: a mediocre player (*slang*).

Pass: drop; also, in Jackpots before the draw, same as *check*.

Pass and back in: enter a pot after having passed.

Pass and out: 1, the rule that a player who once passes must drop out of the deal. 2, any form of poker in which no player is allowed to check free; in every turn he must bet or call or drop. Called also *Pass-out*.

Pat: without drawing a card.

Pat hand: a hand that is held intact, the player refusing to draw; a straight, flush, or full house.

Patience poker: Poker Solitaire; played by dealing twenty-five cards from the top of the pack and placing them in a 5 × 5 square so as to make poker hands in horizontal and vertical rows.

Peek poker: seven-card stud.

Peep-and-Turn: Mexican stud.

Pelter: same as *kilter*.

Penalties: royalties.

Penny Ante: a game in which the ante or limit is one cent; broadly, any game for insignificant stakes.

Percentage: advisability, based on sagacious judgment; more purely, probability expressed in

hundredths; also, an advantage accruing to the house; edge.

Philosopher: European term for a card cheat.

Pigeon: the best card one could draw to improve his hand.

Pig in the Poke: Wild Widow.

Piker: a cheapskate; a player who bets too little.

Pile: a player's entire supply of chips; stack.

Pink: of the same color—"they're all pink," signifying a flush (*slang*).

Pip: any of the large suit symbols ♠, ♡, ◇, ♣ printed on the face of a card (excluding index marks).

Pistol Pete: Pistol stud.

Pistol stud: five-card stud with a first betting interval after the hole cards are dealt.

Play: 1, call; stay in. 2, betting in general.

Play back or **Play behind:** guarantee a table stake beyond the stack one has on the table; the effect is the same as though the additional chips were also on the table, but some house rules do not permit such guarantees to be honored.

Player: 1, any participant in a game. 2, an active participant, as distinct from one who was dealt out or has dropped.

Poch or **Pochen:** an early game having some features of modern poker (*pochen* in German means to bluff).

Poker Solitaire: Patience poker.

Pool: pot.

Poque: an obsolete card game with betting on hands, similar to poker. (See *Poch.*)

Position: the relative seating of the players, a factor of tactical importance.

Pot: 1, the accumulation of all chips bet on the outcome of any one deal. An active player is said to be "in the pot." 2, the period beginning with the deal and first betting interval and ending when there has been a showdown and the winner is decided.

Pothooks: nine-spots.

Pot limit: limitation of any bet or raise to the number of chips in the pot at the time the bet, or raise, is made.

Poverty poker: the rule that a player's losses are limited to one or two stacks; thereafter he may draw chips from the banker and his further losses are shared by the other players.

Premiums: royalties; bonuses paid for certain exceptional hands.

Previous bet limit: same as *Bet the raise.*

Primero: one of the oldest known card games, possibly of Spanish origin, having some features akin to poker.

Procter and Gamble: a dealer's choice game: Each player receives four cards face down, and a three-card widow is dealt to the table. Its cards are turned up one by one, with a betting interval after each; the last such card, and all other cards of the same rank, are wild.

Progressive Jackpots or **Progressive poker:** draw poker in which jacks or better are required to open, with the proviso that if a pot is passed out, queens or better are required, then kings, then aces, and sometimes two pairs after that. Rarely, the requirements go progressively down again to aces, kings, queens, finally jacks.

Puppyfoot: the club ace; any club.

Rabbit: a poor player.

Rabbit hunting: looking through undealt cards to see what would have shown up if—

Raise: 1, bet more than is necessary to call. 2, the amount by which a bet exceeds the amount necessary to call.

Rake-off: the percentage of the stakes taken as a fee by a house or club.

Rangdoodles: an increase in the limit and (usually) a round of jackpots, after any player has held an unusually good hand— full house, or sometimes four-of-a-kind, or better.

Rank: the ordinal position of a card in its suit, determining what card beats another.

Readers: marked cards.

Redeal: a new deal by the same player, after an irregularity in dealing.

Redskin: any face card.

Represent: to play and bet as though one has some particular strong holding.

Reraise: raise, after having been raised in the same betting interval.

Rickey de Laet: a form of Mexican stud in which the rank of each player's hole card is wild for him.

Ride along: accept a free ride.

Riffle shuffle: the shuffle executed by butting the ends of two packets together and interlacing the cards while riffling them with the thumbs.

Roll: turn (a card) face up.

Roodles: 1, any special pot with increased antes or stakes. 2, rangdoodles.

Rotation: the progress of the turn to deal, the distribution of cards in the deal, and the right to bet, which move from player to player to the left.

Rough: in Lowball, relatively unfavorable; as, 6-5-4-3-2 is "a rough six," whereas 6-4-3-2-A is "a smooth six."

Round: once to, or by, each player: In dealing, a round of cards is the service by the dealer of one card to each active player in rotation; a round of deals is one deal by each player in the game. In betting, a round is one turn to bet for each active player, so that a betting interval may consist of one or more rounds.

Round-the-corner straight: a special hand, five cards in sequence if the sequence is considered continuous, with the ace above the king and below the deuce, as in 2-A-K-Q-J. It beats three-of-a-kind, loses to a straight.

Round the world: Cincinnati with the rank of the lowest hole card wild for the holder.

Routine: straight flush.

Royal flush: an ace-high straight flush, the highest possible hand without wild cards.

Royalties: payments collected by a player who holds any of certain high hands, in addition to whatever he wins in regular play.

Run: straight.

Run a pot: make a planned bluff, from the earliest play to the final betting interval.

Runt: 1, any hand less than one pair. 2, the hand 7-5-4-3-2 in two or more suits, the lowest possible, except in Lowball.

Sandbag: to check with a strong hand, in the hope that another player will bet and can be raised.

School: (British) a group of persons who customarily supply the personnel for a game.

Scooping: swinging.

Screwy Louie: same as Anaconda, except that each player passes two discards to the active player nearest his left.

Second: the card next under the top card, which should legally be dealt.

Second-dealing: a card sharper's trick of dealing the second card from the top of the pack, rather than the top card, when he wants to give the top card to a different player.

See: meet (a bet); call the bet of another player.

Serve: deal, especially in giving additional cards at draw poker.

Session: the period between the time when a game begins and the time when play is discontinued; also, from a player's point of view, the time during which he is playing.

Seven-card Flip: a game in which each player is dealt four cards down and may turn up any two of them, after which regular seven-card stud is played.

Seven-card stud: one of the basic stud poker games, each player receiving seven cards in all and finally selecting five of them.

Seven-toed Pete: seven-card stud.

Shark: 1, an expert player. 2, a cheat.

Sharp, Sharper: a player who cheats as a profession.

Shed: to discard.

Shifting Sands: same as Mexican stud except that each player's hole card (at the showdown) and all cards of the same rank in his hand are wild.

Shill: an employee of the house who plays to make up a game.

Short call: a call with fewer chips than the amount of the bet; possible when playing table stakes.

Short pair: 1, in jackpots, any pair lower than jacks. 2, a pair lower than another player is known to have.

Short studs: (British) five-card stud poker.

Shotgun: draw poker with betting intervals after the third and fourth cards are dealt, as well as the usual ones.

Shove 'em Along: same as Take It or Leave It.

Show: 1, have exposed on the table, in stud. 2, expose (one's hand) in the showdown.

Showdown: comparison of the full hands of all active players, to determine which wins the pot.

Shuffle: mix the cards together preparatory to dealing.

Shy: short, said of a pot to which additional antes are due or of a player who owes chips to the pot; light.

Side bet: any bet that does not concern the outcome of the pot; as, a bet on which of two or more players hold the highest spade.

Side card: an unmatched card in a poker hand, of significance only in breaking ties.

Side money or **Side pot:** a pot separate from the main pot, formed by continued betting after a player has put all his chips into the main pot.

Sight: a final call; a right to be in the showdown.

Simultaneous declarations: in high-low poker with declarations, the procedure whereby all players select their declarations before any player's declaration is revealed.

Sit in: become a player in a game.

Six-card stud: stud poker in which a player is dealt six cards and selects any five for the showdown.

Skeet: a special hand, nine, five, deuce, with two other cards lower than ten, and no pair. (Some play that one of the other cards must rank between nine and five, and the other between five and deuce.) Beats three-of-a-kind, loses to a straight. Some play that a skeet flush beats four-of-a-kind, since a skeet beats three-of-a-kind.

Skip straight: a special hand, a series of cards once separated in rank, as Q-10-8-6-4. Beats three-of-a-kind, loses to a straight. Some play that the ace may rank high but not low in a skip straight. Skip straights may not go "round the corner."

Sky's the limit: any game with no maximum bet or raise.

Slick: smooth.

Smooth: relatively good, as "a smooth seven" (7-4-3-2-A) in Lowball.

Snowing: milking.

Southern Cross: a dealer's choice game: Five face-down cards to each player and nine cards in the center, face down, in a 5 × 4 cross; turned up one by one, with a betting interval after each. A player selects his hand from his own hand plus either crossbar. It is sometimes ruled that the center card of the cross and other cards of its rank are wild.

Special hand: any hand which has winning rank only by agreement of the players, but not one of the traditional and universal poker hands.

Spit-in-the-Ocean: a traditional draw poker variant, based on the old French game Bouillotte.

Split openers: discard part of a combination that qualified the hand to open the pot.

Spot: Pip.

Spot card: any card of rank 10, 9, 8, 7, 6, 5, 4, 3, or 2.

–Spot: suffix added to the number of a card for clarity, as *four-spot, eight-spot.*

Spread: expose; show, at the showdown.

Squeeze: look only at the extreme edges of (the cards in one's hand).

Squeezers: playing cards that have corner indices, so that they can be read by squeezing. (*Note:* prior to this century, most playing cards did not have corner indices.)

Stack: 1, the number of chips a player takes from the banker at one time. 2, a pile of chips; all the chips a player has on the table.

Stake: the money or chips with which a player enters a game.

Stand: refuse to draw additional cards (= stand pat).

Standard pack: 52 cards; 13 of each suit: spades, hearts, diamonds, clubs; in each suit A, K, Q, J, 10, 9, 8, 7, 6, 5, 4, 3, 2. (*Note:* at least one joker is included with each pack manufactured.)

Stand-off: tie; two or more identical high hands, which divide the pot equally.

Stand pat: play one's original hand without discarding and drawing, though entitled to do so.

Stay or **Stay in:** remain in the current deal or pot; meet a bet; call, except in the final betting interval.

Stormy Weather: a Spit-in-the-Ocean variation in which three cards are dealt to the center.

Straddle: 1, a blind raise of a blind bet. 2, make a blind bet of double the previous blind bet.

Straight: a hand of five cards in sequence, including two or more suits.

Straight flush: five cards of the same suit in sequence.

Straight poker: closed poker with no draw, only one betting interval, after five cards have been dealt to each player.

Stranger: a player or would-be player unknown to persons already playing in the game.

Streak: a run of good or bad luck.

String bet: chips put into the pot in more than one installment, as a bet or raise.

Stringer: straight.

Stripped deck: a pack from which certain cards or ranks of cards have been removed.

Strippers: cards cut on the bias, or shaved for concavity or convexity, used by cheats.

Strip poker: poker (any form) in which each loser in a pot must remove an article of clothing: a jocular, lewd game.

Stud poker: one of the principal forms of poker, the principal form of open poker, with all cards dealt face-up except one or more hole cards, which are revealed in the showdown.

Suit: any of the four sets of 13 cards each in the standard pack: spades, hearts, diamonds, clubs.

Sweeten the pot: ante again (to a pot not opened).

Swinging: in high-low poker with declarations, declaring for both high and low.

Table: 1, the group of players who compete together, including both active and inactive. 2, the showing cards of all active players in stud poker; board.

Table stake: all the chips a player has in front of him.

Table stakes: a method of placing a limit on betting, whereby the limit is fixed, for and against each player, at his table stake.

Take It or Leave It: a five-card stud game in which each player may refuse the first upcard dealt to him in any round and pass it to his left-hand neighbor, receiving instead another card which he must keep; a player may also refuse, and pass to his left, a card passed to him. If a player accepts a card passed to him, he is dealt no card in that round. If all refuse a card, it becomes dead.

Takeout: the number of chips a player takes or is required to take from the banker at one time.

Take the lead: 1, make the first voluntary bet or raise in a bet-ting interval. 2, make the last or only voluntary raise in a betting interval.

Tap: 1, rap on the table to signify a pass or a waiver of the cut. 2, bet the whole amount of chips in front of oneself. 3, make a bet that requires another player to bet all his chips, or drop.

Tap out: bet all one's chips.

Tennessee: a dealer's choice game: Five cards are dealt to each player, face down, then the dealer turns up five cards, one at a time, with a betting interval after each. In the showdown, each player selects the best hand from his five plus the exposed five cards.

Tens-High: a game (often played in Jacks Back) in which the highest hand wins the pot but any hand higher than a pair of tens is foul.

Texas Tech: same as Double-Barreled Shotgun.

Thirty Days: three tens.

Three-card Monte: three-card poker.

Three-card poker: any of various poker variants in which a hand consists of three cards.

Three Forty-five: an eight-card game with the first three cards dealt down, the next four up, the last down; five-spots are wild.

Threes: three-of-a-kind.

Three-of-a-kind: three cards of the same rank in one hand.

Three-toed Pete: three-card poker.

Throw off: discard.

Tiger: 1, same as Cat; see *Big Cat, Little Cat.* 2, Blind opening.

Tight: (of a game or player) conservative; cautious.

–Timer: designating the number of cards that will fill a hand: thus, a bobtail straight is an *eight-timer,* since any of eight cards will make it a straight.

Trey: any three-spot.

Tricon: three-of-a-kind.

Trio: three-of-a-kind.

Triplets: three-of-a-kind.

Trips: triplets; three-of-a-kind.

Turn: a player's opportunity, in due rotation, to deal, receive cards in the deal or draw, or bet.

Turn down: drop while holding (specified cards); fold.

Twin Beds: same as Bedsprings, except that the cards are turned up alternately from the two rows, and a hand may be selected from a player's cards plus the five cards of either row. The last card turned, and other cards of the same rank, are sometimes ruled to be wild.

Two-card poker: any poker variant in which the best two-card combination wins the pot. (See *Hurricane.*)

Two pairs: a pair of one rank, a pair of a second rank, and a fifth card unmatched.

Under the guns: in draw poker, said of the first player in turn to bet voluntarily before the draw.

Unlimited poker: any poker game in which there is no limit on the amount of a bet or raise.

Up: 1, already in the pot, as an ante or bet. 2 (of a player), having anteed. 3, higher than a lower-ranking pair in the same hand, as *queens-up.*

–Up, as, **Aces-up:** a hand of two pairs, the higher pair being specified.

Upcard: a card dealt to a player properly face up.

Utah: = Cincinnati.

Valet: a jack (French).

Vigorish: the amount charged by the house to permit one to play, taken either by an hourly fee or by cutting the pot.

Welch: refuse to pay a lost bet; also, issue a challenge, then withdraw when it is accepted.

Whangdoodles: 1, rangdoodles. 2, roodles.

Wheel: in Lowball, the lowest possible hand, 5-4-3-2-A, regardless of suits; bicycle.

Whipsawed: 1, caught between two players who raise and reraise each other, and unwilling to drop or yet to call continued raises. 2, having twice faced the same alternative, made different choices, and been wrong each time.

Whiskey poker: a variant of draw poker in which a player may end the play when he wishes an immediate showdown; so called because once often played in bars to decide who would pay for the drinks.

Whore: queen.

Widow: extra cards dealt to the table to be available to all players.

Wild card: a card whose holder may designate it as representing any rank and suit.

Wild game: 1, any form of poker in which certain cards are wild. 2. a game in which players make bets not justified by their hands.

Wild Widow: a Spit-in-the-Ocean variant in which one card is dealt face-up to establish the rank of wild cards but cannot itself be used by any player.

Window: the card whose face is exposed at the end of a player's hand.

Window dressing: letting a card "in the window" be seen, for its deceptive effect on other players.

Wired: back-to-back; said of a pair in the first two cards in stud poker.

Woolworth: 1, two pairs, tens and fives. 2, a game in which fives and tens are wild. 3, a special hand, ten-high, five-low, with no pair, which beats three-of-a-kind, but loses to a straight. 4, almost any variant or rule involving the cards or numbers five and ten.

X Marks the Spot: same as Southern Cross, except that five cards are laid out in a 3 × 2 cross.

You Roll Two: seven-card-stud in which each player is dealt four cards down and turns up any two of them, after which regular seven-card stud is played.

INDEX

Ace kicker, 82
Acepots, 106
Actions at Lowball, 130
Advanced strategy:
  High-Low, 173
  Lowball, 139
Age, 32
Ambigu, 188, 237
American Brag, 255
Anaconda, 209
Analysis, 77
Announcement in turn, 247
Announcement out of turn, 247
Ante, 9, 15, 28, 45
Any bobtail to open, 106
Arkansas flush, 256
As, 7, 235, 236
As Nas, 7, 235, 236
Australian Poker, 24
Automatic bluff, 139

Banker, 19
Baseball, 203
Baseball family, 188, 202
  Baseball, 203
  Baseball with five cards, 202
  Dr. Pepper, 203
  Football, 203
  Four Forty-Four, 203
  Four Fifty-Two, 203
  Heinz, 203

Three Forty-Five, 203
Woolworth, 203
Baseball with five cards, 202
Basic principle of Poker, 7
Basic variations of Stud games, 204
  Eight-card Stud, 208
  Four-Flush Beats a Pair, 205
  Joker Stud, 204
  Kankakee, 207
  Low Hole Card Wild, 209
  Mexican Stud, 205
  Pistol Stud, 204
  Rickey de Laet, 205
  Seven-card Flip, 207
  Seven-card Stud, English style, 207
  Shifting Sands, 205
  Six-card Stud, 206
Beat Your Neighbor, 213
Bedsprings, 195
Best Flush, 256
Bet above limit, 247
Bet of nothing, 16
Bet or Drop, 31
Bet out of turn, 248
Betting, 15, 34, 244, 247, 251
Betting interval, 15
Betting irregularities, 247
Betting limit, 19, 35, 254
Betty Hutton, 257
Bicycle, 124, 257
Big bobtail, 257

Big cat, 33
Big dog, 33
Big Poker, 257
Big tiger, 33
Blaze, 257
Blind, 32
Blind and Straddle, 27
Blind opening, 24, 32, 100, 222
Blind tiger, 32
Block system, 257
Bluff, 236
Bluffing, 61, 79, 139
Bobtail, 106, 257
Bouillotte, 237
Brag, 8, 235, 238
Braggers, 238
Brandeln, 258
Brelan (game), 188, 237
Brelan (hand), 237
Brelan carré, 237
Buck, 46, 236
Bug, 19, 124, 241
Bust, 153
Butcher Boy, 213

California Lowball, 258
Call, 15
Call a sight, 20
Canadian style, 148
Card exposed, 249
Card memory, 77
Cards, 18, 241
Cards Speak, 145, 150
Cat, 26, 241
Catbird's seat, 161
Cat flush, 259
Check, 16
Chestnuts, 52, 53
Chicago, 259
Chips, 19, 44
Choice-pots, 259
Cinch hand, 259
Cincinnati, 193
Cincinnati Liz, 194
Closed Poker, 23, 187, 188, 201
Code of behavior, 47
Code of play, 46
Coffeehousing, 47
Coffin, George S., 65, 195, 203, 236,
    256, 264, 268
Coin-matching, 229
Cold hands, 259

Commerce, 235, 238
Common card, 187
Concession of a pot, 249
Conquian, 235
Consecutive declaration, 161
Contract Poker, 260
Criss-Cross, 197
Cut, 242

Dead cards, 253
Dead's man's hand, 260
Deal, 242
Dealer's choice, 46, 185
Dealer's choice games:
    Baseball family, 202
    classification of games, 187
    Closed Poker games, 188, 201
    Knock-Poker family, 198
    Spit-in-the-Ocean family, 188
    Stud Poker games, 202
    Stud Poker games variations, 204
Dealer's obligations, 35
Dealer's option, 261
Declaration, 145
Designation of wild cards, 248
Deuces-wild, 39, 103
Discards, 29
Dividing the pot, 146
Dr. Pepper, 203
Dog, 26, 33, 102, 241
Dog flush, 261
Doors open, 155
Doors shut, 155
Double-barreled Shotgun, 211
Double-ended straight, 261
Doubling limit, 261
Down-the-River, 35
Draw, 8, 17, 249
Draw out of turn, 250
Draw Poker, 16, 23, 24, 27, 81, 104,
    105, 123, 181, 187, 218
Draw Poker, High-Low, 181
Draw Poker for High, 81
Draw Poker for Low, 123, 137, 223
Draw Poker with the Bug, 104
Draw Poker with the Joker, 105
Drop, 15
Dutch flush, 238
Dutch straight, 262

Eight-card Stud, 36, 208
Eldest hand, 28

Ellinger, Maurice, 257, 262
English Poker, 24
English Stud, 148
Ethics, 18, 36, 54
Etiquette, 54
Evolution of Poker, 235
Exposed card, 246, 253

False openers, 30, 250
Finger Poker, 262
Five-card Stud, 25, 34, 107, 224
Five-of-a-kind, 19, 242
Five-suit Poker, 263
Fixed limit, 19
Flash, 263
Flat Poker, 263
Flip, 205
Flush, 14, 243
Flux, 237
Football, 203
Fortune Poker, 195, 203
Foster, R. F., 235
Four-flush, 26, 106, 205, 263
Four-flush beats a pair, 205
Four-flush to open, 106
Four Forty-Four, 203
Four Forty-Two, 203
Four-of-a-Kind (game), 214
Four-of-a-kind (hand), 14, 243
Freak draws, 85
Freak games, 25
Freak-pots, 263
Freezeout, 263
Frezon, 238
Full hand, 264
Full house, 14, 243

Game theory situation, 230
Garbage, 264
Ge, 237
Gile, 237
Gilet, 237
Gillet, 237
Gleek, 264
Gruesome Twosome, 264

Have a sight, 8
Hand misstated, 248
Heinz, 203
Help Me, Neighbor, 264
Hickok, Wild Bill, 260
High-Low Draw Poker, 181

High-Low Poker, 26, 143
High-Low with Declarations, 160
High-Low "with Fists," 161
High Poker, 81
Hilo, 265
Hilo-Picolo, 265
History of Poker, 7, 235
Holding it in the window, 143
Hole card, 17, 34
House rules:
  chips and stakes, 44
  games to be played, 46
  money, 43
  players, 43
  rules of play, 46
  time limit, 42
Hoyle, Edmond, 265
Hurricane, 202

Imperfect pack, 246
Impossible call, 253
Incomplete hand, 251
Incorrect hand, 246
Incorrect pack, 245
Inside straight, 266
Installment bets, 247
Insufficient bet, 247
Ironclad hand, 266
Iron duke, 266
Irregularities: 22, 245
  in betting, 247
  in dealing Stud, 252
  in the draw, 249
  in Knock Poker, 199
  in showdown, 248

Jacoby, Oswald, 57, 65, 236
Jackpots, 23, 28, 94
Jacks Back, 266
Jacks or Better to Open, 94
Joker, 18, 241
Joker Poker, 266
Joker Stud, 204

Kankakee, 207
Kilter, 266
King, Jack, 76
Kings Back, 266
Kitty, 18
Knock Poker, 198
Knock Poker family, 187, 198
Ku Klux Klan, 267

Lamebrain Pete, 194
Lamebrains, 193
Larsen, Swen A., 262, 264, 265, 266
Laws, 17, 36, 240
Laws of Poker, 240
    betting limits, 254
    Draw Poker, 249
    general laws, 240
    irregularities, 245
    Stud Poker, 251
Limiting the draws, 29
Limits on raises, 22
Little bobtail, 267
Little cat, 33
Little dog, 33
Little tiger, 33
Long Studs, 267
Lowball, 25, 123, 137, 223
Low Draw Poker, 118, 123, 137, 223
Low Hole Card Wild, 208
Low Poker, 25, 117
Low Stud Poker, 119

Matching coins, 229
Mathematical theory of games, 229
Mathematics, 57, 222, 229
Memory, 77
Memory in Stud Poker, 78
Mexican Stud, 205
Middle straight, 268
Mike, 201
Minnie, 268
Miscellaneous (dealer's choice) games
    209
Misdeal, 245
Mississippi River Steamboat Poker, 8
Mistrigris, 268
Mites and lice, 268
Modern Hoyle, The, 236
Money-management, 72, 127
Money transactions, 43
Monkey flush, 268
Monte, 202

Natural cards, 19
Neumann, John von, 229
New York Stud, 268
Nickel ante, 45
Nits and buggers, 268
Nits and lice, 268
No-pair hand, 15, 243

Nothing, 129
Number of players, 43
Nut, 129

Object of Poker, 14, 241
Obsolete Poker games, 236
    Ambigu, 237
    As, 236
    As Nas, 236
    Bouillotte, 237
    Brelan, 237
    Brag, 238
    Commerce, 238
    Gile, Gilet, Gillet or Trionfetti, 237
    Poch or Pochen, 239
    Poker with the Buck, 236
Odds at Blind-Opening Draw Poker,
    222
Odds at Draw Poker: 218
    drawing 3 cards to a pair, 219
    drawing 2 cards to a pair and ace
        kicker, 219
    drawing 2 cards to triplets, 219
    drawing one card to triplets, 220
    other draws, 220
Odds at Draw Poker for low, 137, 223
Odds at Five-card Stud, 224
Odds at Lowball, 137, 223
Odds at Seven-card High-low Stud, 227
Odds at Seven-card Stud (High), 226
    against making a full house or better,
        226
    against making a flush, 227
    against making a straight, 227
Odds at Stud Poker, 224
Office hours, 268
One-card draw, 93
One pair, 15, 243
One-end straight, 268
Open-end straight, 269
Open Poker, 23, 202, 269
Opening requirements at Lowball, 130
Optimum strategy, 230
Option, 148
Origin of Poker, 7, 235
Overhead, 73

Pack, 18, 241
"Painted," 119
Pass and back in, 23
Pass and Out (game), 32
Pass and out (play), 24

Pass-out, 31
Pass out of turn, 248
Pat hand, 269
Pat-hand bluff, 66
Patience Poker, 269
Pedro, 205
Peek Poker, 269
Peep-and-Turn, 205
Pelter, 269
Penalties, 18, 22, 240
Penny Ante, 269
Percentage tables, 215
Pig-in-the-Poke, 191
Piquet pack, 237
Pistol Pete, 270
Pistol Stud, 204
Playing position, 70
Poch (game), 239
Poch (hand), 239
Pochen, 8, 235, 239
Point, 237
Poker, object of, 14, 241
Poker chestnuts, 52
Poker hands, 14
Poker hands possible in:
    52-card pack, 216
    52-card pack, deuces wild, 217
    52-card pack, Joker as "Bug," 217
    40-card pack, 218
    32-card pack, 218
Poker probabilities, 215
Poker Rum, 235
Poker Solitaire, 270
Poker with the Buck, 236
Poque, 8, 235
Position, 68
Positional bluffing, 135
Pot, 14
Pot limit, 20
Preliminaries to the Poker game, 17
Prime, 238
Primero, 270
Probabilities in Poker, 215, 216, 221
Procter and Gamble, 195
Professional game defined, 24
Progressive Jackpots, 31, 107
Progressive Poker, 271
Proving openers, 30
Psychology, 61

Raise, 15
Rank of cards, 241

Rank of Poker hands, 14, 33, 49, 144,
    242
Redeal, 245
Representation, 166, 174
Reviewing the draw, 30
Rickey de Laet, 205
Risk strategy, 128
Rough, 124
Round-the-corner straight, 271
Round the World, 194
Routine, 272
Royal flush, 14, 242
Rules of play, 46
Rum, 235
Run, 272

Sandbag, 37
Sandbagging, 24, 55, 95, 171
Scooping, 145
Screwy Louie, 272
Seating, 241
Selection (High-Low), 148
Semi-bluffing, 124
Seven-card Flip, 207
Seven-card High-Low Stud, 149, 227
Seven-card Stud, 17, 25, 35, 114, 226
Seven-card Stud, English style, 207
Sevens rule, 125
Seven-Toed Pete, 35
Shifting Sands, 205
Short pair, 272
Short Studs, 272
Shotgun, 209
Shove 'em Along, 212
Showdown, 14, 145, 245
Showing openers, 250
Shuffle, 242
Shuffling the discards, 29
Side pot, 20, 147, 254
Simultaneous declaration, 160
Six-card High-Low Stud, 147
Six-card High-Low Stud, Cards Speak,
    158
Six-card Stud, 36, 206
Skeet, 26, 273
Skip straight, 26, 273
Smooth, 124
Southern Cross, 197
Special games, 25
Special hands, 26
Special house rules, 47
Spit-in-the-Ocean, 39, 189

Spit-in-the-Ocean family, 187
  Bedsprings, 195
  Cincinnati, 193
  Cincinnati Liz, 194
  Criss-Cross, 197
  Lamebrain Pete, 194
  Procter and Gamble, 195
  Round the World, 194
  Southern Cross, 197
  Spit-in-the-Ocean, 189
  Stormy Weather, 192
  Tennessee, 198
  Twin Beds, 196
  Wild Widow, 191
  X Marks the Spot, 197
Splitting openers, 29, 250
Stakes, 44, 126
Stand pat, 29
Stormy Weather, 192
Straddle, 32
Straight, 9, 14, 243
Straight Draw Poker, 31, 97
Straight flush, 14, 242
Straight Poker, 27, 236
String bets, 247
Strip Poker, 274
Stud Poker, 9, 16, 23, 25, 34, 107, 119,
  188, 224, 251
Stud Poker for High, 107
Stud Poker for Low, 119
Swinging, 145

Tables of percentages, 215
Table stakes, 20, 254
Take It or Leave It, 212
Tennessee, 193
Tens-High, 275
Texas Tech, 211
Theory of bluffing, 68

Theory of games, 229
Three-card Monte, 275
Three-card Poker, 202
Three Forty-Five, 203
Three-of-a-kind, 14, 243
Three-toed Pete, 275
Tiger (game), 32
Tiger (hand), 26, 33
Time limit, 18, 42
Transfers, 43
Tricon, 237, 276
Trio, 276
Trionfetti, 237
Twin Beds, 196, 276
Two-card Poker, 201
Two pair, 14, 243

Under the guns, 69
United States Playing Card Company,
  236
Unlimited Poker, 276
Unmade hand, 130
Utah, 193

Von Neumann, John, 229

Wheel, 117, 149
Whiskey Poker, 200, 235
White check, 31
Wild-card games, 18, 26
Wild cards, 9, 18, 241
Wild Widow, 191
Window, 142
Woolworth, 203
Wrong number of cards, 249

X Marks the Spot, 197

You Roll Two, 277

ABOUT THE AUTHOR

IN THE FIELD OF CARD GAMES, *the name of Albert Morehead is probably the foremost one of this century. Mr. Morehead took over the mantle where Hoyle doffed it; as a matter of fact, all modern "Hoyles" were either written or co-authored by him. He is perhaps best known as the man who so brilliantly wrote* The New York Times's *daily Contract Bridge column for many years, but his penetrating knowledge of all other card games was equally expert. This fact is attested to by the impressive number of book titles (over 40) which he has authored, co-authored, or edited over the years. Apart from Contract Bridge, these books include masterly works on Poker, Gin Rummy, Canasta, Samba, and every other card game down to and including the many forms of Solitaire.*

Through it all, Poker was his favorite game and he felt he knew even more about that one than all the other games on which he was the acknowledged world authority. The Complete Guide to Winning Poker, *completed shortly before his death, is by far his most ambitious book on the subject, embracing everything that he had written in earlier years and adding much new material. It will stand as the final word on the game of Poker for years to come.*